PERCEPTION AND ACTION IN MEDIEVAL EUROPE

PERCEPTION AND ACTION IN MEDIEVAL EUROPE

Harald Kleinschmidt

THE BOYDELL PRESS

First published 2005
The Boydell Press, Woodbridge

ISBN 1 84383 146 5

The Boydell Press is an imprint of Boydell & Brewer Ltd
PO Box 9, Woodbridge, Suffolk IP12 3DF, UK
and of Boydell & Brewer Inc.
668 Mt Hope Avenue, Rochester, NY 14620, USA
website: www.boydellandbrewer.com

A CIP catalogue record for this book is available
from the British Library

Library of Congress Cataloging-in-Publication Data
Kleinschmidt, Harald, 1949–
    Perception and action in medieval Europe / Harald Kleinschmidt.
        p. cm.
    Summary: "Study of the changing nature of the perception of an action
and the action itself, and how thought-processes altered radically in the
Middle Ages" – Provided by publisher.
    Includes bibliographical references and index.
    ISBN 1–84383–146–5 (hardback : alk. paper)
    1. Perception – History – To 1500. 2. Act (Philosophy) – History –
To 1500. 3. Civilization, Medieval – Psychological aspects. I. Title.
    BF311.K6263 2005
    121'.34'0940902 – dc22   2005005788

This publication is printed on acid-free paper

Printed in Great Britain by
Athenaeum Press Ltd., Gateshead, Tyne & Wear

Contents

List of Illustrations

Abbreviations

CCCM	*Corpvs Christianorvm*. Continvatio mediaevalis
CCSL	*Corpvs Christianorum*. Series Latina
EETS OS	Early English Text Society. Original Series
EETS ES	Early English Text Society. Extra Series
Mansi	Johann Dominicus Mansi, *Sacrorum Conciliorum nova et amplissima collectio* [repr. (Graz, 1960)]
MGH AA	Monumenta Germaniae Historica, *Auctores antiquissimi*
MGH Cap.	Monumenta Germaniae Historica, *Capitularia regum Francorum*
MGH Chron.	Monumenta Germaniae Historica, *Deutsche Chroniken*
MGH Conc.	Monumenta Germaniae Historica, *Concilia*
MGH DD	Monumenta Germaniae Historica, *Diplomata regum et imperatorum Germaniae*
MGH Epp.	Monumenta Germaniae Historica, *Epistolae [in Quart]*
MGH, Epp. Sel.	Monumenta Germaniae Historica, *Epistolae selectae*
MGH Font.	Monumenta Germaniae Historica, *Fontes iuris Germanici antiqui in usum scholarum*
MGH Leges	Monumenta Germaniae Historica, *Leges*
MGH, Libri mem.	Monumenta Germaniae Historica, *Libri memoriales et necrologia*
MGH, LL nat. Germ.	Monumenta Germaniae Historica. *Leges nationum Germanicarum*
MGH Necr.	Monumenta Germaniae Historica, *Necrologia*
MGH Poet.	Monumenta Germaniae Historica, *Poetae latini aevi Carolini*
MGH SS	Monumenta Germaniae Historica, *Scriptores*
MGH, SS. rer. Germ.	Monumenta Germaniae Historica, *Scriptores rerum Germanicarum in usum scholarum*
MGH, SS rer. Merov.	Monumenta Germaniae Historica, *Scriptores rerum Merovingicarum*
PG	Jacques-Paul Migne, *Patrologiae cursus completus*. Series Graeca
PL	Jacques-Paul Migne, *Patrologiae cursus completus*. Series Latina
RS	[Rolls Series] *Rerum Britannicarum Medii Aevi Scriptores*

Introduction

On the day before his battle against Cadwallon (or Catlon), King of the Britons, King Oswald of the Northumbrians, had a vision while lying in his tent on the campsite close to the battlefield. In his vision Oswald saw St Columba, the Irish missionary to Northumbria, descending from heaven. The saint appeared to touch the clouds with his head, radiating with the beauty of an 'angelic form'. The saint spoke to the king, giving him courage and promising him happiness and victory over Cadwallon. Oswald woke up, left his tent and reported the vision to his counsellors. The counsellors heard the report with comfort and relief and promised to convert to Christianity after the battle. Indeed, Oswald won the battle after Cadwallon was killed. He returned home victorious and received divine ordination as the 'ruler of all Britain' [*totius Brittanniae imperator*].

Abbot Adomnán of the Irish monastery at Iona, established by St Columba in 563, began his *Life of Columba* with this vision. Columba was one of Adomnán's aristocratic relatives, and Adomnán wrote the *Life* at the very end of the seventh century. He insisted that he had heard of Oswald's vision from his predecessor at Iona, Abbot Failbhe, who in turn reportedly had received news of the dream directly from Oswald. Adomnán introduced Oswald as a ruler over migrants from the continent to whom he referred generically as 'Saxons'. He added the information that at the time of the battle, Oswald and twelve of his followers, who had been baptised while in exile among the Picts, were the only Christians among the Saxons who were then 'darkened by the shadow of heathenism and ignorance'.[1]

Bede, who said he completed his *Ecclesiastical History of the English People* in 731, has his own report on the battle preparations that differs from Adomnán's while confirming some features of Adomnán's version. According to Bede, Oswald set up a cross on the battlefield before the battle began and insisted on holding the cross himself while warriors fixed it in the ground. Oswald sank to his knees after the cross had been placed in the ground, and said a prayer. According to Bede, Oswald and his warriors were in need of divine help in order to triumph over Cadwallon, whom Bede, like Adomnán, styled King of the Britons.[2]

---

1   Adomnán, *Life of Columba*, lib. I, cap. 1, ed. Alan Orr Anderson and Marjorie Ogilvie Anderson (London, 1961), pp. 12–14 [new edn (Oxford, 1991)]. There is an almost verbatim copy of the story in the twelfth-century *Life of Saint Oswald* by Reginald of Durham, ed. Thomas Arnold, *Symeonis Monachi Opera Omnia*, vol. 1 (London, 1882), p. 367.

2   Bede, *Historia ecclesiastica gentis Anglorum*, lib. III, cap. 2, ed. Bertram Colgrave and Roger Aubrey Baskervill Mynors (Oxford, 1969), pp. 214–16 [repr. (Oxford, 2003)].

We can approach Adomnán's and Bede's reports as miracle stories of which there are so many examples in medieval hagiography and historiography. We can then follow the lead of many critical historians,[3] dismiss the report as the fancy creation of gifted and learned monks who had the conversion story of Emperor Constantine in mind and assume that Adomnán had the intention of styling King Oswald as a second Constantine. Bede, for his part, emphasised the cooperation between Oswald and his retainers and pointed out the role of the cross while, in this passage, passing over St Columba in silence. Yet we can also consider Adomnán's and Bede's reports as sources for the world of perceptions and imagined actions in which Adomnán's and Bede's Northumbrian audience lived at the turn of the eighth century. The second option has the advantage of allowing penetration into imagined worlds that are no less real than their manifest and tangible counterparts but whose truth lies in recorded subjective experiences and consciousnesses and not in objectively verifiable contexts.

What do Adomnán and Bede tell us about Northumbrian imagined worlds at the turn of the eighth century? The first observation is that Adomnán proceeded in a rather conventional way when presenting his report. Like many other authors of miracle stories, he emphasised the trustworthiness of the informants on whom he relied. He also followed the conventions by ascribing miracles to the work of saints whom he let act as instruments of divine revelation. Similarly, Bede noted that the battlefield, to which he assigned the Old English name 'Hefenfeld' and the Latin name 'Caelestis Campus', meaning 'heavenly field', was a place where miracles were still taking place in his own day.[4] However, Adomnán made a rare choice when placing reports about St Columba's miracles at the beginning of his life of the saint whereas, in many other cases, the miracle stories were featured at the end of or even in separate texts appended to the lives. Adomnán's arrangement helped associate the saint with the subsequent missionary activities of King Oswald, and emphasised the impact of the Irish Church. While demonstrating his willingness to play with literary conventions, Adomnán put on record his knowledge of hagiographic traditions through his association of Oswald with Constantine. The association is implicit because Adomnán does not name the Roman emperor directly. Yet he did allude to memories of ancient Roman institutions by claiming that Oswald received divine ordination as an 'imperator' in connection with a battle. In the context of the reports, the word is crucial and conspicuous but its meaning is obscure. It could have been understood in its technical meaning as a ruler's title but it could also have been used in a

---

3 Among others, see David P. Kirby, *The Earliest English Kings* (London, 1991), pp. 88–92. For a critical survey of the historiography on St Oswald, see Clare Stancliffe, 'Oswald, 'The Most Holy and Most Victorious King of the Northumbrians', in Stancliffe and Eric Cambridge, eds, *Oswald. Northumbrian King to European Saint*, Paul Watkins Medieval Studies XIV (Stamford, 1995), pp. 33–83.

4 Bede (see note 2), p. 216.

non-technical sense of a person in a position to give out commands. The attribute 'of all of Britain' [*totius Brittanniae*] that Adomnán added to the word 'imperator' does not give more precision. Adomnán introduced Cadwallon as a ruler over Britons at large, although in fact Cadwallon held sway merely over Gwynedd. Nevertheless, Adomnán could have wished to communicate the message that, after his victory over Cadwallon, Oswald succeeded his defeated opponent as the ruler over all of Britain. Yet Adomnán chose to liken Oswald to Constantine, implying that Oswald became ruler over all of Britain as a territory in the same way as Constantine was the ruler over the entire Roman Empire after his victory in 312. It had been customary in the late Roman Empire to stress the military achievements of emperors as victorious military leaders and to ascribe to the army a leading role in selecting candidates for the imperial office. Adomnán may have known this tradition; yet if he did, he obfuscated it by insisting that it was the divinity that empowered and ordained Oswald through the intervention of St Columba and not the army under his command.

Likewise, Bede included Oswald in the group of some fifth-, sixth- and seventh-century insular rulers to whom he ascribed the position of holders of some *imperium* over parts of the British Isles.[5] Hence, Adomnán and Bede played with allusions to rulers, recorded in secular and religious traditions, in the same way as hagiographers and historiographers had done before and were going to do afterwards. Thus Bishop Gregory of Tours described Clovis, King of the Franks, as a New Constantine,[6] and Charles I, King of the Franks, became a New David in the propaganda of Abbot Alcuin of St Martin in Tours.[7] However, Adomnán and Bede were explicit in styling Oswald as a

---

5   Bede, *Historia* (see note 2), lib. II, cap. 5, pp. 148–50. For further material on the Roman tradition of ascribing military virtues to emperors, see Edmund Ernst Stengel, 'Der Heerkaiser (Den Kaiser macht das Heer). Studien zur Geschichte eines politischen Gedankens', in Stengel, *Abhandlungen und Untersuchungen zur mittelalterlichen Geschichte* (Cologne and Graz, 1960), pp. 1–170 [first published in *Historische Aufsätze. Karl Zeumer zum sechzigsten Geburtstag als Festgabe dargebracht von Freunden und Schülern* (Weimar, 1910); also printed separately in an enlarged version (Weimar, 1910)]. It is quite a different matter that tenth-century intellectuals used the same formula as a title for the English kings, probably drawing on Adomnán and Bede. See Harald Kleinschmidt, *Untersuchungen über das englische Königtum im 10. Jahrhundert*, Göttinger Bausteine zur Geschichtswissenschaft LIX (Göttingen, Frankfurt and Zurich, 1979), pp. 64–89.

6   Gregory of Tours, *Historiarum Libri X*, lib. II, cap. 29–30, ed. Bruno Krusch and Wilhelm Levison, MGH, SS rer. Merov. I (Hanover, 1951), pp. 74–6. Bede had similar stories to tell about King Edwin of Northumbria, who allegedly agreed to convert to Christianity if given victory over King Cwichelm of Wessex, and about King Caedwalla of Wessex, whom Bede had pledge to donate to the church one-fourth of the land he intended to occupy in the Isle of Wight. See Bede, *Historia* (see note 2), lib. II, cap. 9, lib. IV, cap. 16, pp. 164–6, 382.

7   For the styling of rulers as 'New David' from the fourth to the twelfth centuries, see Hugo Steger, *David rex et propheta*, Erlanger Beiträge zur Sprach- und Kunstwissenschaft IV (Nuremberg, 1961), pp. 127–9.

second Christ winning over his foes and spreading Christianity with twelve
followers. Hence, for Adomnán and Bede, it appears to have been perfectly
reasonable to take for granted that persons could take roles. This is not surprising in view of the then current meaning of the Latin word *persona* which,
like its Greek counterpart *prosopon*, denoted the theatrical mask rather than
the identity of an individual.[8]

In Adomnán's report, the miracle took the form of a *visus* or *visio* that
Oswald 'saw'. St Columba appealed primarily to the sense of vision although
he also used speech to attract Oswald's attention, issue commands and foretell
the future. The dominant feature in Oswald's vision was the light in which St
Columba descended upon the campsite like an angel. The association of light
with the divine world was a common feature of the theory of perception of
late Antiquity and the early Middle Ages when shining light represented the
ideal of aesthetic perfection.[9] The saint thus acted as the divinity's messenger,
revealed to Oswald a small portion of the divine world and allowed him to
receive support and encouragement from the divinity. The vision was the
medium for the transmission of divine messages that Oswald was given to
execute. Unlike modern psychoanalysts, who use dreams to reconstruct the
past, early medieval hagiographers employed dreams as a means for the perception of the future. Oswald's way towards success began with his perception
of a divine message and ended with his ability to translate his perception into
appropriate actions and execute the divine command. While he did not repeat
Adomnán's statement that most of Oswald's warriors were non-Christians at
the time of the battle, Bede concurred, reporting that Oswald summoned his
fellow warriors to kneel before the cross he had erected, and asked them to
trust in divine assistance.

Adomnán's and Bede's reports thus shed light on standards of perception.
Standards of perception are frequently recognisable expectations about
causes, processes and effects of the use of the senses. Perceivers employ these
standards hoping to be able to control perception. With regard to vision and
audition, the standard of perception determines the patterns of interaction
between the seen or heard persons, artists or musicians or objects as
message-senders on the one side and viewers or listeners as message-receivers
on the other. In Adomnán's and Bede's reports, the standard of perception
consisted of two expectations: first, that perception could have the goal of
allowing the execution of divine will with the help of intervening agents; and,
second, that perception could be translated into actions without the personal
judgements of actors.

Moreover, Adomnán described the miracle in a way that turned the hero
Oswald into the recipient of heavenly energy conferred upon him through the
body of St Columba. The saint's body connected heaven with earth and shed

---

[8] For a discussion of these words, see Harald Kleinschmidt, *Understanding the Middle
Ages* (Woodbridge, 2000), pp. 203–7.

[9] For a discussion, see David Chidester, *Word and Light. Seeing, Hearing and Religious
Discourse* (Urbana and Chicago, 1992), pp. 53–72.

light on most of the campsite, including Oswald's tent. The beams that flew from heaven to earth resembled the liturgy and the pictorial image of Pentecost in the early Middle Ages.[10] The imagery of Pentecost was suitable to the Christ-like figure of Oswald. Oswald could perform Christ's role as a missionary after he had received divine energy and gained victory in battle through the intermediation of St Columba. He fulfilled his duty through the appropriate use of divine grace. Thus Adomnán measured the success of Oswald's actions in accordance with Oswald's willingness and capability to make use of supportive external energy, in this case of divine origin. Bede concurred in styling Oswald 'the most holy and victorious king' and describing him as the recipient of divine grace.[11]

Bede explicitly attributed Oswald's defeat of Cadwallon to the intervention of the divinity which, Bede said, gave victory to its worshippers on the ground of merit in times of their dire need. Although both authors were ordained Christian monks, their reports displayed the activities of groups whose members followed a concept of action that militated against the fundamentals of Christian doctrine. Frequently concepts of action can be recognisable generalisations about motives, processes and goals of the doings of persons in groups. The concept of action featured in Adomnán's and Bede's reports continued to be applicable as long as persons remained integrated into groups like warrior bands, descent and local groups, whose members were tied to each other by bonds of contractual agreements, kin and neighbourhood and adhered to common group-bound religious beliefs and ritual practices. With its quest for universalism, Christianity called into question the particularism of traditional groups. The pre-Christian standard of perception and concept of action were linked to social organisation whereas the Christian standard of perception and concept of action were derived from universal aesthetic and moral principles. The enforcement of the latter provoked a severe change in the former.

The actions of Oswald's entourage of counsellors displayed a further characteristic feature of the early medieval concept of group-centred action. Adomnán let the counsellors pledge to accept Christianity as their religion after receiving victory in battle, following the hagiographic and historiographic traditions about Emperor Constantine and King Clovis.[12] Conversion thus took the form of an agreement between the divinity and human actors. The divinity had to demonstrate its willingness to convey grace through granting victory in battle before human actors were willing to change their religion, that is, desert their former deities in favour of a new one.

---

[10] The Pentecost sequences contained the formula 'Sancti spiritus assit nobis gratia', first recorded in the *Liber Ymnorum* by Notker the Stammerer, ed. Wolfram von den Steinen, *Notkeri Poetae Balbuli Liber Ymnorum* = Steinen, *Notker der Dichter und seine geistige Welt*, Editionsband (Bern, 1948), p. 54. Notker's hymn continued to be popular until the Tridentine Council. For the reproduction of a Pentecost picture, see Kleinschmidt, *Understanding* (see note 8), p. 70.

[11] Bede, *Historia* (see note 2), lib. III, cap. 7, p. 232. For further cases, see Kleinschmidt, *Understanding* (see note 8), pp. 63–72.

Religious affiliation resulted from exposure to divine power that was experienced as helpful for persons and beneficial for the maintenance of groups. In order to attract believers as followers, the Christian divinity became obliged to demonstrate its superior ability and willingness to convey the energy required for the successful conduct of human actions. Believers had to be willing and able to use the emanations of divine grace appropriately and for the accomplishment of morally defensible goals. Oswald and his followers appear to have expected that the accomplishment of goals critically hinged on actors' willingness to adhere to due process and their ability to make use of externally supplied energy.

While Oswald and his followers were described as wanting to enter into some form of particularistic contract with the Christian divinity, the Christian doctrine of divine grace, as argued by St Augustine,[13] started from the assumption that human actors were born as sinful beings and had no choice other than to act sinfully. Hence, their only chance of redemption was to rely on divine mercy. According to this doctrine, the divinity could give mercy at its own discretion but could not possibly be obliged to do so in any way. Against this doctrine, Oswald and his followers modelled their relationship with the divinity in terms of a contract between persons of different rank and expected that the parties to the contract were obliged to honour it. Hence, while Oswald and his retainers derived their religious beliefs from the organisation of the particularistic groups within which they lived, Christian theological doctrine strove to enforce universalistic principles according to which all Christian believers were expected to act.

Modern aestheticians and ethicists have found it hard to penetrate into changing standards of perception and concepts of action. Their approach has been theoretical rather than historical, focusing on the problem of the enforcibility of norms. Modern aesthetic and ethical theories have displayed various assessments about the enforcibility of norms. Whereas, following Kant, most aestheticians convinced themselves that normative aesthetic judgements should not and cannot be enforced and that attempts to do so are unwarranted acts of intrusion into the private sphere of the individual,[14] ethicists were divided over the question of under what conditions moral norms can and should be enforced.[15]

---

[12] See Eusebius of Caesaraea, *Vita Constantini*, lib. I, cap. 28, in *PG*, vol. 20, col. 943. Gregory, *Historiarum* (see note 6), lib. II, cap. 30, pp. 75–6.

[13] Augustine, *Contra duas epistolas Pelagianorum*, lib. IV, cap. 3, 30–1, in *PL* vol. 44, col. 754. Augustine, *De natura boni*, cap. 9, in *PL* vol. 42, col. 554. Augustine, *De civitate Dei*, lib. XIII, cap. 14, lib. XIV, cap. 13, ed. Bernard Dombart and Alphons Kalb, CCSL. XLVIII, 2 (Turnhout, 1955), pp. 395–6, 434–6.

[14] Immanuel Kant, *Vorlesungen über Logik. Logik Philippi* [1772], ed. Preussische Akademie der Wissenschaften, Kant, *Gesammelte Werke*, vol. 24, 1 (Berlin, 1966), p. 359. Kant, *Kritik der Urteilskraft* [Berlin, 1790], newly ed. in Kant, *Werke in zwölf Bänden*, ed. Wilhelm Weischedel, vol. 10 (Frankfurt, 1968), pp. 279–328. Hans-Georg Gadamer, *Wahrheit und Methode*, 5th edn (Tübingen, 1986), pp. 48–87 [first published (Tübingen, 1960)].

[15] Alasdair MacIntyre, *A Short History of Ethics* (London and New York, 1966), pp. 260–1

Why this difference? One answer is that, unlike early medieval hagiographers and historians, modern European theorists of aesthetics and ethics took for granted that perception cannot and should not be regarded as convertible into action. Under this premise, aesthetic judgements did not have to be followed by actions whereas moral judgement had to be so. Thus, if someone's aesthetic judgments failed to be accepted by others, only a few modern adherents to the medieval aesthetics of St Thomas Aquinas would worry.[16] However, if responsible persons made inappropriate or imperfect moral judgements or consciously committed immoral actions and remained unsanctioned, a sense of crisis emerged, and demands for the intensification of social and political control became vocal.

Another answer is to be found in Max Weber's theory of social action as rational action. Weber believed that the rationality of social action must be ascertained through the measurement of the degree to which the action can attain its preconceived goal. Thus, following Weber, rational action was defined as the doings of a person who, stimulated by one or several motives, launched several processes of movements in order to accomplish one or several goals. Through this triad of motives, processes and goals, rational action was taken to be observable and measurable within the situations in which they occurred.[17] These social contexts appeared to allow the observation of actions and measurement of the success to which the actor accomplished the set goal or goals. They allocated high significance to the actors' willingness and ability to mobilise the energies contained in their own bodies. Within the triad of motives, processes and goals, processes obtained an instrumental role, as they seemed to result from motives and to be the means to accomplish goals.[18] Within the framework of Weberian theory, actions in

---

[7th printing (1978)]. MacIntyre, *After Virtue*, 2nd edn (Notre Dame, IN, 1984), pp. 6–22 [1st edn (London, 1981)].

16 Among them Jacques Maritain, 'Beauty and Imitation', ed. Melvin Rader, *A Modern Book of Esthetics*, new edn (New York, 1952), pp. 8–20 [first published (New York, 1935)]. E. Brian F. Midgley, *The Natural Law and the Theory of International Relations* (London, 1975), p. 2. Midgley, 'Natural Law and the "Anglo-Saxons"', in *British Journal of International Studies* 5 (1979), pp. 270–2.

17 Max Weber, *Wirtschaft und Gesellschaft*, 5th edn, Studienausgabe, ed. Johannes Winckelmann (Tübingen, 1980), book I, §1, section 1–2, pp. 1–2. For a study of Weber's concept of action, see Helmut Girndt, *Das soziale Handeln als Grundkategorie erfahrungswissenschaftlicher Soziologie*, Veröffentlichungen des Max Weber Instituts der Universität München I (Tübingen, 1967), pp. 22–34.

18 Thus explicitly Weber, *Wirtschaft* (see note 17), book 1, §2, pp. 12–13. It is true that Wolfgang Schluchter, *Die Entstehung des modernen Rationalismus. Eine Analyse von Max Webers Entwicklungsgeschichte des Okzidents*, rev. edn (Frankfurt, 1998), pp. 23–5 [first published (Tübingen, 1979)], has made much of Weber's concept of *Wertrationalität* by which, he claims, Max Weber understood the pursuit of actions not directed towards the accomplishment of goals but of some immanent value. See also Schluchter, *Die Paradoxie der Rationalisierung. Zum Verhältnis von 'Ethik' und 'Welt' bei Max Weber* (Frankfurt, 1980), pp. 9–40 [first published in *Zeitschrift für Soziologie* 5 (1976), pp. 256–84]. Yet Schluchter overstates Weber's distinction in two respects. The first is that Weber himself admitted *Wertrationalität* as a type of goal-orientation for

which processes were not instrumental to the observable accomplishment of set goals consequently could not count as rational actions.[19] Likewise, if actors believed or tacitly assumed that the goals of their actions were dictated to or imposed upon them by other persons, divine agents or superhuman forces in the physical environment, their actions appeared to follow a non-Weberian rationality because actors disclaimed any involvement in setting the goals of their actions.[20] Positively speaking, twentieth-century theorists of action were concerned with the doings of persons only under three conditions. The first condition was that actors meet the demand to use their own physical and intellectual energies and capabilities for the purpose of setting the goals for their actions. The second condition was that actors launch the processes of their actions in communicative situations where the degree of goal-attainment became intersubjectively measurable. The third condition was that actors accept the premise that the processes of actions were and ought to be instruments to accomplish the set goals.

Theorists of aesthetics approached perception in a different way. They assumed that, if any communication about perceptions occurred, it usually came after the perceptions had been made. Thus, while the judgements about the success of goal-oriented actions could and often would take place while the actions were ongoing, judgments about the appropriateness of perceptions usually took place *post-factum*, if they took place at all. Therefore, modern theorists of perception shared the view that actions, including think-

---

actions only in the limited sense of the degree by which human actions can be directed towards the execution of moral duties or religious commands and noted that actions are seldom purely *wertrational*. The second is that Weber also accepted the principle of goal-orientation of actions also for those types of actions that he categorised as *wertrational*.

[19] According to Weber, *Wirtschaft* (see note 16), book 1, §2, p. 13, actors behave irrationally if they do not consider the consequences of their actions.

[20] Anthropologists and historians have long studied process-oriented actions but have tended to characterise them as magical or superstitious beliefs. Among anthropologists, Evans-Pritchard long dominated the field with his attempt to explain aspects of African thought as a non-standard form of rationality because, so Evans-Pritchard insisted, it is impossible for an observer to pass objective judgements on the verifiability of success or failure of an action. See specifically his definition of magic in Edward Evan Evans-Pritchard, *Witchcraft, Oracles and Magic among the Azande* (Oxford, 1937), p. 9 [reprints (Oxford, 1965, 1968, 1972)]. For a criticism of Evans-Pritchard's views, see: Mary Douglas, ed., *Witchcraft. Confessions and Accusations* (London, 1970). Clifford Geertz, 'Common Sense as a Cultural System', in Geertz, *Local Knowledge* (London, 1993), pp. 78–80 [first published in *Antioch Review* 33 (1975); 1st edn of Geertz, *Local Knowledge* (New York, 1983)]. Eva Gillies, 'Einleitung', in her edn of Evans-Pritchard, *Hexerei, Orakel und Magie bei den Zande* (Frankfurt, 1988), pp. 7–34. For the Middle Ages, similar world-views have been described by Aaron Yakovlevich Gurevich, *Mittelalterliche Volkskultur* (Munich, 1987) [first published (Moscow, 1972); English version (London, 1985)]. Gurevich's interpretations have been challenged by Dieter Harmening, *Superstitio. Überlieferungs- und theoriegeschichtliche Untersuchungen zur kirchlich-theologischen Aberglaubensliteratur des Mittelalters* (Berlin, 1979). Harmening, ' "Magische Volkskultur". Ethnographische Befunde oder literarisches Konstrukt?', in *Mediaevalia Historica Bohemica* 7 (2000), pp. 55–90.

ing, could lead to perceptions whereas perceptions needed to pass the *post-factum* test of adequacy before they could be allowed to stimulate morally defensible goal-oriented actions.[21]

This attitude towards the interconnectedness of perception and action is distinctly European and North American, and modern at that. It was developed only from the end of the eighteenth century, when the postulate became firmly established that aesthetic judgements ought to be recognised as subjective. Yet up until the middle of the eighteenth century, theorists took the opposite assumption for granted that aesthetic judgements could be standardised and were convertible into moral judgements, while conceding the capability of autonomous perceptions and actions to the divinity as well as to human actors.[22] Moreover, late seventeenth- and early eighteenth-century physiognomists and sensualists argued in support of the rationality of aesthetic judgements because they assumed that perception ought to be linked to the metaphysical category of common sense.[23] The fusion of attempts to derive aesthetic judgements from general, although metaphysical standards with the concession of the capability of autonomous action to human actors was already characteristic of the aesthetics and ethics of Albertus Magnus and

---

[21] For the debate on the political theory of actions and the social theory of international relations, see David Easton, *A Framework for Political Analysis* (Englewood Cliffs, 1965), pp. 50–1. Alexander Wendt, *Social Theory of International Politics* (Cambridge, 1999), pp. 67–91.

[22] Giovanni Battista della Porta, *De humana physiognomia*, lib. I, cap. 17 (Hanau, 1593), pp. 55–6 [first published (1586); repr. (Naples, 1986)]. Christian Thomasius, 'Neue Erfindung einer wohl gegründeten und für das gemeine Wesen höchst nöthigen Wissenschaft das Verborgene des Hertzens anderer Menschen auch gegen deren Willen aus der täglichen Conversation zu erkennen', in Thomasius, *Kleine teutsche Schriften* (Halle, 1701), pp. 449–90. Christian Wolff, *Philosophia rationalis sive logica* (Frankfurt and Leipzig, 1732), pp. 641–706 [repr., ed. Jean Ecole, Wolff, *Gesammelte Werke* II/1,3 (Hildesheim, Zurich and New York, 1983)]. Wolff, *Vernünftige Gedanken von den Kräften des menschlichen Verstandes* (Halle, 1754), pp. 219–31 [repr., ed. Hans Werner Arndt, Wolff, *Gesammelte Werke*, ser. I, vol. 1 (Hildesheim, Zurich and New York, 1978)]. James Parsons, 'Human Physiognomy Explain'd in the Crounian Lectures on Muscular Motion for the Year 1746', in *Philosophical Transactions of the Royal Society* 44,1 (1746), supplement. Henry Fielding, 'An Essay on the Knowledge of the Character of Men [1753]', in Fielding, *Miscellaneous Writings in Three Volumes*, vol. 1, Fielding, *The Works* XIV (London, 1967), pp. 279–305. Johann Caspar Lavater, *Physiognomische Fragmente zur Beförderung der* Menschenkenntnis und Menschenliebe, 6 vols (Winterthur, 1775–79). An early critic of physiognomy was Georg Christoph Lichtenberg, 'Über Physiognomik. Wider die Physiognomen. Zu Beförderung der Menschenliebe und Menschenkenntnis [1778]', in Lichtenberg, *Schriften und Briefe*, vol. 3, ed. Wolfgang Promies (Munich, 1972), pp. 256–95.

[23] For example, see Anthony Ashley Cooper, Earl of Shaftesbury, *Sensus communis* [1723], ed. in Shaftesbury, *Standard Edition*, vol. 1, 1 (Stuttgart, 1992), pp. 40–4, 48, 74–6. Francis Hutcheson, *An Inquiry into the Original of Our Ideas of Beauty*, Book I, Section 1, 6, Book II, Section 3 (London, 1725), pp. 4–11, 65–78, 150–78 [repr., Hutcheson, *Collected Works*, ed. Bernhard Fabian, vol. 1 (Hildesheim, New York, 1971)]. Carl von Dahlberg, *Grundsätze der Ästhetik, deren Anwendung und künftige Entwicklung* (Erfurt, 1791), p. 3.

St Thomas Aquinas. Albertus believed that the sense organs were directly connected with that part of the brain that he considered to house the common sense. Thomas insisted on the normativity of aesthetic as well as ethical judgements although at the same time he admitted that human actors were capable of making their own decisions about good and evil in accordance with their conscience. Furthermore, he assumed that perception followed from some 'cognitive power' that persons used more or less aptly and that made perception possible by imposing order on objects with an innate goodness.[24] Thus, between the thirteenth and the eighteenth centuries, aesthetics and ethics joined in the common beliefs that perception and action ought to take place in a predetermined framework of norms and that perceivers as well as actors should, on the one side, develop their decision-making capability, while, on the other, they should subject themselves to a generally acknowledged standard of perception and commit themselves to moral action.

But how could aesthetics and ethics cope with situations in which perceptions were taken to be directly convertible into actions without the intermediation of a conscience and a cognitive power? Which actions were considered to be primarily process-oriented? Which actions were considered to be rational under the condition that the actors believed to be driven by exogenous forces and in pursuit of goals that had been imposed upon them? Answers to these questions can only be provided through the study of the standards of perception and concepts of action that operated in, and portrayed, a world that was different from what modern aesthetic and ethical theories assumed to be the case. First and foremost, the modern notions of aesthetics and ethics appear to be too narrow for this kind of approach. If aesthetics was confined to theories about judgements of beauty in art or in art and nature, the Middle Ages appeared to be a period when aesthetics hardly existed. If ethics was understood to be a theory about judgements of moral action, much of the medieval period seemed to be a dark age when ethics seemingly consisted of the more or less appropriate rumination on the legacy of the philosophy of Antiquity. But the twentieth-century narrow notion of aesthetics is not a given. Alexander Gottlieb Baumgarten, credited with having spread the use of the term, was aware of the fact that its Greek etymon meant 'perception'.[25] Hence, there is no prima facie reason to reject the broad definition of aesthetics as a theory of perception if this definition is helpful in analysing changing standards of perception and if it can allow the description of the processes that lead to narrowing down the term to its current meaning. Likewise, recognising the debt of medieval ethics to the legacy of Antiquity does not exclude the possibility of an inquiry into the changing concept of action in the Middle

---

24 Albertus Magnus, *Liber de memoria et reminiscentia*, cap. 1, in Albertus, *Opera omnia*, vol. 9, ed. August Borgnet (Paris, 1890), p. 97. Thomas Aquinas, *Summa theologiae*, Prima secundae, qu. 27, ar. 1 ad 3, in *S. Thomae Opera omnia*, ed. Roberto Busa, SJ, vol. 2 (Stuttgart, 1980), p. 393.

25 Alexander Gottlieb Baumgarten, *Theoretische Ästhetik*, ed. Hans Rudolf Schweizer (Hamburg, 1983), pp. 10–12 [newly ed. from Baumgarten, *Aesthetica*, vol. 1, pars I, cap. 7, §7 (Frankfurt, 1750)].

Ages, even if innovations have to be sought in sources other than specialised theoretical treatises. The very demand that theory needs to be expounded in written texts in order to qualify as theory turns logocentric because it arbitrarily sets literacy as the standard of communication about theoretical issues. But there is neither historical nor epistemological support for this approach as it wrongly implies that orally communicating groups and persons, who choose not to express their aesthetic and ethical thoughts in writing, although they might have the capability to do so, have neither aesthetics nor ethics.

Through examining the standards of perception and concepts of action extant in a variety of narrative and normative sources as well as from extant artefacts of the Middle Ages, the following five chapters historicise aesthetics and ethics as theories of perception and action by reading them against their various social contexts. Chapter I considers the use of vision and audition in the light of what can be gleaned from pieces of art and music about the interconnectedness of perception and action in the Middle Ages. The scope of this inquiry is not limited to theories of art and music but covers the practical matters of the use of the eyes and ears as sense organs. Chapter II reconsiders standards of perception together with the practicalities of action through a case study from the early eleventh century. The case links the transformation of attitudes toward perception and action among the inhabitants of an early eleventh-century East Saxon village to the contemporaneous change of their social organisation and modes of behaviour. Chapter III continues the study with a survey about what can be ascertained from medieval normative and narrative sources about perception of odour, touch and taste. Chapter IV turns attention towards action and reviews changing concepts of action gleaned from theoretical as well as narrative and normative sources. Chapter V completes the study with a synthesis of the histories of aesthetics and ethics as well as theoretical views on their interconnectedness.

For the Middle Ages, there is no scarcity of sources for such an inquiry, although most extant sources have to be placed in contexts different from those in which they originally appeared. Thus much on the history of aesthetics as a theory of perception can be gleaned from dedication pictures as frontispieces of books even though none of these miniatures was made for the purpose of theorising on perception. Likewise, much evidence on the history of ethics as a theory of action is contained in charters and other legal records whose primary purpose was not the documentation of thoughts on the history of action.

I

Perception and Action:
The Genesis of their Separation as Concepts

Qvi qvis senator cvriam officii cavsa ingrederis,
Ante hoc ostium, privates affectvs omnes abicito iram, vim, odium, amicitiam
Advlationem reipublicae personarum et cvram svbicito nam iniqvis fveris,
Itaqvoqve dei ivdicivm expectv bis atqve svstinebis

Inscription above the entrance to the council chamber
in Tallinn town hall. 1651*

Introduction

Ever since the seventeenth century the followers of John Locke, among European aestheticians, have accepted the premise that perception and action are separate concepts. Perception has appeared as the result of some external 'impression' on the sense organs of the perceiving body. Action has been understood as the response to a received sensory 'impression' impacting on the body from the outside. The belief that the perceiving body should absorb an external sensory 'impression' has connoted perception with passivity, and action as the separate, sequential and active counterpart of perception.[1] However, the sensualist belief in the separateness of perception and action is far from obvious. The question is: how did the sensualist belief come into existence? Put differently: what were the social and cognitive foundations of perception and action up until the end of the seventeenth century, that is, in

---

* Whoever enters this hall as a councillor in official business, should cast away in front of this door all excitements of private life, namely rage, willingness to use force, hate, friendship, flattery, and replace them by the care for city and the people. If you are unfair to someone else, you will be treated similarly before God's Judgement.

[1] John Locke, *Works*, vol. 1 (London, 1823), p. 136 [repr. (Aalen, 1963); another edn under the title *An Essay Concerning Human Understanding*, ed. Alexander Campbell Fraser, vol. 1 (New York, 1959), pp. 121–2]. Anthony Ashley Cooper, Earl of Shaftesbury, *Sensus communis* [1723], ed. in Shaftesbury, *Standard Edition*, vol. 1, part 1 (Stuttgart, 1992), pp. 40–4, 48, 74–6. Francis Hutcheson, *An Inquiry into the Original of Our Ideas of Beauty* (London, 1725), pp. 4–11 [repr. Hutcheson, *Collected Works*, vol. 1, ed. Bernhard Fabian (Hildesheim and New York, 1971)].

the Middle Ages broadly conceived? This chapter presents a history of the changing ways of interconnecting perception with action in the course of the Middle Ages, with a focus on the use of the eyes and the ears. The history of the responses to external 'impressions' on the other sense organs will be reviewed in the third chapter.

Humans select objects to see and hear out of the myriad visible and audible things in the world in accordance with changing standards of perception. Within any given period, the standard of perception may or may not be explicit. If it is explicit, it can be traced in normative or theoretical texts, which are usually laid down in writing. Such texts are usually scrutinised in the context of the history of aesthetic theory. If it is not explicit, it has to be reconstructed from extant pieces of art and music in the same way as the grammar of a spoken language can be reconstructed from its use. Thus pieces of art and music follow a standard of perception, even when explicit norms are not on record. In terms of the history of perception, the processes of making explicit a standard for perceiving art and music reflect in themselves changes of perception. The consequence is that when the standard of perception changes, all those pieces of art and music that physically endure beyond that change will be perceived by viewers or listeners in ways that differ from those at the time of their making. Hence, what artists and musicians perceive and what is perceived as art and music by viewers and listeners, is not constant, but varies across space and time. Thus, whenever the communication between what the artist or the musician wishes to express and what the viewer or listener can perceive is to be successful, visual and aural perception have to follow a certain standard that can facilitate the communication of messages within a defined group at a certain place and within a finite time span. Hence, as pictures can be used to reveal changes of the standard of visual perception, music can provide information about the history of the standard of aural perception. In what follows, pictures are used as evidence for changes of the standard of the visual perception of space, whereas music is discussed as evidence for changes of the standard of the aural perception of time.

Visual perception

The historiography of visual perception has focused on the emergence of mathematically controlled central-point perspective in the course of the fourteenth and fifteenth centuries. Historians and cultural philosophers thus argued that space became visualised first when artists began to create illusions of three-dimensionality in two-dimensional pictures. These historians and philosophers suggested that the illusions of three-dimensional space provided for the only possible representation of space. This suggestion in turn proceeded from the assumption that the concept of space was limited to a continuous ordering device within which the relations of objects and living beings could be depicted in terms of measured distances. However, this assumption

Fig. 1 Stone of Hornhausen, c. 700 AD. Landesamt für Archäologie Sachsen-Anhalt, Museum für Frühgeschichte Halle. A long-haired mounted warrior rides over a ramp above an assembly of two animal bodies facing each other.

is far from obvious, [2] for modern historians and philosophers studying visual perception have often been unwilling to take into account that the definition of space as a continuous ordering device for objects and living beings appeared only in the course of the Middle Ages. The impact of changes of the concept of space on visual perception is thus the issue examined in this section.

A frequently produced type of picture in the early Middle Ages shows a single human figure together with ornaments in the shape of two animal bodies with their heads facing each other. This type of picture was used in stone sculptures, book illuminations and also in pendants such as bracteates and pieces of enamel art. In many cases, the ornamental frame of animal bodies defines the space into which the human figure was placed.[3] Such

[2] See Miriam Schild Bunim, *Space in Medieval Painting and the Forerunners of Perspective* (New York, 1940) [repr. (New York, 1970)]. Hubert Damisch, *The Origin of Perspective* (Cambridge, MA, and London, 1994) [first published (Paris, 1987)]. Jean Gebser, *Ursprung und Gegenwart*, vol. 1 (Stuttgart, 1959), pp. 23–49. John White, *The Birth and Rebirth of Pictorial Space*, 3rd edn (London and Cambridge, MA, 1987) [first published (London, 1957)].

[3] For example, see the displays in *Evangelium Quattuor. Codex Lindisfarnensis*, facsimile edn, 2 vols (Zurich, 1956) [another edn (1960)]. Also ed. by Eric George Millar, *The*

Fig. 2 Christ as the victor over a dragon and a lion. Illumination accompanying Psalm 90, ninth century. Stuttgart, Württembergische Landesbibliothek, MS Bibl. Fol. 23, fol. 107v.

pictures display a specific kind of space that the artist tried to create for the viewer. The artists had space demarcate the activities of a solitary human figure through animal bodies. Consequently, these animal bodies represented forces of the physical environment that appeared to be potentially hostile to human beings.

There were two ways of depicting animal bodies as frames for the activities of human beings. First, animal bodies could be depicted as directing their energies against each other, thereby neutralising them.

Figure 1 displays an aristocrat on horseback, or perhaps even the war god Woden, armed with a spear and a shield. The animal bodies are placed in the bottom part of the picture and remain separate from the horseman. Thus the man rides above the animals without having to encounter or not even knowing of the danger of being attacked by them. The power of the horseman appears to be strong enough to confine the animals to some subterranean part of the world. Already in the ninth century, the Church used the same belief for its portrayal of the figure of Christ as a warrior-band leader and the exemplary winner in struggles against dangerous forces in the physical environment, as the ninth-century picture in Figure 2 shows.[4] In a similar late tenth-century Christian setting, the Danish king Harald had a runic stone made in commemoration for his father Gorm. On one side, the stone was decorated with a picture of Christ as the victor in a struggle with a big worm-like

Lindisfarne Gospels (London, 1923). Partly ed. Janet Backhouse, *The Lindisfarne Gospels*, repr. (London, 2001), pp. 34, 48, 52, 56 [first published (London, 1981)].

4   *Heliand*, vv. 1211b–1278, 4198–4293, ed. Otto Behaghel, 10th edn by Burkhard Taeger, Altdeutsche Textbibliothek IV (Tübingen, 1996), pp. 49–51, 150–3.

Fig. 3 Purse lid from the Sutton Hoo ship burial, early seventh century. London, British Museum. Each ornament on the left and right sides of the bottom row shows a human figure flanked by two animals each with open mouths. They appear to be about to swallow the human figure. Similar ornaments belong to the stock elements of brooches of Salin's style II, contemporary with the Sutton Hoo burial, and they were also featured on sculptured stones.

animal.[5] Still in the twelfth century, a map of the world contained in an English Psalter manuscript displayed two dragons beneath the *ecumene*, that is, literally in the underworld.[6]

But animal bodies could also be depicted as attacking a single human figure that had to defend itself. In this latter case, the animals could be perceived as potentially hostile forces of the environment that could be harmful to humans when they did not direct their energies against themselves (Figure 3). However, early medieval pictures were not merely made for the purpose of representing contemporary perceptions of space and the dangers to which humans could be exposed. It has been noted that some early medieval theologians emphasised the importance of vision and the significance of pictures for the success of the mission. To that end they advocated a middle path between ecstatic forms of picture veneration and the asceticism of iconoclasm. Augustine, for one, defended the didactic use of pictures to visualise ideas correctly through corporeal manifestations.[7] Around AD 600, Pope Gregory I confirmed this task in his letter to Bishop Serenus of Marseille,

---

[5] For a reproduction, see Else Roesdahl, ed., *Wikinger, Waräger, Normannen. Die Skandinavier in Europa. 800–1200* (Mainz, 1992), p. 279.

[6] London, British Library, Add. MS 28681, fol. 9r.

[7] Augustine, *De trinitate*, lib. XI, cap. 1, in *PL* vol. 42, col. 985.

Fig. 4 The enthroned emperor. Frontispiece of the gospel book of Emperor Lothair I, ninth century. Paris, Bibliothèque nationale de France, MS Fonds lat. 266, fol. 1v.

whom he encouraged to ensure that the new and illiterate converts were properly instructed in Christian rules of conduct through pictures.[8] The strategy continued to be applied well into the eleventh century.[9] In the twelfth century, Honorius Augustodunensis defined pictures as 'the literature of the lay people'.[10] The use of pictures was then a standard part of religious service even though Augustine tried to reduce the impact of vision on actions.[11] Thus, late antique and early medieval Christian authors did not contest the view that visual perception was a process through which the picture as the object of perception interacted with the perceiving persons or groups, and did so in such a way that the viewers were led towards predetermined reactions. The specific type of these reactions could identify viewers as members of certain groups and could likewise exclude outsiders. In short, the late antique and early medieval standard of visual perception entailed the expectation that perception was to be translated into predetermined action.[12]

Numerous monastic books with their frequently observed deictic elements confirm the expectation that perception ought to be translated into action. In a few works it was made explicit that the pictures had the task of admonishing their viewers. One is extant in a Gospel Book (Figure 4), which contains a picture of Emperor Lothair I sitting on the throne. The picture focuses on the personage of the emperor and displays only some columns of rudimentary architecture and other manifestations of space. Thus the viewer can neither gather solely from the picture that the throne is placed inside a building nor ascertain what distances exist between the throne and the columns framing it on either side. The emperor is made to sit everywhere or nowhere. A dedication poem facing the picture explains that the viewer should say prayers for the emperor.

In this case, the situational context was liturgical: the Gospel Book appears to have been regarded as a donation by the emperor to the monastery of St Martin in Tours (where the book was kept). In return for the book the

---

8   Gregory I, *Registrum epistolarum*, no. 9, ed. Paul Ewald, Ludo Moritz Hartmann, MGH Epp., vol. 2 (Hanover, 1892–99), p. 208.

9   In 1025, the Synod of Arras renewed Gregory's proposal. See Acts of the Council of Arras, cap. XIV, ed. Mansi, vol. 19, col. 454 (Paris, 1901).

10   Honorius Augustodunensis, *Gemma animae*, cap. 132, in *PL* vol. 172, col. 586.

11   Augustine, *De Genesi ad litteram*, lib. XII, cap. 8, 20, in *PL* vol. 34, col. 461.

12   For the Iconoclast controversy, cf. the *Libri Carolini* lib. III, cap. 23, ed. Hubert Bastgen MGH Conc. Suppl. (Hanover, 1924), pp. 150–5 [to be newly edited by Ann Freeman and Paul Meyvaert (MGH, Conc. Suppl. I)]. The Occidental propaganda against Byzantium maintained that pictures should convey to their onlookers some meaning of historical events and should direct minds from falsehood to truth. But even in Latin Christendom, Pope Gregory's letter to Bishop Serenus received an interpolation that could allow affective forms of picture veneration under papal authority. See Micheel Camille, 'The Gregorian Definition Revisited. Writing and the Medieval Image', in *L'image. Fonctions et usages des images dans l'Occident médiéval*, ed. Jérôme Baschet and Jean-Claude Schmitt (Paris, 1996), pp. 89–108. Jean-Claude Schmitt, 'L'Occident, Nicée II et les images du VIIIe au XIIIe siècle', in *Nicée II. 787–1987. Douze siècles d'images religieuses*, ed. François Boespflug and Nicolas Lossky (Paris, 1987), pp. 271–301.

monks were obliged to say prayers for the emperor after his death. Through
the poetic text accompanying the picture, the monastic readers of the book
were reminded of their obligation. The picture had the task of admonishing
the *illiterati* among the monks of St Martin in Tours to practise the *memoria*
of the emperor as their previous benefactor.[13] Similarly, Emperor Louis the
Pious had a list drawn up of fifty-four monasteries early in the ninth century
that were exempted from their duties to give 'donations' or provide military
service to the emperor but were still obliged to say prayers for the well-being
of the emperor and his sons and for the stability of the empire.[14] In its capacity as a reminder of monastic duties the picture could stand by itself, as it did
not per se need a comment. But a literate and poetically gifted scribe could as
well make an effort to compose some explanatory verses to specify verbally
what was already self-evident from the picture itself, namely that perception
should translate into action.

Early medieval sources abound with references to admonitions that powerful persons directed at less powerful people through gestures, in writing and
in speech. In a few cases, the purpose of the admonitions was specified. For
one, in 789 Charlemagne issued a law called 'general admonition' for the
entire kingdom under his control and declared that it was his purpose to
correct mistakes, prevent lack of decency and make known the rules for the
conduct of life that he considered to be correct.[15] Likewise, in the tenth
century, Bishop Atto of Vercelli wrote an *admonitio* for the priests of his
diocese to remind them of their duty to observe the rules of the Church.[16]
These authoritative instructions were supplemented by the correspondence
among persons of equal rank. Thus, St Boniface and other eighth-century
missionaries of either sex exchanged admonitions and mutually reminded
each other of the necessity to fulfil their duties.[17]

In the early Middle Ages, actors could thus recognise perception as a source
of action. They could do so within a cognitive and normative framework in
which they expected to be able to act efficiently if they could receive a significant share of their energies and physical strength from external forces. These
forces could be superhuman agents, pre-Christian deities, the Christian divinity and its temporal representatives, rulers or other persons of high rank and
unusual power, living and deceased members of kin groups, and friends. Such
an expectation was viable only under the condition that persons were accustomed to assist others against the irksome or evil, awe-inspiring or dangerous
impacts of the physical environment and against outside groups. In other
words, the belief that perception could determine action required the confi-

13 The poem with the headline *Sigilai versus ad Hlotharium imperatorem* has been printed
    separately in Ernst Dümmler, ed., MGH Poet., vol. 2 (Berlin, 1884), p. 671, vv. 23–7.
14 Ed. Alfred Boretius, MGH Cap., no. 171, vol. 1 (Hanover, 1883), pp. 351–2.
15 Charlemagne, 'Admonitio generalis', 23. 3. 789, ed. Alfred Boretius, MGH Cap., no. 22,
    vol. 1 (Hanover, 1883), pp. 53–62.
16 Atto of Vercelli, *Capitulare*, in *PL* vol. 134, col. 27.
17 Michael Tangl, ed., *Die Briefe des Heiligen Bonifatius und Lullus*, nos 9, 23, 27, 61, 64,
    73–5, etc., MGH, Epp. Sel. I (Berlin, 1916).

dence on the part of the actors that perception was subjected to group-bound standards. Consequently, perceived persons or objects and actors were integrated into networks of close social bonds and ties. These particularistic groups formed several types that were vertically arrayed in the sense that they persisted next to and competed with each other. Hence there was no overarching integrative concept of society, and anyone could maintain simultaneous memberships in a variety of different types of group. Within these types of group, be they kin groups, neighbourhood groups, groups by contract or political groups, the ability of certain persons and supernatural or divine agents to admonish and protect others without needing to be admonished or protected displayed their power. Such power frequently allowed outstanding persons, mainly deities in the pre-Christian religions as well as Christ and high-ranking rulers, to confront the physical environment with the hope of success and even without the help of others.

These attitudes predetermined actions that emphasised the dependency of persons on their physical and socio-political environments. It is difficult to overlook the fact that the early medieval pictorial representation of space was closely paralleled by similar perceptions of the physical environment during the early Middle Ages when dense woodlands and marshes surrounded many settlements and were referred to as 'deserts' inhabited by wild beasts and dangerous creatures.[18] The inhabitants of settlements tried to avoid going into or crossing the woodlands alone and preferred to do so in groups, except in cases of emergency. In the early Middle Ages, these attitudes made sense when long-distance migrations and short-distance colonisation movements loomed large. These movements exposed actors to hazards in the hostile and dangerous physical environment, when the weather, plants and animals posed numerous threats. Under such circumstances, the human body was regarded as the recipient of various external influences and pressures that might be negative as well as positive in kind. Actors conducted their lives under the impression that whatever they could or ought to accomplish was possible only in so far as each member of a group acted in agreement with the wishes and demands of senior or powerful members of their group and in accordance with the demands believed to have been released by the divine agency or superhuman forces in the physical environment.

According to this standard of perception, persons experienced themselves as weak and frail. It suggested that the pressures and restrictions that the physical environment posed against human activity could only be resisted or over-

---

[18] For the use of the Medieval Latin word *desertum* for woods, see Abbo of St-Germain-des-Près, 'Sermon 2', in Abbo, *22 Predigten*, ed. Ute Önnerfors, Lateinische Sprache und Literatur des Mittelalters XVI (Frankfurt, 1985), p. 15 [ninth century]. Bartholomaeus Anglicus, *Liber de proprietatibus rerum*, lib. XIV, cap. 51, ed. Georg Barthold Pontanus a Braitenberg (Frankfurt, 1601), p. 620 [thirteenth century; repr. (Frankfurt, 1964)]. English version by John of Trevisa (London, 1495), p. 486 [Trevisa's version, ed. M. C. Seymour (Oxford, 1988)]. The Old English epic of Beowulf describes marshes as the living space of Grendel and Grendel's mother: *Beowulf and the Fight at Finnsburh*, vv. 103–5. ed. Frederick Klaeber, 3rd edn (Lexington, MA, 1950), p. 5.

Fig. 5 A residential hilltop castle; early sixteenth century, from Maximilian I,
Weisskunig (Vienna, 1775), fol. 21. By permission from the Albertina, Vienna.
Such landscape depictions were rare in the Middle Ages because of the
qualitative segregation of spaces.

come through the protection-generating grouping of persons under the
leadership of someone with extraordinary and outstanding capabilities. Many
of these groups were perceived as continuing beyond the lifetime of a person.
If they were political groups, they provided to their members a framework of
politically relevant traditions through which norms and rules of conduct
could be transmitted; if they were kin groups, they incorporated each
member into genealogical networks comprised of living and dead members as
the extant *Libri memoriales*[19] and the custom of burying the dead on kin land
documented.[20]

19 E.g. *Liber memorialis von Remiremont*, ed. Eduard Hlawitschka, Karl Schmid and Gerd
Tellenbach, MGH, Libri mem. I (Munich, 1970).
20 See Barbara Scholkmann, 'Normbildung und Normveränderung im Grabbrauch des

In summary, the early medieval standard of perception comprised, among other things, the principle that perception should translate into predetermined actions that persons were expected to follow the didactic use of pictures. These patterns of action were group-centred in the sense that they were determined by and characteristic of the specific norms and values accepted by particularistically organised groups. They transmitted and reinforced attitudes through which ordinary persons could expect to remain capable of overcoming the hazards of the physical and socio-political environments as long as they remained integrated into groups.

The group-centred standard of perception underwent a dramatic change from the twelfth century. Since then, the standard of perception has become primarily space-centred in various ways. Initially, during the twelfth, thirteenth and fourteenth centuries, space came to be depicted, not as an integrated and continuous field of action, but as the aggregate sum of hierarchically arrayed places with which different qualities were associated. According to this standard of perception, higher places were ranked as the better ones. Therefore, what mattered in this standard of perception was no longer interconnectedness with group-specific action but recognition of hierarchically ordered qualities of places. Put differently, displays of the effectiveness of persons' actions no longer consisted in demonstrations of their power to generate protection and transmit traditions but in their capability to obtain the highest possible position in the hierarchies of places. There were many manifestations of this change.

Within the physical environment, the change from a group-centred to a space-centred standard of perception became manifest in new forms of architecture. From the eleventh century, groups of privileged aristocrats began to move out of farming settlements and established their residences in hilltop castles that were built on uphill locations wherever possible and thus were visibly elevated above the settlements of the peasant farming population. Aristocratic castles were also placed on hills overlooking urban settlements or on artificial mounds where the natural landscape did not offer elevated locations (Figure 5). The same topographical hierarchisation appeared in newly founded urban communities of towns and cities within and north of the Alps. Some of the settlements were built on spurs of elevated land sometimes immediately below a castle, overlooking the open scenery and visible from afar. They also displayed the spatial hierarchy of places by allocating the higher parts to a hilltop castle, a palace and the residence of ruling urban patriciates of traders, while lower-ranking artisans and craftsmen were usually confined to low-lying parts. These arrangements showed hierarchies of ranks among social groups, which were not vertically arrayed, but horizontally stratified. Uphill residences gave to their occupants the possibility to demon-

Mittelalters. Die Bestattungen in Kirchen', in *Prozesse der Normbildung und Normveränderung im mittelalterlichen Europa*, ed. Doris Ruhe and Karl-Heinz Spieß (Stuttgart, 2000), pp. 93–117.

Fig. 6 Three ladies watching a knightly tournament, thirteenth century. Codex Manesse, Heidelberg, University Library, Cod. Pal. Germ. 848, fol. 42r: 'Her Albrecht von Haigerloch'.

strate the success of their actions in terms of accumulating capital and political power.

Likewise, pictures ceased to be the instruments for translating perception into action and, instead, became instruments for visualising hierarchies. One of the best indications for this change comes from the thirteenth-century *Manesse* manuscript held by Heidelberg University Library. A number of its illuminations display arrangements within which human figures are placed into hierarchically arrayed groups and communicate among themselves through gestures. Figure 6 displays a knightly tournament in which a group of female figures placed on the upper level of the picture make gestures of sympathy towards male figures on the lower level. The gestures suggest that the persons on the upper level provided encouragement and sympathy to the persons on the lower level. In the case of this, as in the case of other pictures of the same manuscript, the fighting knights were displayed as receiving support from the women watching the tournament from above. However, the knights were neither depicted as threatened by potentially dangerous forces of the environment, nor were they shown using their own physical strength and bodily energy to overcome obstacles presented by the physical world. Instead, they were made to direct their energies against each other and compete for the position of the strongest in what is depicted as an exclusively human-made environment. Moreover, the artist does not seem to have made an effort to include the viewers of the picture, who are hardly expected to translate into action what they perceived in the picture. That is to say, the artist may have intended to convey to the viewer the impression that female sympathisers could strengthen the fighting power of males but there was no indication that viewers were expected to articulate similar sympathies. Hence these pictures fulfilled the task of giving a visual display of spatial hierarchies. This visualisa-tion of spatial hierarchies produced a new type of message sent by the artist to the viewer. Artists no longer expected viewers to generate predetermined reactions when looking at the picture; instead, artists positioned viewers as observers of interactions among persons in different hierarchically arrayed spaces without being themselves involved. Pictures began to address the viewers with words to convey their messages. These messages appeared in writing in the picture. More straightforwardly, reports of visions could contend that visionaries and otherwise gifted persons could hear crucifixes speaking to them.[21]

The depiction of spatial hierarchies appeared even more explicitly in other pictures from the same time period. Figure 7, taken from a mid-thirteenth-century manuscript of the Old Testament, consists of four scenes arrayed from the top left to the bottom right. At the top left, King David sits on a throne and directs a war, whereas the other three parts represent battle scenes. David's throne is elevated above the ground, and the king points with his right arm above the head of a servant kneeling before him. To the right of the kneeling servant one sees the rear sides of two horses bearing knights. The knights on horseback turn back towards David to receive his commands. Architecture indicates that David's throne is located inside a building, whereas the knights in whose direction he points appear to be outside. David's crowned head is raised far above that of the kneeling servant and is

---

21 Thus the eleventh-century virgin Irmgard of Süchteln (near Cologne) was reported to have been commanded by the crucifix in the church of San Paolo fuori le mure in Rome to greet the crucifix in Cologne Cathedral when returning home. The life of Irmgard was written in the fourteenth century. The fact that the crucifix of San Paolo was made c. 1310–c. 1320 supports the argument that the vision does not belong to Irmgard's life-time but to the time of the writing of her life. See Otto Lehmann-Brockhaus, *Schriftquellen zur Kunstgeschichte des 11. und 12. Jahrhunderts für Deutschland, Lothringen und Italien*, nr 2516 (Berlin, 1938), p. 540. Likewise, Thomas of Celano's Life of St Francis of Assisi reports that the saint saw how the lips were moving while the cru-cifix at San Damiano was speaking to him. See 'Fr. Thomae de Celano vita secunda S. Francisci', lib. VI, cap. 10, in Thomas de Celano, *Vita prima et vita secunda S. Francisci Assisiensis* (Quaracchi, 1926), pp. 136–7.

Fig. 7　King David fights a war. Ms containing the Old Testament, thirteenth
century. New York, Pierpont Morgan Library, MS 638, fol. 41r.

only slightly lower than the heads of the two mounted knights. The picture
thus represents the relations between the king and the knights in proportions
that differ from what would be considered appropriate in modern representations of space. No indication of the distances between the king and the
knights is given, and no obvious dividing line demarcates the inside of the
building with the royal throne from the outside battle scenes. The size and
height of the figures are without proportion in that the king, while seated on
the throne, appears to be almost as tall as the mounted knights and, at the
same time, elevated far above the kneeling servant, who occupies the space in
between the king and the knights. Hence this artist gave preference to the

depiction of spatial hierarchies wherein the king as the holder of the highest secular office appeared as the dominant feature in the picture. Moreover, in the battle scenes, close mêlées of knights in action are shown, and one or two horses are interspersed into each battle scene, appearing as overriding features.

Because artists displayed space as an aggregate of hierarchically ordered places in the twelfth and thirteenth centuries, perception was then focused on the world of tangible realities that were ordered in space according to their qualities or the relative degree of importance that artists assigned to them. Viewers no longer interacted with the picture in such a way that predetermined actions could be expected in consequence of their perceptions. Instead, the viewers themselves objictified the pictures as part of the outside world of tangible realities. Thus the previously close interconnectedness between perception and action was severed, and perception began to exist as an autonomous activity in its own sake.

The widest possible extension of this new standard of perception in pictorial art was already accomplished during the early thirteenth century with the monumental *mappaemundi* drawn for ecclesiastical, mainly monastic, institutions. In these world maps, the entire world became objictified as a hierarchical order of past and present places before or below the divinity. Hugh of St Victor wrote an instruction on map-making in which he demanded that terrestrial paradise as the place of the origin of humankind should be located in the East as the uppermost part of the *mappamundi* closest to the divinity.[22] Various levels of hierarchy were distinguished by the relative distance between the divinity at the highest point of the map, usually above the world and any other location of a place in the map. Indeed, as Hugh of St Victor demanded, terrestrial paradise is usually to be found in the upper part of the *mappaemundi* within the *ecumene*. The space below paradise was mostly inhabited by strange creatures and was interconnected with the rest of the *ecumene* through the four rivers allegedly flowing out of paradise according to the Old Testament (*Genesis* 2). The upper half of a *mappamundi* was usually allocated to Asia, whereas Africa and Europe shared the lower part. Sometimes, as in the example shown in Figure 8, the centre of the world was occupied by the city of Jerusalem, below which one could perceive the Mediterranean Sea as the inland lake of the Roman Empire of Antiquity. The lower end of the *mappamundi* was sometimes marked by Hercules's pillars as the symbol of the end of the world. The round shape of the world appeared

---

[22] Hugh of St Victor, *De arca Noe mystica*, cap. XIV, in *PL* vol. 176, col. 700. Similarly Vincent of Beauvais, 'De Asia et eius capite quod est paradisus', in Vincent, *Speculum naturale*, lib. XXX, cap. 2 (Douai, 1624), col. 2400. Earlier verbal descriptions of visible images of the earth, such as by Isidore of Seville, *Etymologiarum sive originum libri XX*, lib. VIII, cap. 11, 61, ed. Wallace M. Lindsay (Oxford, 1911) [repr. (Oxford, 1985)], and by Theodulf of Orleans, 'Carmen XLVII', ed. Ludwig Traube, 'Theodulfi Carmina', in: MGH Poet., vol. 1, ed. Ernst Dümmler (Berlin, 1881), pp. 547–8, used the simile of mother nature.

Fig. 8 World map (*mappamundi*, T-O format), thirteenth century, Hereford
Cathedral.

like an expanded letter O, while the borders among Africa and Europe in the
lower part and Asia in the upper part resembled the letter T.

This type of *mappamundi* did not only depict the world in its spatial
dimension as the inhabitable *ecumene* but also its temporal dimension as
sacred history. Paradise marked the beginning of human history, seen as the
sequence of four world empires spanning the period between the expulsion
from paradise and Judgement Day. According to the late and post-Roman
understanding of sacred history, the Roman Empire was the last of these
world empires.[23] Hence, the Roman Empire was located opposite paradise,
that is, at the bottom of the world map. Thus, the combination of spatial and

---

[23] Following St Jerome's commentary on the Book of Daniel. See Jerome,
Commentariorvm in Danielem Libri III [IV], cap. I, 2. 31–35, ed. Francisco Gloria,
CCSL. LXXV A (Turnhout, 1964), 793–5.

Fig. 9 Ambrogio Lorenzetti, View of a city, first half of the fourteenth century. Siena, Pinoteca Nazionale.

temporal elements of the hierarchical ordering of the world[24] led to a picture of the *ecumene* in which Asia occupied the highest level, in proximity to the divinity, while Europe was at the lowest position, most remote from the divinity. The *mappaemundi* thus visualised the perception of the world as the divinely willed and hierarchically ordered aggregate sum of places through which humankind was journeying from paradise to Judgement Day. The *ecumene* appeared as the universal theatre of human action without human-made borders and with only the divinely willed natural boundaries.

However, in the fourteenth century, the hierarchical ordering of spaces with different qualities and the visualisation of these hierarchies in depictions of space began to get out of date. They began to be complemented by efforts to display space as integrated and continuous to the extent that its permeability could be visible in pictures. Already before the middle of the fourteenth century, Ambrogio Lorenzetti, a member of the Sienese school of painters, displayed the city within its environment. He chose the bird's-eye perspective to depict the location of the city with roads leading to and away from it and made no attempt to visualise hierarchies (Figure 9). At about the same time,

---

[24] Such hierarchies were described explicitly in philosophical tracts concerning the ordering of the world, among them the thirteenth-century *Sententiae* by Bonaventure, II *Sententiae* [Petri Lombardi], dist. 12 a. 2 q. 1 arg. 4, dist. 13 a. 2 q. 2, fols 302b, 321a–321b, ed. Clemens Baeumker, *Witelo. Ein Philosoph und Naturforscher des XIII. Jahrhunderts* (Munster, 1908), pp. 398–9 [repr., ed. Ludwig Hödl (Munster, 1991)].

Fig. 10 Ambrogio Lorenzetti, *The good government*, 1337–1339. Siena, Palazzo Pubblico.

the same painter created a series of fresco allegories of good and bad government, which he placed into a city as its architectural framework (Figure 10). In these allegories, Lorenzetti rendered urban space permeable so as to allow viewers an estimation of the distances between the depicted human figures and architectural structures. For example, viewers could catch a glimpse of a teacher instructing school children inside a building, watch merchants offering their goods in an adjacent building, and observe women dancing in an open space within the city. The houses appeared to be built on a rather steep slope, which may have been an appropriate representation of the city of Siena

for whose city hall the frescos were painted. The architecture of the city followed the stereotypical pattern of locating the residences of the more affluent
citizens in the upper part. But the painter placed no additional emphasis on
depicting further spatial hierarchies. Instead, he depicted the space in the city
as integrated, continuous and permeable. Admittedly, the painter sought to
make visually explicit sets of messages. For example, he tried to display the
well-governed city as an example of good government in general. In this
limited sense of conveying messages, this picture was devised as a means of
prompting predetermined reactions among the viewers, namely to accept the
city as the model of good government. Similarly, mid-fourteenth-century
Saxon city law placed courts under divine control and stipulated that courtrooms be furnished with pictures of the Last Judgement to remind judges of
their duty to pass fair verdicts. Although some of these paintings were
destroyed or covered in areas where the Reformation took root, the demand
that they should be created continued to prevail elsewhere in the sixteenth
century.[25] Similarly, pictures of infamy that were shown in town halls and
other public buildings continued to display to debtors and potentially disloyal
citizens what their fates were going to be.[26] Lastly, the large number of votive
pictures dedicated to saints attests to the continuing trust in the power of pictures. At first glance, the purpose of these pictures might be regarded as a
variant of the early medieval interconnectedness of perception and action.
However, there is a fundamental difference. When looking at early medieval
pictures, viewers were expected to act in specific preconceived ways. Yet the
late medieval painters made no attempt to determine viewers' actions by
means of the messages that they associated with their pictures. Instead, they
strove at most to provide moral guidance that left a substantive variety of
choices for action to those viewers if they chose to act in accordance with such
guidance.

Thirteenth-century scientists went beyond this standard of perception and
tried to boost the formation of new theoretical as well as empirical attitudes
towards space. They began to define the environment as the space in between
objects, that is, as a continuum in which objects exist and living beings can
move.[27] Simultaneously, some towns and cities began to open themselves up

25 For example, see the allegory of good government designed for the Regensburg town
hall by Melchior Bocksberger, c. 1573/74. Museen der Stadt Regensburg. Detail printed
in Susan Tipton, *Res publica bene ordinata. Regentenspiegel und Bilder vom guten Regi-
ment. Rathausdekorationen in der Frühen Neuzeit*, Studien zur Kunstgeschichte. CIV
(Hildesheim, 1996), p. 555, Pl. 29.

26 On the legal regulations concerning pictures in courtrooms, see Alexander von Daniels
and Franz Freiherr von Gruben, ed., *Das sächsische Weichbildrecht. Jus Municipale
Saxonicum*, art. XVI, vol. 1 (Berlin, 1858), col. 256. Ulrich Tengler, *Leyenspiegel*
(Strasbourg, 1530), fol. XVIIr [first published as *Layen Spiegel. Von rechtmässigen
ordnungen in Bürgerlichen und peinlichen regimenten* (Augsburg, 1509)].

27 See Albertus Magnus, *De caelo et mundo*, lib. III, cap. 1, lib. III, cap. 2, in *Alberti Magni
Opera omnia* V, 1, ed. Paul Hossfeld, (Munster, 1971), pp. 55–9. Roger Bacon,
Perspectiva, Distinctio III, cap. 1, ed. David C. Lindberg, *Roger Bacon and the Origins of
Perspectiva in the Middle Ages. A Critical Edition and English Translation of Bacon's*

to their rural environments, intensifying their ties with neighbouring villages through trade and migration and making use of nearby woodlands. Town and city councils strove to establish themselves as lords over neighbouring villages and other urban communities, wealthy urban inhabitants bought private land outside the towns and cities, and merchant companies as well as municipal governments established trade and political networks. Already in the late thirteenth century the trading network comprised the entire tri-continental 'Old World' of Africa, Asia and Europe. Individuals began to penetrate into awkward woodlands and mountain areas, and they dared to do so alone. One particularly famous example is a letter that Petrarch sent to his teacher Francesco Dionigi di Borgo San Sepolcro c. 1355. In his letter Petrarch reported on his experiences of climbing Mount Ventoux in southern France. He described the landscape as permeable although he had in fact been warned of all sorts of risks and dangers before starting the expedition. He disclosed his surprise when, upon reaching the mountain peak, he became aware of the openness of the landscape and the indefiniteness of space.[28] The letter is noteworthy because Petrarch recorded the experience of having been told that no one had ever climbed the mountain before. Thus, throughout the thirteenth and fourteenth centuries, an unprecedented degree of human penetration across and into space occurred and made it difficult to support the previous perception of space as aggregates of hierarchically ordered places with different qualities.

Therefore, the perception and depiction of space as integrated, continuous and permeable were incompatible with the previous visualisation of space as the aggregate sum of qualified places. This was so because artists could only depict space in this new way, if they dissociated from qualities or assessments of importance what was situated in the upper or lower portions of their pic-

---

Perspectiva with Introduction and Notes (Oxford, 1996), pp. 326–9. John of Rodington, In libros sententiarum. Ms. Biblioteca Apostolica Vaticana lat. 5306, fol. 8ra, ed. Katherine Tachau, *Vision and Certitude in the Age of Ockham. Epistemology and the Foundations of Semantics. 1250–1345* (Leiden, 1988), p. 227. Strangely, Christoph Wulf, 'Auge', in Wulf, ed., *Vom Menschen. Handbuch Historische Anthropologie* (Weinheim and Basle, 1997), p. 449, categorises Albert the Great's theory of vision as purely Aristotelian and Roger Bacon's as Platonian and Alhazenian.

28 Francesco Petrarca, Epistolae familiares, lib. IV, cap. 1, in Petrarca, *Epistoli*, ed. Ugo Dotti (Turin, 1978), pp. 118–34 [repr. (Turin, 1983)]. Although descriptions of the openness of the landscape are rare before the fourteenth century, Petrarch's report has usually been seen against the background of the literary images of Antiquity to which he referred in his letter, and it has been argued that his view of the landscape was shaped by these images rather than by his experience. See Giuseppe Billanovich, 'Petrarca und der Ventou in *Petrarca*, ed. August Buck, Wege der Forschung. CCCLIII (Darmstadt, 1977), pp. 444–63. Xenja von Ertzdorff, 'Reisende berichten. Schriftliche Kommunikationsmuster im Wandel. Bergbeschreibungen mit Panoramablick und das "historische Fenster" in der Landschaft', in *Kommunikationsformen im Wandel der Zeit. Vom mittelalterlichen Heldenepos zum elektronischen Hypertext*, ed Gerd Fritz and Andreas H. Jucker (Tübingen, 2000), pp. 239–42. Karlheinz Stierle, *Petrarcas Landschaften. Zur Geschichte ästhetischer Landschaftserfahrung*, Schriften und Vorträge des Petrarca-Instituts XXIX (Krefeld, 1979).

tures. Depicting space as integrated, continuous and permeable demanded that the order of the picture be constructed on an imaginary focal point outside the picture, so that a central perspective emerged that could create to the viewer the illusion of some three-dimensional 'depth' of the visualised space.

Correspondingly, Cennino Cennini cast his explication of the technique of central-point perspective into the description of the way to paint mountains.[29] Leonardo da Vinci followed him and other fifteenth-century theorists of painting, such as Piero della Francesca[30] and Leon Battista Alberti,[31] when he metaphorically described the central-point perspective in the following way:

> Perspective is the visible law according to which – as all experience confirms – all things send their images in pyramidal lines to the eye; and bodies of the same size will form a pyramid with a more or less accurate angle depending on their distances. It seems to me that pyramidal lines are lines that depart from the outside boundaries of the objects, merge at a distance and lead to one single terminal point. A point shall be what cannot be divided at any place and the terminal point of the pyramidal lines is that which is located in the eye and which receives all tips of the pyramids.'[32]

From the fifteenth century, the central-point perspective has dominated artists' attitudes toward space in Europe. The new standard promoted the perception of the physical environment as allowing, if not requesting, persons to trespass over boundaries and move across integrated and continuous space through the use of their own physical energies. By the sixteenth century, the perception of integrated and permeable space as open for human trespass reached a stage in which the openness of space could be depicted even in cases where it was recognisably contrary to experience, as in the etching shown in Figure 11. The etching shows a port city located on the shores of an ocean

---

29 Cennino d'Andrea Cennini, *Il libro del' arte* [c. 1437], cap. LXXXVIII, transl. by Daniel V. Thompson, *The Craftsman's Handbook* (New York, 1950), p. 57.

30 Piero della Francesca, *De prospettiva pingendi. A facsimile of Parma, Biblioteca Palatina, Ms 1576* [c. 1450], Documents of Art and Architectural History. Ser. II, vol. ` New York and Williamstown, 1992), fol. 4r.

31 Leon Battista Alberti, *De pictura praestantissima* (Basle, 1540), pp. 38–41 [repr. (London, 1976); another edn by Hubert Janitschek, *Kleinere kunsttheoretische Schriften*, Quellenschriften für Kunstgeschichte und Kunsttechnik des Mittelalters und der Renaissance XI (Vienna, 1877), p. 79], who defined painting as a 'window through which we look at the world'.

32 Leonardo da Vinci [Francesco Melzi], MS A, fol. 3r (Paris, Bibliothèque nationale de France, formerly Milan, Biblioteca Ambrosiana). Leonardo's scattered remarks on painting were converted into a book manuscript probably by Melzi, heir to Leonardo's manuscripts, and appeared under the title *Trattado della pittura*. (Paris, 1651). For an edn see Carlo Pedretti and Giorgio Baratta, ed., *Leonardo e il libro di pittura* (Rome, 1997). Similarly at the same time: Jean Pelerin, *De artificiali perspectiva* (Tulli, 1505). For a later reflection of Leonardo's description, see Joachim von Sandrat, *Teutsche Academie der edlen Bau-, Bild- und Mahlerey-Künste* (Nuremberg, 1675), p. 90.

Fig. 11 Theodore de Bry, View of the port of Seville, sixteenth century. Seville, actually located on the Guadalquivir River and accessible from the open sea only at high tide, is portrayed as a coastal settlement, presumably because it was the starting point for Columbus's first voyage as well as for scores of sixteenth-century European migrants for their journeys westwards across the ocean. From Theodore de Bry, *Americae pars quarta* (Frankfurt, 1594), pl. I. Göttingen, Niedersächsische Staats- und Universitätsbibliothek, 4 Itin. I, 3848.

with ocean-faring vessels arriving at and departing from its harbour. It is included in a best-selling book published in 1594 by Theodore de Bry on transatlantic migration, and takes notice of the fact that during the sixteenth century most European migrants to America left from the city of Seville. Consequently, the publisher identified the coastal port city as Seville. However, the picture does not take into account the fact that Seville is located on the Guadalquivir River and is accessible from the open sea only at high tide.[33] The publisher was aware of the location of the city and still used an incompatible image. This can be surmised because, in the caption, he admitted that the scene did not agree with the actual topographical conditions of Seville, and excused himself with the argument that the etcher did not have an appropri-

---

[33] Therefore, other sixteenth-century pictures display Seville as a port city on riverbanks; for example, the mid-sixteenth-century painting by Alonso Sanchez Coello of Columbus's departure from Seville in 1498.

ate model to depict Seville correctly. If this was so, the printer could have chosen an impression of any city as his model. However, as his choice fell on a coastal port city, he confirmed that what mattered to him first and foremost in the case of Seville was the visualisation of accessibility to open sea rather than the display of the actual topography. Accessibility to the open sea was a typical feature in sixteenth-century illustrations of the continent of Europe and was also reflected in the contemporary exceptionalist theory that Europe differed from the rest of the world because of its openness to the sea. Thus the image of Europe's accessibility to the open sea can be found in the marginal additions to the global map printed in the collection of travel reports by Simon Grynaeus in 1532. These marginal additions symbolise the continents and have been attributed to Hans Holbein, the Younger. One of the symbols shows Europe in the form of a coast of the open sea viewed from a building with two columns. A walking traveller named VARTOMA approaches the sea-shore. The name corresponds with Ludovico de Varthema who travelled to India on his own early in the sixteenth century, joined Portuguese service in India, returned to Portugal in 1508 and published a book on his journey in 1510.[34] European openness to the sea was frequently referred to in the descriptions of the world by the Venetian scholar Giovanni Botero.[35]

Summary of visual perception

The history of the standard of visual perception during the Middle Ages displays fundamental changes in the patterns of interaction between artists as the senders and viewers as receivers of messages. During the early Middle Ages, artists and viewers shared the belief that the viewers' perceptions ought to be translated into predetermined actions. Perception was then group-centred, and pictures were not merely means of transmitting messages but media in the genuine sense of the word. That is to say that they were the instruments that were considered capable of inducing their viewers to perform predetermined actions. During the twelfth century, the innate relationship between perception and action was severed when artists began to place priority on depicting spatial hierarchies. Perception was no longer focused only on the maintenance of group integration but obtained the further purpose of visualising different qualities of places in space. The diffusion of the central-point perspective in the fifteenth century finalised the process through which perception gradually became focused on permitting

---

[34] The Holbein map is the frontispiece to Symon Grynaeus, *Novus orbis regionum ac insularum veteribus incognitarum* (Basle, 1532). Ludovico de Varthema's report has been edited by Lincoln Davis Hammond, *Travelers in Disguise. Narratives of Eastern Travel. Poggio Bracciolini and Ludovico de Varthema* (Cambridge, MA, 1963). Folkert Reichert, ed., *Reisen im Orient. Ludovico de Varhema*, Fremde Kulturen in alten Berichten II (Sigmaringen, 1996).

[35] On Botero, see Aldo Albònico, *Il mondo americano di Giovanni Botero* (Rome, 1989).

orientation in space, and the role of pictures was reduced to that of transmitting non-verbal messages.

Aural perception

This section will focus on changes in experiences of time and aural perception throughout the course of the Middle Ages, drawing on evidence from music performances and the theory of music. Although equal in importance with the pictorial arts, music as a medium of aural perception can be briefly dealt with here, because the major changes of the standards of aural perception coincide with similar changes of the standards of visual perception.

As far as we know, much of the performance of music in the early Middle Ages was enacted for the purpose of provoking certain effects on the performers as well as the audience.[36] St Augustine, who tried to control these effects, admitted that songs could incite religious fervour in his mind.[37] Similarly, Cassiodore believed in the positive effects of the singing of psalms.[38] Further sources, among them ninth- and even eleventh-century ecclesiastical canons, showed that early medieval aural perception, similar to visual perception, was regarded as a means of provoking or stimulating predetermined actions among churchgoers.[39]

The staunch resistance by Church authorities to singing and dancing performances in churchyards and in or near religious buildings, their denunciation of such practices as frivolous or even 'magical' and their invocation of divine punishments for singing in churchyards and in religious buildings was reflected early on in a number of narrative sources. Thus Venantius Fortunatus has the story of a fifth-century nun in the convent of St Radegundis who heard dancers sing songs that she had composed some years earlier. The performance must have taken place in proximity to the nunnery, and Venantius did not forget to mention that the nun was embarrassed about the record of her previous seemingly unholy doings.[40] Still early in the eighth century, Bede reported the capability of Caedmon, a well-known singer, to

---

[36] Isidore of Seville, Etymologiarum, lib. III, cap. 17 (see note 17). Anicius Manlius Torquatus Severinus Boethius, *De musica*, in *PL*, vol. 63, col. 1169. For stimuli believed to be related to aural perception, see Gregory I (see note 7), p. 200. MGH Poet., ed. Ernst Dümmler, vol. 2 (Berlin, 1884), p. 671, vv. 23–7.

[37] Augustine, 'Sermo CCCXI', cap. 5, in *PL*, vol. 38, col. 1415.

[38] Cassiodore, *Expositio in psalmos*, Ps. XCVII, ed. Marcus Adriaen, CCSL. XCII (Turnhout, 1958), p. 878.

[39] Synod of Mainz [813], cap. 48, ed. Albert Werminghoff, MGH Conc., vol. 2, part 1 (Hanover, 1906), p. 272. Regino of Prüm, *Liber de synodalibus causis et disciplinis ecclesiasticis*, lib. I, cap. 304; lib. I, cap. 398; lib. II, cap. 5,55; lib. II, cap. 390, ed. Friedrich Wilhelm Hermann Wasserschleben (Leipzig, 1840), pp. 24; 145; 180–1; 213; 363 [repr. (Graz, 1964)]. Burchard of Worms, *Libri Decretorum XX*, lib. II, interrogatio 54, 46, in *PL*, vol. 140, cols 577, 579.

[40] Venantius Fortunatus, *Vita Sanctae Radegundis*, cap. 82–3, MGH AA, vol. 4, part 2 (Hanover, 1881), pp. 47–8.

perform not only 'frivolous and vain songs' but also Christian songs.[41] Lay songs must still have been popular in ninth-century monasteries, as Otfrid of Weissenburg justified his translation of the Gospels into Old High German with the argument that he wanted to distract the monks from the practice of memorising lay songs.[42] The resistance can only be understood through a number of assumptions. First, clerics must have expected that these songs and dances could have important effects upon persons. Second, they must have presupposed that these effects had ecclesiastical significance. Owing to the lack of sources, it remains unspecified what triggered the criticisms of these effects. However, the resistance by church authorities invites the conclusion that these effects were connected with rituals over which the Church tried to place itself in charge. Because the Church issued particularly strong warnings against music performances in churchyards used as graveyards,[43] it is reasonable to assume that the effects that were believed to emanate from songs and dances were connected with the cult of the dead. If so, such enactments of effect-provoking songs and dances may have been intertwined with the pre- and early Christian belief that kin groups were comprised of the living and the dead. The belief included the demand that the living had to communicate with the dead and that songs and dances were the media through which this communication was maintained. Thus, the rigid Church prohibition against singing and dancing in graveyards made sense under the assumption that songs and dances could provoke responses from the dead and that, by consequence, early medieval aural perception, like visual perception, was believed to stimulate predetermined reactions among the recipients of messages within groups. Hence, the standard mode of aural perception implied that in the early Middle Ages group-centred perception could directly be transformed into predetermined group-related action.

However, regarding music performances, the Church authorities were at the centre of a conflict. On the one hand, they opposed the effect-provoking capacity of aural perception when it may have been interconnected with pre-Christian forms of the cult of the dead. On the other hand, they employed it for their own purposes in other cases. In the late seventh century, St Aldhelm, who served as Abbot of Malmesbury and later as Bishop of Sherborne until he died in 705, had the habit of standing in the middle of much-frequented bridges that farmers had to cross on the way to their fields. There he sang Christian songs in order to remind newly converted believers of their obligation to attend Sunday mass services in a nearby church.[44] At that time, not every settlement had its own church and not every parish church

---

[41] Bede, *Historia ecclesiastica gentis Anglorum*, lib. IV, cap. 22[24], ed. Bertram Colgrave and Roger Aubrey Baskervill Mynors (Oxford, 1969), p. 414 [repr. (Oxford, 2003)].

[42] Otfrid of Weissenburg, *[Epistola] ad Liutbertum*, MGH Epp., vol. 6, no 19, ed. Ernst Dümmler (Berlin, 1902), p. 166. Cf. Fidel Rädle, 'Otfrids Brief an Liutbert', in E.-J. Schmidt, ed., *Kritische Bewahrung. Beiträge zur deutschen Philologie [Festschrift Werner Schröder]* (Berlin, 1975), pp. 213–40.

[43] See above, note 39.

[44] See William of Malmesbury, *De gestis pontificum Anglorum*, cap. 190, ed. Nicholas

had its own resident priest, and many newly converted Christians were forced to walk to neighbouring settlements in order to perform their religious duties. Some may have been negligent or may have needed a stimulus that could motivate them to go to church, and Aldhelm seems to have been convinced that singing was the proper method to accomplish this goal. Even though Aldhelm's motivation for singing was recorded only in a twelfth-century statement, it is indirectly supported by the evidence of ecclesiastical canons. Already in the fifth century, Bishop Martin of Braga felt obliged to distinguish between the commands of the Credo as sacred incantations that he recommended, on the one hand and, on the other, diabolic charms and songs that he tried to suppress.[45] In 816, the Council of Aix-la-Chapelle repeated that singers should make efforts to control the effects of their performances through the modesty, purity and seriousness of singing.[46] Thus the effects of music performances were welcome as long as they remained attached to Christian contents. As late as in the tenth century, a description of the organ in the cathedral church of Old Minster, Winchester, confirmed that, even within Christian liturgy, an aural perception existed according to which music was expected to spark reactions among the attendants of the mass services.[47]

Likewise, the custom of preserving group-centred oral traditions that secular professional singers recited accompanied by a harp was practised in pre- and early Christian times. The custom appeared as a musical art within kin groups as well as among the high-ranking lay residents of monasteries up to the ninth century and perhaps even into the tenth. Such musical performances are mentioned in the epic of *Beowulf*, which may have been composed late in the ninth or early in the tenth century,[48] and are also reflected in a late eighth-century letter by Alcuin, Abbot of St Martin in Tours, in which he angrily attacked the monastic custom of singing lay songs.[49] It appears that these performances were extemporised although they may also have followed orally transmitted patterns. Even in the twelfth century, Gerald of Wales noted the Welsh custom of singing songs not in unison but, as he thought, in uncoordinated voices.[50] The fact that the Church initially tolerated the enactment

---

Esterhazy Stephen Armytage Hamilton, RS LII (London, 1870), p. 336 [repr. (New York, 1964)].

[45] Martin of Braga, *De correctione rusticorum*, cap. 16, pars 26, ed. Claude W. Barlow, *Martini episcopi Bracarensis Opera omnia*, Papers and Monographs of the American Academy in Rome XII (New Haven, 1950), p. 199.

[46] Council of Aix-la-Chapelle [816], cap. CXXXVII: 'De cantoribus', ed. Albert Werminghoff, MGH Conc. vol. 2, part 1 (Hanover, 1906), p. 414.

[47] Wulfstan Cantor, *Narratio metrica de Sancto Swithuno*, vv. 137–56, ed. Alistair Campbell, *Frithegodi monachi Breuiloguium Vitae Beati Wilfredi et Wulfstani Cantoris Narratio metrica de Sancto Swithuno* (Zurich, 1950), pp. 69–70. Similarly *Vita Sancti Oswaldi archiepiscopi Eboracensis*, ed. James Raine, *Historians of the Church of York*, vol. 1, RS LXXI (London, 1879), pp. 464–5 [repr. (New York, 1964)].

[48] *Beowulf*, vv. 89–98 (note 18), pp. 4–5.

[49] Alcuin, ep. 124, ed. Ernst Dümmler, *Epistolae Karolini aevi*, vol. 4 (Berlin, 1895), p. 183 (MGH Epp. 6.)

[50] Gerald of Wales, *Topographia Hibernica*, lib. III, cap. 11, ed. James Francis Dimock,

of oral traditions, not only among kin groups, but also in the monasteries and could not in all cases prevent the enactment of *carmina turpia* (dirty songs) in churchyards used as graveyards, showed these forms of aural perception as a widespread standard. The songs may have mainly been recitations of oral traditions when sung in kin groups or among retainers of rulers. But they were also transmitters of Christian doctrine when employed by the clergy. Hence they reflected a standard of perception in which kin and other types of groups played a paramount role in message transmission.

However, this standard of aural perception stood against the principles enshrined in the Gregorian chant, which had been used since the seventh century as a part of the liturgy. Initially, this choral may have allowed some extemporisation and polyphonic elements, but, apparently during the ninth century, an initiative gained ground that aural perception in Sunday services and the monasteries should be subjected to the norms of the Christian liturgy. The result of this initiative seems to have been that monks were instructed to sing liturgical texts in accordance with written notational instructions and avoid any irregularities in extemporised performances. The oldest extant samples of such instructions date from the late ninth-century *Musica enchiriadis* (or *Liber enchiridiadis de musica*), which prescribed a selection for the performance of only such musical sounds (*phthongi*) that fell within certain fixed intervals.[51] Consequently, the handbook permitted two parallel voices only if they followed the strict rules that were subsumed under the concept of *diaphonia*. *Diaphonia* meant that two voices, accompanying each other, should execute one choral song (*cantus*) at different voice levels (*concentu dissono*).[52] Thus, the handbook allowed monastic polyphony only under two conditions. The first was that the unity of the choral song remained intact; and the second that the sequence of sounds followed certain prearranged time intervals. Explicitly, the handbook likened the notation of musical sounds to the writing of texts, the parallel being that, as texts consisted of well-ordered sequences of letters, music consisted of well-ordered sequences of sounds.[53] Characteristically, the sequences into which liturgical aural perception came to be ordered were finite, with the earliest explicit rules for the conclusion of the sequence being recorded from the early eleventh century.[54] When, from c. 1100, a variety of voices were once again allowed to sing coordinated but distinct *cantus* within these finite sequences, the

Giraldi Cambrensis Opera, vol. 5, RS XXI (London, 1867), pp. 153–5 [repr. (New York, 1964)]. Gerald, *Descriptio Kambriae*, lib. I, cap. 13, ed. James Francis Dimock, *Giraldi Cambrensis Opera*, vol. 6, RS XXI (London, 1868), pp. 189–90 [repr. (New York, 1964)].

51 Hans Schmid, ed., *Musica et scolica enchiriadis una cum aliquibus tractatibus adiunctis recensio nova*, cap. 2 (Munich, 1981), pp. 6–7.
52 See Michael Richter, *The Formation of the Medieval West. Studies in the Oral Culture of the Barbarians* (Dublin, New York, 1994), pp. 108–10. Michael Walter, *Grundlagen der Musik des Mittelalters* (Stuttgart, 1994), pp. 234–8.
53 Schmid, ed., *Musica* (see note 51).
54 Guido of Arezzo, *Micrologus*, cap. 18, ed. Josef Smits van Waesberghe (Rome, 1955), pp. 196–208.

diaphonia became reinterpreted as a *duplex cantus*, which was joined together into consonances.[55] Hence the *cantus* was then no longer restricted to one voice that was accompanied in an orderly manner by another, but two or subsequently several *cantus* could coexist within a finite sequence of sounds.

The performance of finite temporal sequences demanded measurability. This was understood as implying the task of numerically specifying the relative length of the coordinated sounds as parts of a temporal sequence. From the thirteenth century, scientists made substantial efforts to fix the mathematical proportion between the various relative lengths of the sounds, and turned coordinated *cantus* into pieces of 'measurable music' that had to be 'composed' ahead of their performance.[56] The 'compositions' were to consist of notations and pauses through which time could be marked. The scholarly effort to orient aural perception towards the measurement of sequences of sounds was in accordance with the simultaneous reception of the Aristotelian philosophical concept of astronomical time during the thirteenth and fourteenth centuries.[57] Music became recognised as a 'science of time' which, in the fifteenth and sixteenth centuries, comprised mathematics, astronomy and chronology as well.[58]

The orientation of aural perception towards the measurement of temporal sequences reduced the significance of incalculable music elements such as spontaneous action and enhanced the formulation of rigorous rules for music composition. However, around 1500 there were also instances of uncomposed pieces of music as vagrant songs and of unorthodox compositions that were subsumed under the term *frottole*[59] But it was only with the beginning of opera performances at the end of the sixteenth century that the rigid abstractionism that informed the standard of late medieval music composition began to soften.

In summary, from the tenth century the enactment of Church-controlled music performances abandoned the task of stimulating predetermined reac-

---

55 In the so-called Montpellier *organum tract*, s. v. 'diaphonia', ed. Hans Heinrich Eggebrecht and Frieder Zaminer, *Ad organum faciendum. Lehrschriften der Mehrstimmigkeit in nachguidonischer Zeit* (Mainz, 1970), pp. 46–7.

56 Johannes de Muris, *Notitia artis musicae* [1321], ed. Ulrich Michels, *Die Musiktraktate des Johannes de Muris* (Wiesbaden, 1970), p. 49. Franco de Colonia, *Ars cantus mensurabilis*, ed. Gilbert Reaney and André Gilles (Dallas, 1974), p. 26.

57 See Udo Reinhold Jeck, *Aristoteles contra Augustinum. Zur Frage nach dem Verhältnis von Zeit und Seele bei den antiken Aristoteleskommentatoren, im arabischen Aristotelismus und im 13. Jahrhundert*, Bochumer Studien zur Philosophie. XXI (Amsterdam and Philadelphia, 1994). Philip Alperson, ' "Musical Time" and Music as an "Art of Time" ', in *Journal of Aesthetics and Art Criticism* 38 (1980), pp. 407–17. J. D. Kraus, 'Studies of Time and Music', in *Journal of Music Theory* 7 (1985), pp. 72–106. Anthony Grafton, *Joseph Scaliger*, 2 vols (Oxford, 1983).

58 Johannes Tinctoris, *Terminorum musicae diffinitorum* (Treviso, 1495), fol. biir [repr. Documenta musicologica, Ser. I, vol. 37 (Kassel, 1983)]. Pietro Pontio, *Ragionamento di musica* (Parma, 1588), p. 2 [repr. Documenta musicologica, Ser. I, vol. 16 (Kassel, 1959)]. Joseph Justus Scaliger, *Opus novum de emendatione temporum* (Paris, 1583), p. 294.

59 Ottaviano Petrucci, Frottole, ed. Rudolf Schwarz (Leipzig, 1934–35).

tions from the audience and became focused on observing ordered finite temporal sequences of sounds. From then on, musicians no longer assumed that their performances could have impacts on their audience in anything but a diffuse affective sense.[60] Hence, in the cases of both visual and aural perception, perception and action have been separate since the twelfth century.

Conclusion: Visual and aural perception

The history of aural perception is similar to the history of visual perception. In the early Middle Ages, visual as well as aural perception was expected to translate into action, but this innate interrelationship between perception and action was severed between the tenth and the twelfth centuries. In both cases, the conceptual separation of action from perception was concomitant with the reorientation of the focus of visual perception from group to space and of aural perception from group to time. In both cases, the process through which perception and action became separated was initiated by the Church whose authorities were suspicious of the beliefs in the power-generating influence of pictures and music performances. The new standard of perception in the late Middle Ages conditioned the theoretical demand that priority should be given to picture-making according to the rules of central-point perspective and to musical performances on the basis of composed or prearranged sequences of sounds. The new standard of perception was congruent with the new conception of space and experiences of time that emerged between the eleventh and the thirteenth centuries, and redefined space and time as indefinite and continuous ordering schemes that were placed beyond human control. In turn, the new conception of space and experiences of time advanced the separation of perception from action not only in terms of practice but eventually in theory as well. But that is the story of the separation of aesthetics from ethics. Before the variegated facets of this story can be comprehended it may be appropriate to describe first a case showing the practical consequences of the changing relationship between perception and action. The dramatic and traumatic experiences of the inhabitants in a small village in early eleventh-century East Saxony cast a spotlight on this change.

---

[60] For an early theory of musical affection, see Epifaura Ferdinandi, *Centum historiae seu observationes et casus medici* (Venice, 1621), pp. 266–8.

II

The Transformation of Perception in the Early Eleventh Century: Dance Historical Records from the Village of Kölbigk in East Saxony

Chorea est circulus cuius centrum est diabolus*

A dance with dramatic consequences

The changes that affected the conditions of life in agricultural settlements at the turn of the millennium have long been recognised.[1] They were first described in terms of economic history and have subsequently been scrutinised by historians of science, technology and the environment,[2] the family,[3] institutions,[4] communication,[5] cities,[6] and thinking.[7] But the effects that

---

*   The dance is a circle whose centre is the devil.

1   Marc Léopold Benjamin Bloch, *Feudal Society*, 2 vols, repr. of the English version of 1961 (London and New York, 1989) [first published (Paris, 1939–40)], esp. vol. 1, pp. 59–71. Guy Bois, *The Transformation of the Year One Thousand* (Manchester and New York) [first published (Paris, 1989)]. Cf. the critical response by Dominique Barthélemy, *La mutation de l'an mil a-t-elle eu lieu?* (Paris, 1997).

2   Grenville Astill, and John Langdon, ed., *Medieval Farming and Technology. The Impact of Agricultural Change in Northwest Europe* (Leiden, 1997). Bernd Herrmann and Rolf Sprandel, ed., *Determinanten der Bevölkerungsentwicklung im Mittelalter* (Weinheim, 1987). Herrmann, ed., *Mensch und Umwelt im Mittelalter*, 3rd edn (Stuttgart, 1987) [first published (Stuttgart, 1986)]. Ernst Schubert and Bernd Herrmann, ed., *Von der Angst zur Ausbeutung. Umwelterfahrung zwischen Mittelalter und Neuzeit* (Frankfurt, 1994). Uta Lindgren, ed., *Technik im Mittelalter*, 3rd edn (Berlin, 1998) [first published (Berlin, 1996)].

3   Georges Duby, *Hommes et structures du Moyen Age* (The Hague, Paris, 1973). Duby, *The Three Orders* (Chicago and London, 1980). Jacques Heers, *Le clan familial au Moyen Age* (Paris 1974). Karl Schmid, *Gebetsgedenken und adeliges Selbstverständnis im Mittelalter* (Sigmaringen, 1983).

4   Gert Melville, ed., *Institutionen und Geschichte*, Norm und Struktur I (Cologne, Weimar and Vienna, 1992). Doris Ruhe and Karl-Heinz Spieß, ed., *Prozesse der Normbildung und Normveränderung im mittelalterlichen Europa* (Stuttgart, 2000).

5   Harald Kleinschmidt, 'Wordhord onleac. Bemerkungen zur Geschichte der sprechsprachlichen Kommunikation im Mittelalter', in *Historisches Jahrbuch* 108 (1988), pp. 37–62.

Notes 6 and 7 opposite

these changes had on standards of perception and concepts of action have been neglected, perhaps because few sources are available. Yet reports of one conspicuous event provide details that allow some insight into the perceptual and behavioural dimensions of the changes early in the eleventh century. The reports are now extant in three main early recensions of which two appear to have been composed by authors who were themselves involved in the event.[8] The event occurred in the East Saxon village of Kölbigk (or Cölbigk, district of Bernburg, Saxony-Anhalt) during the reign of Emperor Henry II (1002–24), probably in 1015.[9] According to one recension, a group of thirteen men and three women, among them the daughter of the local priest, gathered together in the yard in front of the church of St Magnus the Martyr[10] on Christmas Eve at a time when mass service was about to begin. They formed a circle, held hands and began to enact a round dance while singing a series of ballads. These ballads were called *chorolla* (carol) in the recension, which also contains the text of three-line verse. A soloist as the leading voice sang the first two lines while the third one was a refrain sung by the group together:

Equitabat Bovo per silvam frondosam	Bovo was riding on horseback through the green wood,
Ducebat sibi Merswinden formosam	He wedded the beautiful Merswind
Quid stamus? Cur non imus?	Why do we stand? Why do we not move?

Bovo and Merswind are mentioned in the report as the names of two dancers, Merswind being identified as the daughter of the local priest. The dance appears to have been a round dance, perhaps accompanied by ecstatic jumps. As it stands, the ballad was suitable to a round dance in which the refrain was

6   Evamaria Engel, *Die deutsche Stadt des Mittelalters* (Munich, 1993). Hagen Keller, *Adelsherrschaft und städtische Gesellschaft in Oberitalien. 9–12. Jahrhundert* (Tübingen, 1979). Christian Meier, ed., *Die Okzidentale Stadt nach Max Weber* (Munich, 1994). Ulrich Meier, *Mensch und Bürger* (Munich, 1994). Ernst Pitz, *Europäisches Städtewesen und Bürgertum. Von der Spätantike bis zum hohen Mittelalter* (Darmstadt, 1991), pp. 287–390.

7   Harald Kleinschmidt, 'Thinking as Action. Some Principal Changes in Medieval and Early Modern Europe', in *Ethnologia europaea* 27 (1997), pp. 1–20.

8   Report by Theodericus, Paris, Bibliothèque nationale de France, MS lat. 6503, fol. 61. The codex was preserved in the monastic library of Echternach where it had probably been written. Printed in Edélestand du Meril, *Etudes sur quelques points d'archéologie et d'histoire littéraire* (Paris, 1862), pp. 498–502. *Miracula S. Edithae Wiltoniensis.* Printed in Edward Schröder, 'Die Tänzer von Kölbigk', in *Zeitschrift für Kirchengeschichte* 17 (1897), pp. 126–30.

9   In a *Life* of Archbishop Heribert of Cologne, contained in MS Brussels, Bibliothèque Royale Albert Ier 8515, fol. 116rb–vb, the date 1013 is given. See Lantbert von Deutz, *Vita Heriberti. Miracula Heriberti. Gedichte. Liturgische Texte*, ed. Bernhard Vogel, MGH, SS rer. Germ. LXXIII (Hanover, 2001), p. 52. I am grateful to Dr Bernhard Vogel of Erlangen University for this reference.

10 The patron saint is, apparently independently, identified in the *Annales Stadenses* (see below, note 12) and in the report included in William of Malmesbury's *Gesta regum Anglorum*, §174, ed. William Stubbs, vol. 1, RS XC (London, 1887), p. 204 [repr. (New York, 1964)].

sung jointly by all dancers immediately before they began to dance. According to the recension, the almighty divinity intervened after the dance had begun. The divinity inflicted a ban upon the group members who could then not stop dancing but had to continue during day and night without eating or drinking until Christmas Eve of the following year. On that night, they were relieved from the ban through the intervention of Archbishop Heribert of Cologne. They fell into a deep sleep that continued for several days and from which some never woke up again. The surviving members of the group left Kölbigk in search of new homes, while they continued to be ill with painful spasms. For many years they wandered through Europe and lived on collecting alms. One group member eventually arrived at the monastery of St Edith in Wilton, Wiltshire in order to find a cure for his spasms. The monastery preserved one recension of the report in its collections. Another Kölbigk victim of divine wrath knocked on the gate of the monastery at Hersfeld as late as in 1038 seeking a similar cure.[11] The surviving dancers and singers were legally entitled by Church licence to beg for and receive alms from private persons and Church institutions. Thus, as it stands, the report described how singing a song and dancing in a churchyard provoked divine wrath and severely punished the singers and dancers.

Another recension of the report, which may have been written in the monastery at Echternach, notes that its text had been dictated by Bishop Bruno of Toul, later Pope Leo IX (1048–54).[12] It thus presents a perspective on the dancing event that was informed by Church attitudes. From late Antiquity,[13]

---

11 *Lamperti monachi Hersfeldensis opera*, ed. Oswald Holder-Egger, MGH, SS rer. Germ. [XXXVIII] (Berlin, 1894), p. 351. Lampert explained that the event had occurred twenty-three years before the man appeared at Hersfeld.

12 This recension has been preserved in Paris, Bibliothèque nationale de France, MS lat. 9560, which contains homilies of Gregory I. The manuscript was in the monastery of Echternach at the time when the version of the Kölbigk legend was entered. This transmission has led Jean Schroeder ['Zur Herkunft der älteren Fassung der Tanzlegende von Kölbigk', in Michael Borgolte and Herrad Spilling, ed., *Litterae medii aevi. Festschrift für Johanne Autenrieth zu ihrem 65. Geburtstag* (Sigmaringen, 1988), pp. 183–9] to surmise that the literary versions of the legend originated at Echternach. Schroeder's assumption, however, stands against the fact that there are independent records of the Kölbigk event in the eleventh and thirteenth centuries. The eleventh-century record is extant in annals written by Lampert of Hersfeld on his monastery. See above, note 11. Thirteenth-century records are contained in *Annales S. Blasii Brunsvicensium maiorum fragmenta*, ed. Oswald Holder-Egger, MGH SS, vol. 30, 1 (Hanover, 1896), p. 17. *Chronica minor auctore minorita Erphordiensi*, ed. Oswald Holder-Egger, MGH SS, vol. 24 (Hanover, 1879), p. 188. *Annales Stadenses*, ed. Johann Martin Lappenberg, MGH SS, vol. 16 (Hanover, 1859), p. 313. For references to the Kölbigk event in Scandinavian records, see Dag Strömbäck, 'Kölbigk och Hagra', in *Arv* 17 (1961), pp. 27–8.

13 Augustine, *Sermo* CCCXI, cap. 5, in *PL* vol. 38, col. 1415. Moreover, Augustine, *Confessiones*, lib. X, cap. 3, ed. James J. O'Donnell (Oxford, 1992), p. 138, insisted that singing in a church building was a grave sin if it was more moving than the contents of the poem sung. Similarly Bishop Caesarius of Arles, 'Sermo CCLXVI', cap. 4, in *PL* vol. 39, col. 2239. Likewise, Childebert, King of the Franks, *Constitutio*, in *PL* vol. 72, col. 1122, prohibited dancing on holy days, at Easter and Christmas and during religious

Church as well as lay authorities expressed their strong reservations about dancing and condemned certain kinds of dances as relics of 'pagan' beliefs. They also enacted prohibitions against dancing on specific occasions, such as holy days and religious festivals, specifically at Easter and Christmas, and tried to ban the holding of feasts together with dancing in church buildings. These reservations had not waned by the seventh century when, according to the *Life of St Eligius* (the Bishop of Noyon), the saint received praise for a prayer through which he had begged for the divine punishment of dancers.[14] Disapproval continued to be strong in the eighth and ninth centuries when bishops and councils enforced prohibitions of dancing and Raban Maur wrote a critical remark against *ioca inutilia* (useless jokes),[15] and in the early eleventh century, they induced Bishop Burchard of Worms to protest the enactment of such performances as an evil 'magical practice' that reminded him of 'pagan' rituals and, he believed, militated against Christian practices.[16] Thus the Echternach recension of the report on the Kölbigk dancers and singers was in line with a long tradition of Church prohibitions against dancing, specifically when performed inside church buildings or in churchyards and at times of regular mass services. In the later Middle Ages the tradition was supplemented by secular prohibitions of dancing in public places in towns.[17] More-

---

festivals. The Council of Auxerre (573/603), MGH Conc., vol. 1 (Hanover, 1893), p. 180, ruled against dancing together with the holding of feasts in church buildings. Subsequently, the Council of Toledo (589), canon XXIII, ed. Mansi, vol. 12, col. 385, and the Council of Châlons-sur-Sâone (639/651), canon XIX, MGH Conc., vol. 1 (Hanover, 1893), p. 212, banned dancing on the occasions of church dedication festivals and commemorations for martyrs. The Council of Toledo (693), cap. 2, ed. Mansi, vol. 19, cols 69–70, prohibited buffoonery, performances of singing, dancing and diabolic games in church buildings, in houses and on streets. The Augustinian tradition of dance criticism was condensed into the phrase 'chorea est circulus cuius centrum est diabolus et omnes vergunt in sinistrum' (the dance is a circle in whose centre is the devil, and all turn to the left) by Jacques de Vitry, Patriarch of Jerusalem (d. 1240), in his Sermones vulgares, Ms Paris, Bibliothèque nationale de France, Lat. 17509, fol. 146, ed. Richard Albert Lecoy de la Marche, *La chaire française au Moyen Age* (Paris, 1886), p. 413. The moralist Guilelmus Peraldus [Guillaume Peyraut], Bishop of Lyons (d. 1275), elaborated on this phrase in his *Summa viciorum seu tractatus moralis edita a fratre Vilhelmo episcopo lugdunensis* (Basle, 1474), fols 442r–3r.

14 *Vita S. Eligii*, cap. 20, ed. Bruno Krusch, MGH, SS rer. Merov., vol. 4 (Hanover, 1902), pp. 710–11.

15 *Capitularium Benedicti*, MGH Leges, vol. 2, part 2 (1837), p. 83. *Commonitorium cuiusque episcopi*, in *PL* vol. 96, col. 1378 (eighth century). Council of Rome (826), canon XXXV, MGH Conc., vol. 2 (1906), p. 581. Statutes of St Boniface (745), canon XXI, Homily of Pope Leo IV (847–55), cap. XL, ed. Mansi, vol. 9, col. 999; Council of Mainz (813), canon XLVIII, ed. Mansi, vol. 1, cols 74, 895. Raban Maur, *De magicis artibus*, in *PL* vol. 110, cols 1095, 1102–3.

16 Burchard of Worms, *Libri decretorum XX*, lib. II, interrogatio 54, 46, in *PL* vol. 140, cols 577, 579.

17 Caesarius of Heisterbach, *Dialogus miraculorum atque magnum visionum*, Distinctio IV, cap. 11, ed. Joseph Strange, vol. 1 (Cologne, 1851), p. 183 [repr. (Ridgwood, NJ, 1966)], has the story about a priest who loved dancing and music in the church and even joined dancing parties wearing the holy cross. According to Caesarius, he received divine pun-

over, up to the nineteenth century, references to the Kölbigk event were used to repeat and reinforce these prohibitions in the context of moral education.[18]

It seems that dancing performances of the Kölbigk type were common as the texts of the report take it for granted that the dance was enacted on the spot without any previous instructions. Because the texts of the report contain no explanation why the dancers chose to perform the dance in the Kölbigk churchyard, it is not possible to decide whether the location was deliberately chosen by the dancers or whether the dances were enacted accidentally by a group of persons who had initially gone to the church in order to attend mass on Christmas Eve. Evidently, the authors of the various recensions were not interested in motives for, but in processes of, action. In any case, it seems safe to conclude that it was the dancing performance in the churchyard that was believed to have provoked divine wrath, and not dancing as such, and it appears to have been perfectly sensible to the ecclesiastical author of the Echternach recension that dancing in churchyards used as graveyards carried with it the risk of divine punishment. That Church authorities were eager to convey this message can also be inferred from the fact that they did much to spread the news about the Kölbigk dancers throughout western and northern Europe. The event has subsequently been linked with the annual procession of the jumping saints at Echternach on Whit Sunday.[19] But that may have been a retrospective association from the late Middle Ages.

Although none of the early recensions explicitly referred to graves, it is likely that the Kölbigk dancers and singers enacted their performance on graves. From the late seventh century at the latest, the Church made efforts to establish its sacred buildings and their immediate surroundings as burial grounds and to prevent members of kin groups from using kin land to bury their dead. As a result, rural church buildings became flanked with graves if the interments did not take place directly in their interior. Nevertheless, kin members appear to have retained their belief that the dead remained

ishment because dancing was the work of the devil. For secular prohibitions against dancing by town councils, see the fifteenth-century Nuremberg policing order against 'frivolous dances' in *Nürnberger Polizeiordnungen aus dem XIII bis XV Jahrhundert*, ed. Joseph Baader, Bibliothek des Litterarischen Vereins in Stuttgart LXIII (Stuttgart, 1861), pp. 90–1 [repr. (Amsterdam, 1966)]. For moralising rhetoric against dancing under church influence, see Melchior Ambach, *Von Tantzen. Vrtheil auss Heiliger Schrift vnnd den alten Christlichen Leren gestellt* (Frankfurt, 1543). Florian Daul, *Tantzteuffel* (1569) [repr. (Leipzig, 1978)]. Johann Münster, *Ein gotseliger Tractat von dem ungotseligen Tantz. Dem Sohn Gottes zu ehren und seiner Kirchen zum besten. Dem Teufel aber zum trotz und der welt abzubrechen gestellt* (Heilbronn, 1594), p. 63 [another edn (Hanau, 1607)].

18 *Anhaltisches Magazin* (1828), p. 407 [contains a report on Kölbigk-style Christmas celebrations which is drawn on the childhood memories of a then old man]. Christian Heinrich Broemel, *Fest-Täntze der ersten Christen* (Jena, 1701), p. 34. Cyriacus Spangenberg, *Adels-Spiegel*, vol. 1, book 12, cap. 8 (Schmalkalden, 1591), fol. 403v [for the year 1373]. Joachim Hildebrand, *De nuptiis veterum christianorum liber* (Helmstedt, 1661), p. 4.

19 For a modern description, see Alex Langini, *La procession dansante d'Echternach* (Echternach, 1977).

Fig. 12 Matthäus Merian, *The Kölbigk dancers.* Printed in Joachim Ludwig Gottfried, *Historica chronica* (Frankfurt, 1632), part 6, p. 14. Göttingen, Niedersächsische Staats- und Universitätsbibliothek, 4° H.un.II, 276:6.

members of their widely dispersed extended double-descent groups. For they developed the much-criticised custom of gathering in such graveyards to communicate with the dead by singing songs and dancing on the graves to which reference was made in the previous chapter. The assumption that the Kölbigk villagers retained the same belief may explain the strong response by the Church authorities against the dancing and singing event and their efforts to prevent its repetition by exhibiting the unhappy consequences of infringements of Church rules. Thus the Kölbigk dancers and singers appear to have called into question the Church monopoly of control over the cult of the dead. Their tragic fate seems to have raised sympathies among their contemporaries. They were willing to support the victims of divine wrath through alms which allowed some of them to survive for more than a decade. The Kölbigk event can thus hardly have been beyond imagination in the early eleventh century. The seventeenth-century picture shown in Figure 12 still reflects this attitude. It depicts a graveyard with the dancers in the foreground and a bone-house in the background, a cleric stepping out of the church building gesturing at the dancers and a dog barking at them.

Similar events are on record from later times, namely at Erfurt in 1239,[20]

---

[20] See Nicolas de Siegen, *Chronicon ecclesiasticum*, ed. Franz Xaver von Wegele (Jena, 1855), pp. 354–5. Johannes Lindner, 'Excerpta Saxonica, Misnica et Thuringiaca ex

Fig. 13 Pieter Bruegel, the Elder, *Dancing sickness*, 1564. Albertina, Vienna.

when children lapsed into dancing; at Liège in 1274; at Cologne and several other places along the Rhine and the Moselle in 1374,[21] when men and women were reported to have danced in a frenzy and to have had illegitimate sexual relations; in Zurich apparently in 1418; in Brescia in 1466; and in Dresden as late as in 1555, when groups of persons were imprisoned who had

monachi Pirnensis', ed. Johann Burchard Mencke, *Scriptores rerum Germanicarum praecipue Saxonicarum*, vol. 2 (Leipzig, 1728), col. 1531. For a later review of the Erfurt case, see Christian Heinrich Broemel, *Choreas sacras veterum Christianorum sigilatim Erffurti & Arnstadiae institutas epistola* (s. l., 1695).

21 Cf. for Liège, Johann Pistorius, *Rerum familiarum Belgicarum Chronicon magnum* (Frankfurt, 1654), fol. 319. For the dances on the Rhine and the Moselle, see *Die Chroniken deutscher Städte*. Köln, vol. 3 (Leipzig, 1877), p. 715 (s. a. 1374). Johannes Geerbrand of Leyden, 'Chronicon de comitibus Hollandiae et Zelandiae', lib. 31, cap. 36, ed. Franciscus Swertius, *Rerum Belgicarum annales, chronici et historici de bellis, vrbibus, situ e moribus gentis antiqvi recentioresqve scriptores*, vol. 1 (Frankfurt, 1620), p. 299 [also separately published]. Gobelinus, 'Personae Cosmodrom', Act. 6, cap. 69, ed. Heinrich Meibom, *Scriptores rerum Germanicarum*, vol. 1 (Helmstedt, 1688), p. 286. *Magnum Chronicon Belgicarum*, s. a. 1374, ed. Barthold Georg Struve, *Scriptores rerum Germanicarum*, vol. 3 (Regensburg, 1726), p. 348. Peter of Herentals, *Vita Gregorii XI*, ed. Etienne Baluze, *Vitae Paparum Avenionensium*, vol. 1 (Paris, 1693), p. 483 [also printed in Justus Friedrich Carl Hecker, *Die Tanzwuth* (Berlin, 1832), pp. 186–7]. Radulphus de Rivo, *Gesta pontificum Leodinensium*, cap. IX: De Ioanne de Arckel, cap. IX, in Johannes Chapeavillus, ed., *Gesta Pontificum Leodinensium scripserunt auctores praecipui*, vol. 3 (Liège, 1616), pp. 19–23. Spangenberg, *Adels-Spiegel* (see note 18). Tilemann Elhen von Wolfhagen, *Die Limburger Chronik*, s. a. 1374, ed. Arthur Wyss, MGH Chron. IV,1 (Hanover, 1883), p. 64. Cornelius Zantflict, 'Leodinense Chronicon', s. a. 1374, ed. Edmund Martène and Ursin Durand, *Veterum scriptorium et*

Fig. 14 *The Tarantula dance.* From Athanasius Kircher, *Phonurgia nova* (Kempten, 1673), p. 206. Hannover, Niedersächsische Landesbibliothek , K–A 7026.

been found dancing in churchyards and on graves, naked or in nightgowns and with swords.[22] In these cases, reporters writing in retrospect associated heretical or at least anti-clerical tendencies with the events. For the late fourteenth-century chronicler Tilemann Elhen von Wolfhagen, for one, the Cologne dancers of 1374 were the devil's servants, and their doings were forecasts of the apocalypse.[23]

But some private authors and secular institutions responded differently around 1500. In 1518, the Strasbourg city council organised a procession for a group of dancers to a nearby chapel of St Vitus with the argument that the

monumentorum historicorum, dogmaticorum, moralium amplissima collectio, vol. 5 (Paris, 1729), p. 301 [repr. (New York, 1968)]. Cf., for a report on dancing in churches and on churchyards, Giraldus Cambrensis, *Itinerarium Cambriae,* lib. I, cap. 2, Giraldus, *Opera,* vol. 6, ed. James Francis Dimock, RS XXI (London, 1890), p. 32 [repr. (New York, 1964)].

22 Stadtbibliothek Zürich, Ms U 55, Usteri Manuscripts, s. a. 1418, and Anton Salomon Vögelin, *Geschichte der Wasserkirche in Zürich* (Zurich, 1848), p. 13 (on women dancing in one of Zurich's churches, apparently in 1418). Leo of Rozmital, *Ritter-, Hof- und Pilgerreise 1465–1467* (Stuttgart, 1844), p. 121. Johannes Falke, *Geschichte der Kurfürsten von Sachsen* (Leipzig, 1868), p. 332. Wilhelm Katner, *Das Rätsel des Tarentismus* (Leipzig, 1956), p. 79. S. Sieber, 'Der Schwerttanz, besonders in Mitteldeutschland', in *Mitteldeutsche Blätter für Volkskunde* 7 (1932), p. 20. Cf., for a twentieth-century parallel, Adam Ritzhaupt, *Die 'neue Schar' in Thüringen* (Jena, 1921). Ulrich Linse, *Barfüssige Propheten. Erlöser der zwanziger Jahre* (Berlin, 1983), pp. 97–123.

23 Tilemann, *Limburger Chronik* (see note 21), p. 64.

saint might be able to cure the dancers, while it took strong punitive measures against persons appearing to join the event for their own pleasure. Thus, the Strasbourg city council resorted to a medical interpretation rather than assuming the violation of ecclesiastical canons.[24] Medical interpretations of dancing performances as cases of the so-called St Vitus dance or the 'dancing sickness' were also reflected in pictures that displayed such dancing scenes. An early case is to be found in a drawing by Pieter Bruegel of 1564,[25] which shows frenzied women dancers from Brussels being forcefully led away by men (Figure 13). A later source illustrates a disease called 'the tarantula dance' that was reportedly often performed in southern Italy, in reference to the proverbial sting of the tarantula (Figure 14).

Since the sixteenth century, the dancing occurrences have also been scrutinised in the context of astrological and medical theories that connected the 'dancing sickness' with epilepsy and muscular or nervous irregularities.[26]

24   Strasbourg Archives municipales, MS R 3, fol. 72. Strasbourg, Bibliothèque de l'Université, Chronicle of the Imlin family, s. a. 1518, printed in Ludwig Witkowski, 'Einige Bemerkungen über den Veitstanz des Mittelalters und über psychische Infection', in *Allgemeine Zeitschrift für Psychiatrie und psychisch-gerichtliche Medizin* 35 (1879), p. 594. Andreas Goldmayer, *Strassburgische Chronika*, s. a. 1518 (Strasbourg, 1636), pp. 69–70. Michael Kleinlawel, *Strassburgische Chronik*, s.a. 1518 (Strasbourg, 1625), pp. 130–1. Johann von Königshoven, *Die aelteste teutsche so wol allgemeine als insonderheit elsassische und straßburgische Chronicke*, ed. Johannes Schilter (Strasbourg, 1698), pp. 1087–90. The editor Schilter erroneously dated the event into the year 1418. Wilhelm Rem, *Chronika newer Geschichten*, ed. Friedrich Roth, Die *Chroniken der deutschen Städte*, vol. 25: Augsburg, vol. 5 (Leipzig, 1896), s. a. 1518, p. 88.

25   See Axel L. Romdahl, 'Pieter Brueghel der Ältere und sein Kunstschaffen', in *Jahrbuch der Kunsthistorischen Sammlungen des Allerhöchsten Kaiserhauses* 25 (1905), Pl. XXI, pp. 135–6.

26   Goldmayer, *Chronika* (see note 24), who adduced evil-forecasting constellations as the reason for what he took to be irregular behaviour of the dancers. For the medical interpretation, see the list of doctoral dissertations and other academic publications in the Bibliography and the following sections in general works, such as 'St. Veits-Tantz', 'Tanzkranckheit', in Johannes Heinrich Zedler, ed., *Grosses vollständiges Universal-Lexicon aller Wissenschaften und Künste*, vols 41, 46 (Halle and Leipzig, 1744–45), cols 1758–62, 1011–14. 'Diverses observations de physique générale', in *Histoire de l'Académie royale de science de Paris* (1702), pp. 16–18. Georgio Baglivi, 'Dissertatio VI de anatome, morsu et effectibus Tarantulae', in Baglivi, *Opera omnia medico-practica et anatomica* (Lyon, 1704), pp. 599–640. Stephan Blancard [Steven Blanckaert], *Lexicon medicum tripartitum*, new edn, vol. 1 (Leipzig, 1777), p. 286. Theodorus Corbeius, *Pathologia* (Nuremberg, 1647), liber II, sectio 2, cap. 8, p. 208. William Cullen, *First Lines of the Practice of Physic*, new edn, vol. 2 (Edinburgh, 1812), pp. 198–201 [first edn in Latin (Leiden, 1779); first edn in English (Edinburgh, 1788–94)]. Wilhelm Friedrich Dreyssig, *Handbuch der Pathologie der chronischen Krankheiten*, vol. 1 (Leipzig, 1796), pp. 335–47. Desiderius Erasmus, 'Enarratio psalmi', cap. XXXVIII, in Erasmus, *Opera omnia*, ed. Johannes Clericus, vol. 5 (Leiden, 1704), col. 419 [repr. (Amsterdam and Tokyo, 1969)]. Johann Christian Fritsch, *Seltsame, jedoch wahrhafftige theologische, juristische, medizinische und physikalische Geschichte so wohl aus alten als neuen Zeiten*, vol. 3 (Leipzig, 1733), p. 541. Georgius Horstius, *Observationum medicinalium singularum libri IV priores. Hic accessit Epistolarum et consultationum medicinarum*, vol. 1 (Ulm, 1628), Epistolarum p. 374. Paracelsus [i.e. Theophrastus Bombastus von

However, the medical interpretations of the events came in retrospect, replacing the more serious worries of medieval moralists that dancing and singing in churchyards were punishable infringements of divine law and ought to be banned.

As the report on the Kölbigk event appears to relate the infliction of divine punishment on dancers and singers specifically to performances in churchyards as graveyards, the event itself can be interpreted against the background of the more general antipathy that Church institutions displayed against dancing and singing as elements of lay culture. The report represents an early eleventh-century countryside world in which aural perception was believed to translate into predetermined actions and music was polyphonic and uncomposed. In this world, persons continued to believe that music could and ought to trigger predetermined actions among the audience, but they were discriminated against and punished for their belief. Hence the specific question needs to be answered: why, in the high Middle Ages, were dancing and singing in graveyards as parts of churchyards regarded as crimes provoking divine wrath? The question leads to a consideration of shifting patterns of action and changing rules for membership in groups.

Responses by villagers and Church authorities

Kinship structures transformed during the tenth and eleventh centuries. This process reduced the matrilinear element in the widely dispersed double-descent kin groups of the early Middle Ages and strengthened the position of male household chiefs at the expense of women, the elderly and

Hohenheim], *Artzney*, Buch 7: Von den Kranckheiten, die der Vernunft berauben, Tractat I, cap. 3, Tractat II, cap. 3: Von S. Veits Tantz, in Paracelsus, *Opera* (Strasbourg, 1616), vol. 1, pp. 491, 501. Joannes Schenck von Grafenberg, *Observationum medicarum rariorum liber primus* (Basle, 1581), observatio 234 de mania, pp. 280–2. Johann Storch, *Von Kranckheiten der Weiber*, vol. 2 (Gotha, 1748), pp. 227–46. Thomas Sydenham, *Schedula monitoria de novae febri ingressu* (London, 1686). Johann Ernst Wichmann, *Ideen zur Diagnostik*, vol. 1, 3rd edn (Hanover, 1827), pp. 365–400. Ernst Conrad Wicke, *Versuch einer Monographie des großen Veitstanzes und der unwillkürlichen Muskelbewegung nebst Bemerkungen über den Taranteltanz und die Beriberi* (Leipzig, 1844). Thomas Willis, *Pathologiae cerebri et nervosi generis specimen in quo agitur De Morbis Convulsis et de Scorbuto*, cap. VII (Oxford, 1667), pp. 90–2 [reprinted in Willis, *Opera omnia*, vol. 1 (Geneva, 1680), separate pagination]. Paracelsus (as above) believed that the disease was a consequence of excessive sexual desire and suggested that it should be cured with food prohibition and imprisonment in a dark room. In Zedler's *Großes vollständiges Universal-Lexikon aller Wissenschaften und Künste*, vol. 41 (Halle and Leipzig, 1744), cols 1801–3, s. v. 'Tarantel', one finds a verbal description of the dancing sickness and the suggestion to employ musicians for medical treatment. The *Histoire* (as above) of the French Académie explains that the bite of the tarantula causes tensions of the nerves equal to the tensions to which the cords of musical instruments are subjected. It recommends the playing of musical instruments with similar vibrations as a cure. Similarly Michael Praetorius, *Syntagma musicum*, vol. 1 (Wittenberg, 1614), pp. 226–30 [repr. Documenta musicologica XV (Kassel, 1959).

the young. The male household chiefs began to perceive as beneficial for themselves the fragmentation of the larger kin groups into smaller communities of kin-related residents at a given place and considered less relevant their collateral relations with people residing elsewhere.[27]

This process began in the tenth century within the ruling kin groups and was supported by bishops and abbots because it was congruent with the long-term goals of reducing the importance of kin groups within and outside the Church.[28] It brought together into a fragile coalition secular rulers on the one side and bishops as well as abbots on the other. It was a coalition of mutual benefit. The ordained clergy could free themselves from domination by the aristocratic kin groups, and the secular rulers could raise their position above that of the aristocracy with the approval of the Church.[29] Bishops could be encouraged to perform a liturgy by which a circuit around a cemetery came to demarcate a sacred area and banned intrusion.[30] In this way, high-ranking church officials obtained power to outline areas over which the Church not only had proprietary but also legislative rights. While it remains unclear whether there was such a sacred area around or near the church in Kölbigk, it follows from the logic of the reports on the incident that the singers and dancers committed an action that was punishable because, among other reasons, it occurred on sacred ground. Thus an element of territorialisation became recognisable that added to church control over land and people and, consequently, reduced the control of groups over their members.

The report on the Kölbigk dancers and singers thus portrays the rural countryside as a world in transition. On the one side, the cult of the dead could still be linked to the enactment of songs and dances in villages at the time, as Bishop Burchard of Worms confirmed. The customary practice of communicating with the dead thus seems to have provoked the dancers and singers to choose the churchyard as their performance site, possibly amid graves. Except for the ballad refrain, however, we do not know what kind of songs were sung and thus cannot determine whether they contained kin or

---

27 For a collection of studies on the reduction of matrilinearity in the early Middle Ages, see Schmid, *Gebetsgedenken* (see note 3). A ninth-century case of the continuing existence of extended kin group structures is recorded in Asser's *Life of King Alfred*, cap. 23, ed. William Henry Stevenson (Oxford, 1904) [repr., ed. Dorothy Whitelock (Oxford, 1959)], who mentions that Alfred's mother Osburh preserved vernacular traditions in a 'book', the contents of which Alfred was made to learn by heart. Although nothing is known about what Alfred learned, it is safe to conclude that at least some of the traditions belonged to Alfred's kin group. Hence, around the middle of the ninth century, women could still act as transmitters of kin tradition, and the transmission of tradition was considered to be essential to the perseverance of the kin group.

28 For details, see Harald Kleinschmidt, *Understanding the Middle Ages* (Woodbridge, 2000), pp. 89–119.

29 Leo Santifaller, *Zur Geschichte des ottonisch-salischen Reichskirchensystems* (Vienna, 1954) [2nd edn (Graz, Vienna, Cologne, 1964)].

30 The *Pontifical romano-germanique du dixième siècle*, ed. Cyrille Vogel and Reinhard Elze, vol. 1 (Vatican City, 1966), pp. 192–3, describes the liturgy.

other oral traditions.[31] Yet, elsewhere, contemporary eleventh-century sources[32] display continuing reliance on kin relations still strong enough to induce rural kin groups to act in defence of their members and to seek revenge for their slain relatives.

By contrast, according to the Kölbigk report, the singers and dancers found it difficult to return to normal life in their village because they could not receive the supportive energy that they may have expected from the priest or their locally residing kin members. Unlike earlier or contemporary sources, the Kölbigk report exhibits a conspicuous lack of inclination on the part of the kin groups to take care of their fatally ill members. Instead, the kin members who resided in Kölbigk expelled the surviving singers and dancers, who were then forced to move to other places where they had to rely on church alms. Thus the sources on the Kölbigk dance record the process of narrowing down the rural kin groups that refused to take responsibility for the actions of their members and began to pass social welfare obligations to Church institutions.[33] Admittedly, the extant reports on the Kölbigk event came exclusively from ecclesiastical sources and may therefore reflect the vantage point of the Church. But the news of the Kölbigk event spread widely across Europe, and the vagrants who claimed that they were victims of the event, or who simply bandwagoned, were able to tour Europe as licensed beggars. Hence, the story must have contained credible elements and could be related to the real-world experience in the eleventh century, of which the ongoing transformation of social relations was an integral part.

In the early Middle Ages, one and the same person could simultaneously be a member of a kin group, a neighbourhood group, a contractual group and a political group. The coexistence of and competition among these types of group offered some possibilities for the choice of membership. For example, someone dissatisfied with his or her kin group could opt out of this type of group and join a militarily active contractual group. Likewise, persons could

---

[31] In this context, much has been made of the name of the adjacent place Bernburg, which may be connected to Dietrich of Bern. The *Annales Quedlinburgenses*, ed. Georg Heinrich Pertz, MGH SS, vol. 3 (Hanover, 1839), p. 31, an eleventh-century source, do in fact record the existence of traditions about Dietrich of Bern in East Saxony at the time. But it is too far-fetched a source to support the assumption that the Kölbigk singers and dancers actually commemorated Dietrich of Bern.

[32] Burchard of Worms, *Lex familie Wormatiensis ecclesie [Hofrecht]*, cap. 30, ed. Heinrich Boos, *Urkundenbuch der Stadt Worms* (Worms, 1886), pp. 43–4.

[33] This can be confirmed from Regino of Prüm, *Liber de synodalibus causis et disciplinis ecclesiasticis*, lib. II, cap. 5, ed. Friedrich Wilhelm Hermann Wasserschleben (Leipzig, 1840) [repr. (Graz, 1964)], at the end of the ninth century, which refers to the vengeance of kinsmen 'which we call *faida*', *faida* is an early medieval word for the feud. Likewise, the early eleventh-century *Hofrecht* of Bishop Burchard of Worms (see note 32) mentions that, within one year, thirty-five persons had been killed and that these occurrences forced the bishop as the local lord to take action and enforce the law. Hence the decline of the law-enforcing capability of the kin groups ushered in a state of insecurity where criminal homicide surged and where traditional means of control failed.

purposefully renounce kin membership in order to join a religiously active contractual group.[34]

However, at this time, persons could instead have become outcasts as individuals without any membership in any type of group. Surely, kin groups could expel members,[35] although this seems to have occurred only rarely. If such expulsions happened, the victims had the options of seeking admission to different kin groups, or of establishing or joining a contractual group. Early medieval rulers, however, neither had the sophisticated bureaucracies nor the legitimacy to expel members of the political group under their control. The English word 'outlaw' only first appeared in the eleventh-century laws of Cnut.[36] Rules for the expulsion of a person from a group or the withdrawal of group protection from a person were thus conspicuously absent from early medieval written legal records, and it is likely that there were no written rules because many kin groups transmitted their own rules orally.[37] This argument can be confirmed by the use of the two most frequent Old English words for peace, namely *frith* and *sib*. Both words denoted protection provided by kin groups, among others, and the word *sib* itself is a kin-group term. Peace was thus understood as a condition under which a person could enjoy the protection and friendship of his or her kin. In Old English, persons from whom groups had withdrawn their protection were referred to as *wineleas*, people without friends, and described as people whose only remaining friends were wolves and whom the wolves could tear to pieces.[38]

From the eleventh century, not only the kin groups declined in consequence of their shrinking size and power, but also the neighbourhood and contractual groups lost much of their importance. From the high Middle Ages, the activities of the neighbourhood groups were confined to the articulation of discontent and the militarily active contractual groups waned after secular rulers became invested with more wide-ranging rights to administer adjudication centrally over the resident population under their control during the late tenth, eleventh and twelfth centuries. With the declining significance of kin, neighbourhood and contractual groups since the tenth and eleventh centuries, the choices that persons had among competing types of group were greatly reduced, and the number of outcasts increased.

---

34 For example, see *Das Hildebrandslied*, vv. 18–19, ed. Hartmut Broszinski, 2nd edn (Kassel, 1985), s. p. *Vitae Bonifatii archiepiscopi Moguntini*, cap. 1, ed. Wilhelm Levison, MGH, SS rer. Germ. [LVII] (Hanover, 1905), pp. 5–6.

35 *Wulf and Eadwacer, The Wife's Lament*, ed. George Krapp and Elliott van Kirk Dobbie, in *The Exeter Book* (New York and London, 1936), pp. 170–80, 210–11.

36 The pre-Alfredian insular laws know of expulsion only in cases of aliens with deviant behaviour. *Laws of Wihtred*, §§4, 28; *Laws of Ine*, §20, ed. Felix Liebermann, *Die Gesetze der Angelsachsen*, vol. 1 (Halle, 1903), pp. 12, 14, 98. *Laws of Cnut*, part II, §31, sect. 2, ed. Liebermann, ibid., p. 338.

37 An exception is represented in the *Divisio Regnorum* of 806, cap. 6–20 [in MGH Cap., vol. 1, ed. Alfred Boretius (Hanover, 1883), no 45, pp. 128–30], wherein the Carolingian royal kin group laid down its own rules for hereditary succession while employing the means of a written legal text.

38 *Exeter Gnomic Verses*, vv. 146–7, 173, ed. Krapp and Dobbie (see note 35), pp. 161, 162.

Characteristically, Old English *frith* and *sib* acquired new meanings or were replaced by the Anglo-Norman word *pees* (from Latin *pax*) in the eleventh century. The word *frith* and its variants in other Germanic languages, together with their new medieval Latin derivative *fredum*, no longer denoted protection by a specific group. Instead, *frith* and *fredum* referred to the peace that territorial rulers guaranteed through the enforcement of statutory or common law, or straightforwardly meant a fine payable to the ruler. The term *sib* continued as a kin term in derivatives or compounds like *sibling* while it was replaced as a simplex by the word *family*, which was of Latin origin. Hence, peace became considered to be enforcible upon everyone living in a given territory regardless of group membership. Infringers of the peace faced capital punishment, imprisonment in the hilltop castles where the rulers resided, or expulsion. The wolf's head became the synonym for the gallows.[39] Persons who had committed serious crimes were expelled, forfeited their lives or were regarded as the ruler's personal property.[40] According to the Kölbigk report, it was the divinity, and not human-made institutions of rule, which inflicted punishment on the dancers and singers. Again, the report represents a transitional stage. At Kölbigk, these institutions were strong enough neither to prevent unruly behaviour nor to punish infringers. Likewise, the kin and neighbourhood groups no longer had the power to control the behaviour of their members. Still, however, the local kin groups were given the responsibility of expelling the surviving singers and dancers. After apparently extensive wanderings, the expellees could neither find a new place to settle nor could they join another kin group or a new contractual group and, henceforth, they spent their vagrant lives in solitude. They were turned into outcasts because they no longer had the possibility of opting for another type of group. They did not seek relief from relatives outside Kölbigk, if such persons were available at all. Hence, the only institution to take care of them was the Church.

Conclusion

The report on the Kölbigk singers and dancers has been described here as sources for attitudes and beliefs rather than as a record of events. The difficult and important question whether the report contains accounts of events that actually took place has not been asked. This has not been done because it makes more sense to recast the focus on the evidential value of the report as sources for the process of the fundamental transformation of European culture during the high Middle Ages. The Kölbigk report sheds light on the transformation of standards of perception and types of group characteristic

---

[39] *Old English Riddles*, no. 55, v. 12, ed. Krapp and Dobbie (see note 35), p. 208.
[40] In many a hilltop castle, the prison as the dungeon was located in proximity to a ruler's or lord's chamber. Cf. Bronislaw Geremek, *Inutiles du monde. Truands et misérables dans l'Europe moderne (1350–1600)* (Paris, 1980), pp. 29–32.

of a rural settlement, whose population tried to continue early medieval conventions and were punished for doing so. The report can thus be placed at the centre of perceptual, behavioural and social changes. It depicts a transformation from a standard of aural perception according to which communicated messages were expected to translate into predetermined actions into a standard of aural perception that severed perception from action. It discloses the reduction of the possibilities of choice that a person had among coexisting and competing types of group and the increased potential for vagrancy and outcast existence.

Whereas this and the first chapter described the transformation of the interconnectedness between perception and action with regard to vision and audition, the following chapter will widen the focus and link the medieval history of the perception of smell, touch and taste to harmful or beneficial impacts that persons believed they could receive from their physical and social environments.

III

Impacts from the Environment:
The Perception of Smell, Touch and Taste

Das Best am Tanzen ist, daß man
Nit immerdar nur geht voran
Und auch beizeit umkehren kann*

Sebastian Brant

Introduction

Smell, touch and taste are transient. We have no direct access to the evaporated sense of smell, the bygone impression of touches and the distant flavour of tastes. Smell can disappear as fast as the spoken word, a touch can pass on as if it were a sudden impression causing pain, a taste can be as unstable as an emotion leaving behind a strong desire. We prefer metaphors to describe these sensations, and only if these descriptions are turned into records and are handed on from generation to generation can we have a chance to know them at a later point of time. We do not have general measurements of the intensity of smells, touches and tastes. These sensations are channelled through the mind and they are, consequently, specific to persons and cultures. Nevertheless, we often pass standard judgements about smells, touches and tastes. Few will dislike the scents of spring and avoid exposure to them. Few will appreciate being touched by unknown people in open, yet crowded places. Few will despise the taste of well-selected seasonal spices. Do these perceptions of smell, touch and taste change and, if so, how have they changed from those in the past?

In studies published during the 1930s and 1940s, historians such as Lucien Fèbvre[1] and sociologists such as Norbert Elias[2] provided answers to these

---

* The best about dancing is that one does not always have to move forward but can also turn around.

[1] Lucien Fèbvre, *Rabelais et le problème de l'incroyance au XVe siècle* (Paris, 1962), pp. 461–8 [first published (Paris, 1942)].

[2] Norbert Elias, *Über den Prozess der Zivilisation*, vol. 1, 19th edn (Frankfurt, 1995), pp. 110–263 [first published (Basle, 1939)]. Elias's theory was severely attacked by ethnologist Hans Peter Duerr who attempted to show that there was no increase in affect

questions. They agreed that in the course of the sixteenth, seventeenth and eighteenth centuries marked but gradual changes took place in the standards of the perception of smell, touch and taste, yet they disagreed about the direction in which the changes occurred. Fèbvre found that the intensity of smell perception gradually declined during the sixteenth and seventeenth centuries and was reinforced during the eighteenth century. Elias observed, among other things, two processes going on simultaneously during the early modern period. The first process was the increase in the refinement of tastes. The second process was a decline of the frequency of and an increase in the sensitivity towards touch. According to Elias, the early modern culture of the courts of rulers produced new standards of taste perception through the introduction of a wider range of flavours, more elaborate cooking procedures, the professionalisation of cooks and the sophistication of table manners. Elias believed that the increase in the refinement of taste was part of a more fundamental process of what he termed 'affect control'. In his view, increasing 'affect control' was also responsible for the changes in attitudes towards touch. Thus, while Fèbvre diagnosed a temporary decline of the sensitivity towards smell, Elias sensed a steadily increasing sensitivity towards touch and taste. Yet both scholars left important questions unanswered. What are the standards for the measurement of some 'increase' or 'decline' of the perception of smell, touch and taste? Fèbvre used the standard of his own time. Measuring the evidence of his sources against his standards of perception led him to believe that the intensity of smell perception had temporarily waned. But did contemporaries of the early modern period have the same perception and did they use Fèbvre's standard? Fèbvre did not know because he did not enquire.

Likewise, Elias admitted only his own standard of 'affect control' as a valid measurement for some increase or decline of what appeared to him as a sensitivity towards touch and taste. But what if contemporaries of the early modern period had their own standards, that is, if they believed that they were actually controlling their 'affects' where Elias thought they did not? In this case, an answer is possible only if the sources are allowed to display their own specific standards of perception and the subjective consciousness of actors at the time. Therefore, much as these studies were remarkable at their own time

control in European history and, among others, used sources on medieval bathing as evidence. Contrary to Elias, who claimed that there had been fewer constraints against the display of the nude body in the Middle Ages than in early modern Europe, Duerr insisted that medieval sources on the display of nudity, such as the joint bathing of men and women, were not to be taken as literal descriptions of actual practice but as warnings against indecent behaviour. The controversy did not lead to a better understanding of the history of perception because Elias was preoccupied with demonstrating progress in history, whereas Duerr limited his scope to the goal of destroying Elias's evolutionism. See Hans Peter Duerr, *Nacktheit und Scham*, in Duerr, *Der Mythos vom Zivilisationsprozess*, vol. 1 (Frankfurt, 1988), pp. 38–73, 356–70 [repr. (Frankfurt, 1994). Duerr, *Intimität*, in Duerr, *Der Mythos vom Zivilisationsprozess*, vol. 2 (Frankfurt, 1990), pp. 11–24, 270–360, 365–75, 477–552.

because their authors were aware of the possibility of conceptual changes, the lack of attention to changes of standards of perception prevented their authors from stepping beyond mere contentions about increase and decline. The lack of awareness of changing standards of perception helps to explain the contradictory and perplexing result of the work of both scholars, namely that the sensitivity towards smell should have declined while the sensitivity towards touch and taste should have increased during the same period. Could Fèbvre and Elias have both been correct?

The way out of the dead end of attempting to measure what is not measurable is to ask different questions. One possible question is how persons experienced their interactions with their physical and social environments while being exposed to smells, touches and tastes. Smells, touches and tastes generate sensations through physical impacts on the body, namely through the air we breathe, the external impressions on the skin we receive, and the food we take in. Fèbvre and Elias took for granted that these interactions should follow universal principles. Thus Fèbvre assumed that smells should trigger strong responses by perceivers and was, consequently, surprised to note that, at times, his sources failed to record strong responses towards smells. His conclusion was that the weakness of the responses must reflect a weakened sensitivity towards smell. But Fèbvre had no justification for postulating that responses to smells must universally have the strength that he expected. Similarly, Elias believed that persons should control their 'affects' and was surprised when he found that, at times, persons appeared to be less willing to act in accordance with his demand. For example, he claimed that the use of knives and forks as eating tools represents an increase of 'affect' control but had no justification for his claim. Instead, he was at a loss to say why his standards of 'affect' control have to be universally respected. Upon closer inspection, then, Fèbvre's assumption and Elias's belief represented standards of perception current in twentieth-century European societies rather than principles of universal validity. Behind the appearances of waxing and waning sensations lurk changing standards of perception. This chapter approaches the perception of smell, touch and taste as a changing instrument through which persons could reveal their attitudes towards their physical and social environments.

Sealing off the body against its environment: the history of smell perception

Smells whose emission human actors can hope to control may emerge from settlements or human and animal bodies. Throughout the Middle Ages, and up to the eighteenth century, very little had been recorded about smell perception in the majority of settlements that were agricultural in kind. Only from the later eighteenth century did it become customary for intellectual observers to accept a divide between cities and the countryside and to relate this imagined divide to smell perception. The image of smelly villages emerged as a heterostereotype[3] that was superimposed upon the countryside by inhabitants of urban communities. For example, in his description of the French countryside published in 1777, René-L. Girardin denounced villages as *cloacs* (cesspools), and thereby he gave expression to the conceit that village life did not conform to the then-emerging urban standards of air purification. These standards were new and not widespread in the second half of the eighteenth century. They included the demands that rules of hygiene should be observed and human and other waste should be properly removed inside the towns and cities.[4] The rural farming population at the time did not share these urban standards of air purification. Instead, it seems to have taken for granted that smells would emanate from human settlements. Yet the lack of explicit records of smell perception among the farming population makes it impossible to confirm this assumption. Nevertheless, if the human settlements were experienced as smelly and as long as such experience was taken for granted, there was no conceivable specific reason why such smell perception should be given specific attention in any record and why efforts should have been made to control smell emission.

Late medieval philosophers already provided proof of evidence for this observation by claiming that smell perception had less significance for humans than for animals. For one, Vincent of Beauvais insisted in the thirteenth century that humans were less capable than animals of detecting differences of smell. He assumed that the organ in charge of smell perception was the brain itself and reduced the nose to a mere tube linking the brain to the physical environment. Despite the frequency of visions of paradise and hell as places characterised, respectively, by good scents and bad smells, he also observed that humans would rarely perceive smells in their dreams and concluded that humans were not accustomed to sense smells because they appeared to him to be guided by reason rather than following the dictates of smell. Albert the Great concurred with his description of the sense of smell without reference to the nose as an organ.[5] A century later, Conrad of Megenberg described the nose as a window to the brain (*nasvenster*) and speculated about its use as an indicator of character.[6] Similarly, when the late

---

3   Heterostereotype is a term denoting typical images that are cast upon individuals or groups by other people, contrary to autostereotypes as typical images that people use by and for themselves.

4   René-L. Girardin, *De la composition des paysages* (Paris, 1777), p. 59. Similarly Jean-Noël Halle, *Recherches sur la nature et les effets du mephitisme des fosses d'asiances* (Paris, 1785), p. 10.

5   Vincent of Beauvais, *Speculum naturale*, lib. XXV, cap. 61, lib. XXV, cap. 68 (Douai, 1624), cols 1813–14, 1818 (Vincent of Beauvais. Speculum quadruplex sive speculum maius. 1.) [repr. (Graz, 1964)]. For evidence on vision, see below, notes 38 and 39. Albertus Magnus, *Summa de creaturis*, cap. II, quaestio 31, in *Alberti opera*, vol. 35, ed. Albert Borgnet (Paris, 1898), pp. 271–2.

6   Conrad of Megenberg, *Das Buch der Natur*, cap. I, ed. Franz Pfeiffer (Stuttgart, 1861), pp. 11–12, 423 [repr., ed. Gerhard E. Sollbach (Frankfurt, 1990)]. The same image of the nose appears in a sketch showing the five senses preserved in the anonymous fourteenth-century Tractatus ad libros Aristotelis introductorius cum commentario

fifteenth-century Nuremberg physician, book collector and publisher Hartmann Schedel felt the need to comment on what he had collected from the literature on monsters, he drew on Conrad of Megenberg's work and associated an overly long nose with the physiognomy of a goat and combined the description of a flat, noseless face with a mouth so small that it only allowed drinking with a straw but no eating.[7]

To what extent the disregard for smell emission also applied to smells emanating from the human body throughout the same period is equally difficult to ascertain. There is no lack of attention to smells in late and sub-Roman sources. But the evidence is ambivalent. Foremost among theologians, St Augustine wrote on the importance of producing sweet scents and of avoiding ugly smells; yet he condemned the Roman habit of bathing and insisted that bathing was a means of purification that monks and nuns should use with great care.[8] Secular sources tell a different story. The evidence of early medieval laws that enforced punishments for the destruction of bathing houses suggests that such buildings were not rare (Figure 15). That they were used becomes clear from the report of a ninth-century historiographer that the warm baths at Aix-la-Chapelle were frequented and that Emperor Louis III took a bath every week.[9] At places in southern Europe, Roman baths remained in use or were even restored. The oldest extant legal record for an urban bathing house north of the Alps appears to be in the twelfth-century town laws of Soest (Westphalia).[10] From the twelfth to the first half of the fourteenth century, bathing houses flourished. The Paris city scribe Nicolas Boileau noted the existence of twenty-six public baths in Paris in 1272.[11] The city of Regensburg alone had ten bathing houses in the fourteenth century of which nine continued to operate in the fifteenth century.[12] There were

interlineari et marginali, MS Prague, Czech Academy of Sciences, formerly Charles University Library, Ms 700 (IV.H.6), fol. 22v. The graph represents a human head and locates the sense of smell (*olfactus*) at the nose. The nose is shown as a pipe connecting the brain with the outside world. The same graph reappeared in print in the eclectic description of the world published by Gregor Reisch, *Margarita mundi*, lib. X, tract. 2 (Nuremberg, 1504), s. p.

[7] See Hartmann Schedel, *Das Buch der Croniken vnnd geschichten* (Nuremberg, 1493), fol. XIIr [repr. (Grünwald, 1975)]. Schedel drew on Megenberg, *Buch* (see note 6), p. 490.

[8] Augustine, *Confessiones*, lib. X, cap. 32, ed. James Joseph O'Donnell, vol. 1 (Oxford, 1992), p. 138.

[9] *Lex Baiwariorum*, lib. X, cap. 3, ed. Ernst von Schwind, MGH, LL nat.Germ., vol. V, part 2 (Hanover, 1926), pp. 386–7. Notker the Stammerer, *Gesta Karoli Magni Imperatoris*, lib. II, cap. 15, lib. II, cap. 22, ed. Hans Frieder Haefele, MGH SS. Rer. Germ. N. S. XII (Berlin, 1959), pp. 80, 93.

[10] See Wilhelm Gail, 'Die Rechtsverfassung der öffentlichen Badstuben', LL.D.diss. (University of Bonn, 1940), p. 23.

[11] Nicolas Boileau, *Le livre des métiers* (Paris, 1879), pp. 628–9.

[12] See Rosa Kohlheim, *Regensburger Beinamen des 12. bis 14. Jahrhunderts. Beinamen aus Berufs-, Amts- und Standesbezeichnungen*, Bayreuther Beiträge zur Dialektologie VI (Hamburg, 1990), p. 162. Helmut Wolff, 'Regensburgs Häuserbestand im späten Mittelalter', in *Studien und Quellen zur Geschichte Regensburgs*, vol. 3 (Regensburg, 1985), p. 175.

Fig. 15 Public bath. From Conrad Kyeser, Bellifortis. c. 1400. Göttingen Niedersächsische Staats- und Universitätsbibliothek, MS philos. 63 Cim, fol. 114r.

numerous barbers in many cities and they even formed professional guilds in some of them.[13]

Bathing did not merely connote pleasure.[14] Mid-twelfth-century songs could also associate bathing with moral or spiritual purification and described it as a kind of foot-washing ritual. Even the luxurious sprinkling of the nude body with lavender after a bath could rank as an attempt to please

13 See Johann Herkules Haid, *Ulm mit seinem Gebiete* (Ulm, 1786), pp. 253–4 [repr. (Ulm, 1984)]. Karl Heffner, 'Über die Baderzunft im Mittel-Alter und später, besonders in Franken', in *Archiv des Historischen Vereins von Unterfranken und Aschaffenburg* 6 (1864), pp. 155–246.

14 Among others, see *Roman de la Rose* by Guillaume de Loiris and Jean de Meung, *Vollständige Ausgabe des Rosenromans für François I. M. 948 aus dem Besitz der Pierpont Morgan Library*, vv. 10089–102, facsimile edn by Margareta Friesen, Codices selecti, series IIIC, vol. 1 (Graz, 1993), fols 92r–94v. Cf. Seifried Helbling, [description of a visit in a bathing house], ed. Alfred Martin, *Deutsches Badewesen in vergangenen Tagen* (Jena, 1906), pp. 148–9 [also ed. Joseph Seemüller, *Seifried Helbling* (Halle, 1886)].

the divinity with a good scent.[15] Perhaps under the impact of the bathing cultures of the Levant and North Africa,[16] literary and pictorial descriptions of bathing in the Occident conveyed the sense of joy and pleasure, likening the bath to the fountain of youth, and medical people suggested bathing as a cure for diseases in a relaxed and joyful atmosphere.[17] From the thirteenth century onwards, scholars compiled lists of spas well-known for their hot springs and therapeutic value,[18] and leisure trips to spas were customary and enjoyed by lay persons as well as clergymen.[19]

[15] See Herrand of Wildonie, *Die poetischen Erzählungen*, vv. 68–98, ed. Karl Friedrich Kummer (Vienna, 1880), pp. 250–1. Thomas Murner, *Ein andechtig geistliche Badenfahrt*, cap. VIII–IX, XIV–XVI (Strasbourg, 1514), pp. 32–9, 56–67 [ed. Ernst Martin, Beiträge zur Landes- und Volkskunde von Elsass-Lothringen II (Strasbourg, 1887), pp. 9–11, 15–18].

[16] For evidence on bathing in Arab sources, see Ibn Hawqal, *Kitāb sūrat al-'ard*, ed. Michael Jan de Goeje, Bibliotheca geographicorum arabicorum II (Leiden, 1874), pp. 73, 111, 138, 140, 177, 184, 210, 224, 432–3 [repr. (Leiden, 1967)] [describes bath-houses in Sus, Cordoba, Mosul and smaller towns in Andalusia, North Africa, Egypt, Syria, Iraq and Khorasan]. Ali 'Ubaid Allāh ibn 'Abd al-'Aziz Al-Bakrī, *Kitāb al-ma'rūf bi-al-masālith wa almamālik*, ed. William de Slane (Algiers, 1857), pp. 17, 20, 28, 29, 40, 56 [repr. (Frankfurt, 1992)] [describes bath-houses in Tunis, Sfax, Monastir, Gabes and other towns in North Africa]. Naser-e Khosraw, *Tahlīl-i Safarnāmah* (Tehran, 1992), p. 108 [describes bath-houses in Cairo]. For evidence recording the use of baths by Occidental traders and travellers in the Levant and North Africa, see *I diplomi arabi del R. Archivio Fiorentino*, ed. Michele Amari (Florence, 1863), p. 258 [treaty of 1173 between Saladin and Pisa including the grant of a bath-house in Alexandria]. *Codice diplomatico della republica di Genova*, doc. 167, 169, vol. 1, ed. Cesare Imperiale di Sant' Angelo (Rome, 1936–41), pp. 206–7, 214–15 [grants to Genoese merchants of a bath-house in Castile in 1146]. *Liber iurium Reipublicae Genuensis*, doc. 236, 989, vol. 1, Historiae Patriae Monumenta VII (Turin, 1854), cols 207–10, 1485–86 [grants of bath-houses in 1162]. *Urkunden zur älteren Handels- und Staatsgeschichte der Republik Venedig*, ed. G. L. F. Tafel and G. M. Thomas, vol. 2 (Vienna, 1856), p. 65 [repr. (Amsterdam, 1964)] [grant of a bath-house in Aleppo in 1207/08]. Olivia Remie Constable, *Housing the Stranger in the Mediterranean World* (Cambridge, 2003), pp. 42, 60, 70–2, 75, 118–20, 124–7, 183–4, 208, 294, 297. Isidoro de Las Cagigas, 'Une traité de paix entre le Roi Pierre IV d'Aragon et le Sultan de Tunis Abu Ishaq (1360), in *Hesperis* 18 (1934), p. 71 [on treaties between Hafsid rulers in Andalusia and Occidental traders on the use of baths, fourteenth/fifteenth centuries]. Julian Raby, *Venice, Durer and the Oriental Mode* (Totowa, NJ, 1982), pp. 55–65 [prints a picture of Damascus showing a bath-house and Occidental traders entering the city]. Jean Sauvaget, 'Une ancienne représentation de Damas au Musée du Louvre', in *Bulletin d'Etudes Orientales. Institut français de Damas* 2 (1945/6), pp. 5–6, 8–9 [prints a picture of Damascus showing a bath-house and Occidental traders entering the city].

[17] See Johann Lange, *Epistolae medicinales* (Basle, 1554), p. 184 [quoted from Adolf Hasenclever, 'Dr. Johannes Lange über seine Reise nach Granada im Jahre 1526', in *Archiv für Kulturgeschichte* 5 (1907), p. 423, n. 1]. Andrea Baccio, *De thermis . . . libri septem*, lib. II, cap. 9, cap. 12 (Venice, 1621), pp. 98–100, 107–10. Anna Rapp, 'Der Jungbrunnen in Literatur und bildender Kunst des Mittelalters', Ph.D. diss., typescript (University of Zurich, 1976), pp. 104–8, 128, 150.

[18] Lists of spas have been on record in the medical literature from the late thirteenth century. See: Aurelius Cornelius Celsus and Leonardu Targa, ed., *De balneis omnia quae extant apud Graecos, Latinos et Arabas* (Venice, 1553), fols 37r–47r, 94r–108v, 191v–194v [a collection of treatises on balneology by Petrus de Tossignano, c. 1250,

Note 19 next page

Thus, a curious tenth-century source showing that not merely monks and nuns but also the lay farming population enjoyed baths did not stand alone. This record is contained in the account of the monastery's affairs by Abbot Ekkehard IV of St Gall. Ekkehard reported an incident in which a traveller from the countryside tried to gain access to the bathing services of the monastery.[20] The traveller pretended to be lame and demanded to be treated by the monks. Under this pretence, he was admitted and well taken care of. But difficulties in communication emerged while the man was sitting in the bathtub. This was so because the monk attending to the traveller communicated in a Germanic dialect whereas the traveller spoke a language based on Latin. As the water in the bathtub was too hot for the traveller, he exclaimed: 'Ei mi, cald est, cald est!' (have mercy on me, it's hot, it's hot). But the monk understood the Latin-based word *cald* in its Germanic meaning and believed that the water was too cold for the traveller. Hence, he poured more hot water into the tub so that, eventually, the traveller could no longer endure the heat and jumped out. The traveller thus had to reveal that he could move well but had sought to bathe solely for his own pleasure.

However, it is unclear whether legal rules and the St Gall incident were connected with perceptions of bodily smells among the peasant farming population. This qualification is essential in the light of other sources recording efforts to reduce the frequency of bathing. True, the St Gall incident does show that in the monasteries regular bathing occurred and that, following St Augustine, monks and nuns believed that bathing could be a therapy whereas

Johannes de Dondis, c. 1350, Antonius Gvainerius, c. 1440, and Bartholomaeus de Montagna, c. 1440]. Giovanni Michele Savonarola, *Canonica Michaelis Sauonarole practica de febribus, de urinis, de egestionibus, de omnis Italie balneis* (Venice, 1561), fols 125v, 133v. Hans Folz, 'Ein puchlin von allen paten die von nature heiss sein [printed (Nuremberg, 1480)', ed. Adelbert von Keller, *Fastnachtspiele aus dem fünfzehnten Jahrhundert*, vol. 3 (Stuttgart, 1857), pp. 1249–65. Clemens von Graz, *Dyss buchlein hat gemacht unnd erfaren Mayster Clement von Gracz von allen paden dye von Natur hayss sind* (Brno, 1495). Baccio (see note 17). Johann Friedrich Zückert, *Systematische Beschreibung aller Gesundbrunnen und Bäder Deutschlands* (Berlin and Leipzig, 1768), pp. 101–333.

19 An early case of a pleasure trip to spas is recorded of the thirteenth-century Abbot Albert of St Emmeram in Regensburg. See Lorenz von Westenrieder, ed., *Beyträge zur vaterländischen Historie, Geographie, Statistik und Landwirthschaft* 8 (1796), p. 115. Poggio di Guccio Bracciolini, secretary to the papal *nuntio* at the Council of Constance (1414–18), reported to a friend in Florence on an excursion he had taken in 1417 to the spa at Baden (Aargau). Poggio gave an impression of the pleasure of the local townsfolk in bathing [in Bracciolini, *Lettere*, ed. Helene Harth, vol. 1 (Florence, 1984), pp. 130–1; also in Lothar Schmidt, ed., *Die Renaissance in Briefen von Dichtern, Künstlern, Staatsmännern, Gelehrten und Frauen*, vol. 1 (Leipzig, 1909), pp. 104–18]. Cf. the later descriptions of the same spa in the travel reports by Pero Tafur, *Andanças é viajes por diversas partes del mundo avidos (1435–1439)*, Colección de libros espanoles raros ó curiosas VIII (Madrid, 1874), pp. 234–5 [English version, ed. Malcolm Letts (London, 1926)]; and Michel de Montaigne, *Journal de son voyage*, ed. Fausta Garavini and Jean Bond (Paris, 1983), p. 98.

20 Ekkehard IV of St Gall, *Casus Sancti Galli*, ed. Georg Heinrich Pertz, MGH SS, vol. 2 (Hanover, 1829), pp. 121–2.

bathing for pleasure in the Roman tradition was regarded as an offence against monastic asceticism. In his early eighth-century *Ecclesiastical History of the English People*, Bede took a similar attitude when he praised Abbess Æthelthryth for taking a bath only twice in a year on the occasion of high church festivals.[21] Likewise, Ruotger, the author of the tenth-century *Life of Bruno*, archbishop of Cologne and brother of Emperor Otto I, emphasised Bruno's habit of using neither soap nor means to brighten his skin for his daily hygiene. Furthermore, Ruotger insisted that Bruno's asceticism as the holder of a high church office differed from the usual practices of lay aristocratic kin groups.[22] The eleventh-century rules for the monks of Hirsau were explicit in allowing full baths only twice a year, namely at Easter and at Christmas.[23]

Monastic asceticism reduced the reputation of lay bathing. From the twelfth century, the pleasurable connotations of therapeutic bathing could nourish the suspicion that public baths were frivolous places.[24] They were not infrequently held to be simple brothels, specifically at places where men and women would sit in the bathtubs together. Theologians, moral philosophers and lawgivers denounced bathing as evil, banned the display of the nude body, spoke out in favour of a morality that devaluated the human mind as frail and the human body as ugly, weak and filled with dirt, generated perceptions of the human body as the source of bad, evil and even dangerous smells, categorised bathing as heretical and an act of resistance against secular and church

---

21 Bede, *Historia ecclesiastica gentis Anglorum*, lib. IV, cap. 19, ed. Bertram Colgrave and Roger Aubrey Baskervill Mynors (Oxford, 1969), p. 391 [repr. (Oxford, 2003)].

22 Ruotger, *Vita Brunonis*, cap. 30, ed. Irene Ott, MGH, SS rer. Germ. N. S. X (Cologne and Graz, 1951), p. 31.

23 William of Hirsau, *Constitutiones Hirsaugienses et Gengenbacenses*, lib. II, cap. 41, in *PL* vol. 150, col. 1101.

24 The frivolous character of the depiction of some bathing scenes is not always appreciated by students of the history of bathing. See, for example, Manfred Kossock, *1492. Die Welt an der Schwelle zur Neuzeit* (Leipzig, 1992), p. 24. Here, the author prints an illumination of a bathing scene in a brothel from the Roman author Valerius Maximus, Factorum et dictorum memorabilium librio novem, cap. 9. The manuscript was written about 1480. Manuscripts of this work frequently displayed a brothel scene together with the section of the text at which the corruption of morals is explained to the emperor. The same intention of depicting frivolous (and thus non-standard) bathing scenes may have been pursued by Hans Bock, the Elder, in his late sixteenth-century painting of a bath in the Swiss Confederacy (Baden in the Aargau or Leuk), held by the PTT Museum, Bern. The picture shows an open-air bath with nudes of either sex in steaming water around a wooden board carrying fruit and drinks. At least two men are pursuing women with recognisably sexual desires. For an interpretation of this painting as a straightforward description of contemporary bathing habits, see Michael Maurer, 'Bilder repräsentieren Geschichte. Repräsentieren Bilder Geschichte?', in Klaus Füßmann, Heinrich Theodor Grütter and Jörn Rüsen, ed., *Historische Faszination. Geschichtskultur heute* (Cologne, Weimar and Vienna, 1994), pp. 76–82. For the satirical description of a bathing house as a brothel, see Ulrich von Hutten's story of the Würzburg canon who had himself entertained by women in a bathtub. The story is in Hutten, *Epistolae obscurorum virorum* and has been edited by Heffner, 'Baderzunft' (see note 13), pp. 212–13.

authorities and brandmarked other bodily joys as evils and temptations of the devil. [25] The pessimistic anthropology peaked in the fourteenth-century equation of the body with a 'nine-holed nightsoil pail',[26] and provoked further decline in the appreciation of bathing. Eventually, in the sixteenth century, Augsburg women could receive praise for watering their bodies only twice in a year and, instead, using perfumes to disseminate good scents,[27] and the philosopher Peter Ramus, who was by no means hostile to the temporal joys of the world, could be proud of taking a bath only once in a year.[28]

Such attitudes appeared to be confirmed by practical experiences from the time of the Black Death. The Umbrian physician Gentile da Foligno, who died

[25] See Walter de Milemete, *De nobilitatibus sapientiis et prudentiis Regum*, cap. XVI, facsimile edn (London, 1913), p. 125 [= fol. 63r]. Jakob Geiler von Kaysersberg, *Von den 15 Staffeln* (Strasbourg, 1517), fol. 35v. For fourteenth-century and later laws preventing the joint bathing of men and women, see J. Bader, ed., 'Badeordnung in dem Glottertal', in *Zeitschrift für die Geschichte des Oberrheins* 19 (1868), p. 249. Ulrich Knefelkamp, *Das Gesundheits- und Fürsorgewesen der Stadt Freiburg im Breisgau im Mittelalter*, Veröffentlichungen aus dem Archiv der Stadt Freiburg VXII (Freiburg, 1981), p. 75. Franz Josef Mone, 'Über Krankenpflege vom 13. bis 16. Jahrhundert in Wirtemberg, Baden, der bairischen Pfalz und Rheinpreußen', in *Zeitschrift für die Geschichte des Oberrheins* 2 (1851), p. 291. Charles Wittmer, 'Bains et baigneurs à Strasbourg au Moyen Age', in *Cahiers alsaciens d'archéologie, d'art et d'histoire* (1961), p. 92. Willi Varges, 'Die Wohlfahrtspflege in den deutschen Städten des Mittelalters', in *Preussische Jahrbücher* 81 (1895), pp. 286–7. Georg Zappert, 'Über das Badewesen in mittelalterlicher und späterer Zeit', in *Archiv für Kunde österreichischer Geschichtsquellen* 21 (1859), p. 82. Duerr, *Nacktheit* (see note 2), uses these laws directly against the belief that men and women could take joint baths. He does not consider the motives that authorities may have had in issuing and enforcing these laws. Their frequency in the fourteenth and fifteenth centuries points towards the existence of a custom that authorities intended to end. Hence, against their explicit intention, the laws contain evidence that bathing customs existed that contradicted the laws. Moreover, as Duerr knows himself, the effect of the laws seems to have been limited, as, early in the seventeenth century, a moralising German physician could still lament an apparently popular practice at places with public open-air baths, according to which men and women would take off their clothes, rush to the bath naked and take the bath jointly. See Hippolythus Guarinonius, *Die greuel der verwüstung menschlichen geschlechts* (Ingolstadt, 1610), quoted in Karl Kochendörffer, 'Zum mittelalterlichen Badewesen', in *Zeitschrift für deutsche Philologie* 24 (1892), pp. 495–6. Apparently, the moralist became angry about the habit in response to the therapy that demanded bathing in a relaxed and pleasant atmosphere, including the satisfaction of sexual desires (see above, note 17). The painting of Abano Terme by Domenico Vandelli of 1761, a spa wellknown for having been visited by Emperor Frederick III in the fifteenth century, could still show the scene of a village with nudes of either sex in an open-air bath near the road to Padua.

[26] Johannes von Tepl [John of Saaz], *Der Ackermann aus Böhmen*, cap. XXV, XVI, ed. Willy Krogmann, 4th edn (Wiesbaden, 1978), pp. 125–6. The idea that ugly substances could emanate from the body is on record elsewhere in the Middle Ages. See Freidank, *Bescheidenheit*, vv. 21, 11–16, ed. Heinrich Ernst Bezzenberger (Halle, 1872).

[27] See *Des Grafen Wolrad von Waldeck Tagebuch während des Reichstags zu Augsburg 1548*, s. d. 7 July 1548, ed. C. L. P. Tross, Bibliothek des Litterarischen Vereins in Stuttgart LIX (Stuttgart, 1861), pp. 221–2.

[28] On Ramus, see Abel Jules-Maurice Lefranc, *Histoire du Collège de France depuis ses origines à la fin du premier Empire* (Paris, 1893), pp. 206–24.

of the plague in June 1348, made 'rotten air' responsible for the outbreak of the epidemic. He argued that such miasmas could enter the body, turn into poison within the body and depart again to seek further victims.[29] Ugly smells from the interior of the earth served as a further reason for the plague. When a severe earthquake hit the eastern Alps on 25 January 1348, the Florentine chronicler Giovanni Villani, before he became himself a victim of the epidemic, connected the disaster with the plague that erupted in Venice less than a month later.[30] Similarly, the Venetian Chronicler Lorenzo de Monacis went to great lengths to describe the city's terrifying stench when the epidemic was at its peak.[31] Consequently, in its comment on the reasons for the Black Death in 1348, the Paris Medical School identified the spread of excessively and thus smelly moist air from India to Europe as the cause of the epidemic. In their diagnoses, the medical doctors and their contemporaries followed Aristotle's lead in assuming that smells were transmitted through moist substances in the air and the water.[32] They concluded that the plague was spreading through the inhalation of excessively smelly air and recommended that urban folk should eat light food, refrain from sexual intercourse and avoid taking baths.[33] Thus they requested abstention and other strategies of asceticism rather than demanding that persons should actively use their own will and energies to control smell emission and to change the environment to their advantage.

Indeed, smell emission from urban settlements was substantial, ubiquitous and perpetual throughout and beyond the Middle Ages. The narrow space within the walled urban settlements, the often insufficient facilities for the appropriate removal of faeces and other waste, the existence within the towns and cities of manufacturing workshops, the manifold traffic of incoming and outgoing traders during markets: all these factors produced smell in the densely populated urban space. Human ordure and material waste could be left on courtyards or streets, an easy though sometimes illegal solution; could be buried in cesspools in the backyards of houses, sometimes in proximity to local wells; or could be piped into nearby streams. When rivers crossed the settlements, they were flanked by the houses of artisans for whom the use of water and water power was essential. Butchers, tanners, dyers and other arti-

---

[29] Gentile da Folignos's *consilium* on the plague has been edited by Karl Sudhoff, 'Pestschriften aus den ersten 150 Jahren nach der Epidemie des "Schwarzen Todes" 1348', in *Archiv für Geschichte der Medizin* 5 (1912), p. 334.

[30] *Cronaca di Giovanni Villani, a miglior lezione ridotta*, lib. XII, cap. 123, ed. Francesco Gherardi Dragomanni, Colezione di storici e cronisti Italiae editi e inediti IV (Florence, 1845), p. 183 [repr. (Frankfurt, 1969); another repr. (Turin, 1979)].

[31] Lorenzo de Monacis, *Laurentii de Monacis Veneti Cretae Cancellarii Chronicon de rebus Venetis ab U[rbe] C[ondita] ad annum MCCCLIV* (Venice, 1758), pp. 314–15.

[32] Aristotle, *De anima*, 443a.

[33] *Report of the Paris Medical Faculty*, October 1348, ed. Robert Hoeniger, *Der Schwarze Tod in Deutschland* (Berlin, 1882), pp. 152–6 [repr. (Vaduz, 1986)]. English version in Rosemary Horrox, ed., *The Black Death* (Manchester and New York, 1994), pp. 158–63.

sans would drain their waste water into the river, which would carry the refuse from city to city.

In a few instances, literary texts have preserved the anxiety that life in such smelly and polluted environments could be dangerous. Boccaccio's *Decameron*, for example, opened with a description of the ugliness of the city at the time of the Black Death. Boccaccio allowed a group of surviving Florentines to leave the city to seek refuge in the less smelly and thus healthier countryside and recorded their pledge to improve the sanitary conditions of the city upon return.[34] Some city authorities considered the stench unbearable, expected that it might cause mental and other diseases, and strove to reduce it. The mayor of London, for one, ordered a comprehensive survey of the filth in the city's streets to be made in 1344 and fined German Hansa merchants in the Steelyard for having dumped waste into the River Thames. In 1349, King Edward III warned that the city should be kept clear of all evil smells to prevent the spread of the plague. When little improvement appeared to occur, the king deplored the city's gruesome filth in 1357 and insisted that the inhabitants be aware of the dangers to their health if the sanitary conditions did not improve. Nevertheless, in 1372, the city felt obliged to issue statutes according to which a fine of four shillings had to be levied on inhabitants who placed refuse before the doors of others, together with a fine of two shillings to be paid by those who threw their refuse out of the window. The statutes were reissued in 1381, 1385 and 1390. On the continent, the council of Cologne ruled in 1353 that waste had to be cleared from the streets during the night to avoid smell pollution; in 1376, the council of Göttingen made efforts to increase the purity of the air in the city by cleaning the waterways running through it, and in 1398, the council decreed that waste should be deposited on the streets for no longer than two successive nights. In the fifteenth century, the council of Nuremberg acted similarly, requesting that waste should not be pumped into a brook running through the city, and demanded that waste that had been dumped into the streets should remain there for no longer than eight successive nights. In the same century, the council of Goslar, north of the Harz, banned the building of stables for swine in the frontyard of houses to reduce the stench. Elsewhere, a few rulers were more lenient. Thus the earl of Württemberg allowed the inhabitants of the capital city of Stuttgart in south-west Germany to cast their waste onto courtyards, provided no one was molested or injured while passing by.[35]

34 Giovanni Boccaccio, *Decameron*, editio princeps (Venice, 1492). English version in Horrox, ed., *Black Death* (see note 33), pp. 26–34.
35 For fears of diseases caused by excessive smell, see Hermann Hoffmann, *Würzburger Polizeisätze. Gebote und Ordnungen des Mittelalters*, no. 363, Veröffentlichungen der Gesellschaft für Fränkische Geschichte, vol. X, part 5 (Würzburg, 1955), p. 182. For London, see the order to prevent butchers from dispersing their waste on to the street [1336], in Reginald Robinson Sharpe, ed., *Calendar of Letter-Books preserved among the Archives of the Corporation of the City of London*, Letter-Book A (London, 1899), p. 183. Also the Royal Order for Cleaning the Streets of the City and the Banks of the Thames [1357], in Henry Thomas Riley, ed., *Memorials of London and London Life* (London,

In the fourteenth century, poets began to praise the beauty of the open countryside with its good scents. In 1387, Geoffrey Chaucer's *Canterbury Tales* opened with an expression of the joy with which 'people from all over England' greeted spring and set out for a rural pilgrimage to Canterbury:

> When with mild rain April has watered March's draft down to the roots and bathed every vein in juice, from whose power the flower grows; after Cephyr with his sweet breath has awakened the tender sprouts in every forest and field; and after the young sun has half completed his course in Capricorn and when the small birds sing melodies (for they sleep all night with open eyes, because nature excites their hearts), then everyone yearns for going on a pilgrimage.[36]

Chaucer put on record the emerging willingness of urban residents to cross the walls of their towns and cities for pleasant and enjoyable journeys. His reference to the sweetness of the wind hinted at the pleasant smell that travellers could encounter on their journeys. This *synesthesia* of taste with smell perception, enshrined in the legacy of Roman Antiquity,[37] also occurred in late medieval visions of paradise where visionaries were recorded to have experienced landscapes in terms of 'sweetness'[38] and as spacious places outside the narrow confines of the towns and cities. On the opposite side, hell was imag-

1868), pp. 295–6. A similar order was given to the inhabitants of the Steelyard, in Rolf Sprandel, ed., *Quellen zur Hansegeschichte*, Ausgewählte Quellen zur Geschichte des Mittelalters XXXVI (Darmstadt, 1982), p. 376. For Cologne, see Walter Stein, ed., *Akten zur Geschichte der Verfassung und Verwaltung der Stadt Köln im 14. und 15. Jahrhundert*, vol. 2, Publikationen der Gesellschaft für Rheinische Geschichtskunde X (Bonn, 1895), p. 23. For Göttingen see Goswin Freiherr von der Rapp, ed., *Göttinger Statuten*, no. 48 (1376), 74, §31 (1398), Quellen und Darstellungen zur Geschichte Niedersachsens XXV (Hanover, 1907), pp. 60, 88. For Nuremberg, see Joseph Baader, ed., *Nürnberger Polizeiordnungen aus dem XIII bis XV Jahrhundert*, Bibliothek des Litterarischen Vereins in Stuttgart LXIII (Stuttgart, 1861), pp. 277–80 [repr. (Amsterdam, 1966)]. For Goslar, see Uvo Hölscher, 'Goslarsche Ratsverordnungen aus dem 15. Jahrhundert', in *Zeitschrift des Harzvereins* 42 (1909), p. 63. For Stuttgart, see Eberhard, Earl of Württemberg, Order of 14 August 1466, ed. Adolf Rapp, *Urkundenbuch der Stadt Stuttgart*, no. 483, Württembergische Geschichtsquellen. N. F. XIII (Stuttgart, 1912), p. 269.

[36] Geoffrey Chaucer, *The Canterbury Tales*, in Chaucer, *The Works*, ed. Fred Norris Robinson, 2nd edn (Oxford and New York, 1974), p. 17. For a parallel to Chaucer, see Heinrich Seuse, *Deutsche Schriften*, ed. Karl Bihlmeyer (Stuttgart, 1907), p. 199.

[37] Cicero, *De oratore*, lib. III, cap. 98–9 [various editions]. Pope Gregory I popularised the usage by including into his *Dialogues* the report about a *visio* in which the visionaries seemed to have been exposed to an unusually sweet scent emitted from a grave. See Gregory I, *Dialogues*, lib. IV, cap. 49, part 5, ed. Adalbert de Vogüé, vol. 3, Sources chrétiennes CCLXV (Paris, 1980), p. 170.

[38] Dante Alighieri, *Divina comedia*, Paradiso, canto VI, vv. 71–80, ed. Natalino Sapegno (Milan and Naples, 1957). Bartholomaeus Anglicus, *Liber de rerum proprietatibus*, lib. XIX, cap. 7, ed. Georg Barthold Pontanus a Braitenberg (Frankfurt, 1601), p. 1145 [repr. (Frankfurt, 1964)]. *Alphabet of Tales*, cap. 603: Paradisus. Paradisi disposicio, ed. M. M. Banks, EETS OS CXXVII (London, 1905), p. 403.

ined as an underground inferno not only with extreme heat and crampedness but also a strong stench.[39]

Smell perception began to change when it came under the impact of the optimistic anthropology that took shape in the Renaissance. While retaining the perception of the body as a source of smell, anthropologists praised the beauty and excellence of the human body,[40] and supported requests for purposeful actions to the ends of preventing smell emission and closing off the body against its physical and social environments. These demands were fuelled by the novel perception of the nose as an organ in itself rather than as a mere tube connecting the brain with the outside world.[41] The art of creating good scents developed into an aspect of the culture of rulers' and aristocrats' courts.[42] Eventually, Johann Joachim Becher, a seventeenth-century scientist who regarded air as an agent of rotting processes, elaborated the use of perfumes into a full-blown scientific theory of air pollution. Following the lead of the fourteenth-century Paris medical doctors, Becher postulated that rotting processes produced air, which contained evil substances and, in turn, produced ugly smells.[43] Seventeenth- and eighteenth-century chemists proposed the further argument that once these rotting gases had left the body, they could provoke fatal infections among those who inhaled the polluted air.[44] Yet this doctrine militated against the inherited appreciation of bathing as a therapy, which was developing into the fully fledged professional field of

39 Dante, *Divina comedia* (see note 38), canto XXX, vv. 1148–60. Robert of Brunne, *Handlyng Synne*, vv. 1385–1400, ed. Frederick James Furnivall. EETS OS CXIX (London, 1901), p. 50.

40 See Giannozzo Manetti, *De dignitate et excellentia hominis*, cap. III [1452] (Basle, 1532) [newly ed. Elizabeth R. Leonard (Padua, 1975), p. 6]. Gianfrancesco Pico della Mirandola, 'Oratio de hominis dignitate' [1493], in Pico, *Opera omnia*, vol. 1 (Basle, 1557), pp. 314–15 [repr. (Hildesheim and New York, 1969)].

41 See Joachim Camerarius [the Elder], *Themata physica de odorum natura et affectionibus*, M.D. diss. (University of Marburg, 1587). Giovanni Battista della Porta, *De humana physiognomia*, lib. II, cap. 9 (Hanau, 1593), pp. 734–78 [first published (1586); repr. (Naples, 1986)]. Conrad Schneider, *Liber de osse cribriformi et sensu ac organo odorato* (Wittenberg, 1655), p. 187.

42 See John Davies, *Nosce Teipsum. On the Soul of Man and the Immortality Thereof* (London, 1599), ed. Edward Arber, *An English Garner*, vol. 5 (Westminster, 1895), p. 174. Michel de Montaigne, 'Des senteurs', in Montaigne, *Essais* [1588], ed. Maurice Rat, vol. 1 (Paris, 1962), p. 348.

43 Johann Joachim Becher, *Physica subterranea* (Leipzig, 1703), p. 558 [first published (Frankfurt, 1669)].

44 See Nicolas de Blégny, *Secrets concernant la beauté et la santé* (Paris, 1688), p. 696. C. Delassone, et al., 'Sur les alterations que l'air éprouve par les différents substances', in *Histoire et mémoires de la Société Royale de Médecine* (1786), pp. 320–6. Claude Léopold Genneté, *Purification de l'air croupissant dans les hôpitaux, les prisons et les vaisseux de mer* (Nancy, 1767). John Howard, *The State of the Prisons in England and Wales*, 2nd edn (Warrington, 1780), pp. 8–9. Joseph Priestley, *Experiments and Observations on Different Kinds of Air* [Lecture delivered to the Royal Society on 28 June 1750] (London, 1774–77).

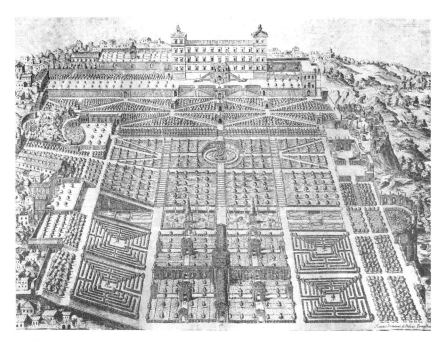

Fig. 16 Specimen of a Renaissance aristocratic residence in the countryside. The Villa d'Este in Tivoli. Etienne de Perac, 1573.

balneology from the fifteenth century.[45] Balneologists demanded that water should be used to remove potentially fatal substances from the body. Remaining unconvinced, the critics continued to take the view that excessive watering

[45] Charters by the Electors Palatinate Frederick I for the bath at Hub in the Ortenau district of Baden, dated 11 August 1475, and Philip for the saline at Kreuznach, dated 7 June 1490, ed. Franz Josef Mone, 'Ueber Armenpflege vom 13. bis 16. Jahrhundert', in *Zeitschrift für die Geschichte des Oberrheins* 2 (1851), pp. 283, 286. Lorenz Fries, *Tractat der Wildbeder* (Strasbourg, 1519). Johann Dryander [Eichmann], *Vom Eymser Bade* (Mainz, 1535) [repr., ed. by Irmgard Müller (Marburg, 1981)]. Dryander, *Arzneispiegel* (Frankfurt, 1547), presents a picture of a steam bath suggested for the treatment of various diseases; reprinted in Martin, *Badewesen* (see note 14), p. 212. For surveys of diseases that were regarded as curable through bathing, see Johann Winter [Guinther], *Commentarius de balneis et aquis medicatis* (Strasbourg, 1565). Georgius Pictorius, *Badenfahrtbüchlein* (Frankfurt, c. 1560) [repr., Bibliotheca Palatina F 3607 (Munich, 1991)]. Martin Ruland, *Hydriatice. Aquarum medicarum sectiones quatuor* (Dillingen, 1568). Ruland, *Vom Wasserbaden* (Dillingen, 1568), pp. 1–16. Leonhardt Thurneisen von Thurn, *Pison. Das erst Theil: Von kalten, warmen, minerischen vnd metallischen Wassern* (Frankfurt an der Oder, 1572). For descriptions of local spas, see, among others, Johann Matthaeus Hessus, *Natürliche wolerfarene Beschreibung dess Marggräfischen Bades Speyer* (1606). Ludwig von Hörnigk, *Wißbad* (Frankfurt, 1637). Johann Wilhelm Mogen, *Neu beschriebener Nider-Selterser Brunnen* (Frankfurt, 1669). De Vigneul-Marville [i.e., Bonaventura d'Argonne], *Mélanges d'histoire et de littérature*, vol. 1 (Rotterdam, 1700), p. 120. Johann Philipp Seip, *Beschreibung der Pyrmontischen Mineral-Wasser und Stahlbrunnen*, 4th edn (Hanover, Pyrmont, 1740).

of the body made the skin more malleable, opened the pores and freed rotting gases with seemingly dreadful consequences for the human and the physical environments.[46] In accordance with the medieval conventions, Nicolas Hoüel, a sixteenth-century medical doctor, argued that the plague was a consequence of the emanation of infectious gases from the body.[47]

Following the new theory, perfumes like *moschus* or *ambra* were widely used, together with creams and powder, in order to seal the body off against the physical and social environments.[48] The theory took a step beyond the late medieval conventions in that it helped develop the demand that individuals should take their own initiative to prevent environmental pollution by containing fatal rotting gases in their bodies.[49] In this way, sixteenth-, seventeenth- and eighteenth-century smell prevention rose to the symbol of the court aristocracy and the higher echelons of the urban population. These groups could thereby indicate their willingness and capability to subject themselves to a moral code and educational standard according to which they were obliged to make their own efforts to control smell emission. Consequently, wealthy members of urban patriciates, high-ranking court aristocrats and territorial rulers invested considerable fortunes to create spacious gardens at their urban residences or to build lavish palaces in countryside parks from the fifteenth century (Figure 16).

By contrast, the absence of the willingness and capability to comply with this novel code of ethical norms and educational standards among the peasant farming population and urban artisans characterised these groups as uneducated folk.[50] In turn, the new standard of smell perception helped establish the platform from which rural settlements and downtown parts of cities could be regarded as smelly areas. Smell perception served as a marker of social status: the higher the social status of a person was, the more onerous became the tasks of keeping the body in good order and preserving the physical and social environments in a stable condition and unmolested by ugly smell. The nose not merely became an important sense organ in its own right but even rose to the status of a means for the accomplishment of adequate behaviour. Late eighteenth-century physiognomists could expect that a well-proportioned nose might serve as the counterpart to the brain and keep the body in balance.[51]

---

46 Robert Boyle, *The General History of the Air* (London, 1692), pp. 212–13. Boyle, 'Experiments and Notes about the Mechanical Production of Odours', in Boyle, *Experiments, Notes . . . about the Mechanical Origine or Production of Diverse Particular Qualities* (London and Oxford, 1676), s. p.

47 Nicolas Hoüel, *Traité de la peste* (Paris, 1573), p. 16.

48 For a general survey, see Eugene Rimmel, *The Book of Parfumes* (Philadelphia, 1867).

49 Already Montaigne, 'Senteurs' (see note 42), p. 349, reported the story that some 'King of Tunis' had the habit of stuffing food with odoriferous substances in order to create a pleasant atmosphere at his court.

50 See Johann Khevenhueller-Metsch, *Feste und Feiern zur Zeit Maria Theresias, 1741–1776* (Vienna, 1987), pp. 62–3, 156–7.

51 Johann Caspar Lavater, *Physiognomische Fragmente*, vol. 1 (Leipzig and Winterthur, 1788), p. 151 [ed. Fritz Aerni (Waldshut, 1996), p. 134]. Lavater, *Hundert*

Fig. 17 Master of the Love Gardens, Feasting in the garden outside a castle. c. 1450. Berlin, Staatliche Museen Preussischer Kulturbesitz, Kupferstichkabinett. Photograph: Jörg P. Anders.

The only areas where the smells of the physical environment were already integrated into settlements in the late Middle Ages were hilltop castles. For example, the early thirteenth-century minstrel Ulrich of Liechtenstein[52] described how he picked flowers for a noble lady whom he served, and that he drank the water she had used for washing her hands. The reference indicates that the use of picked flowers was customary to decorate castle interiors and, apparently, that aristocratic women would habitually wash their hands. The aristocracy appears to have been willing to bring the sweetness of good scents into the barrenness of human settlements, which explains why the feasting garden became a prominent architectural feature of medieval castles (Figure 17).

But in the sixteenth century, the hilltop castles became outmoded. They were then perceived as narrow, cold and sealed off against the outside world by their walls. Thus, they could not compete with the lavish villas and palaces that members of the urban patriciates and territorial rulers built within spa-

physiognomische Regeln, in Lavater, *Nachgelassene Schriften,* ed. Georg Geßner, vol. 1 (Zurich, 1802), p. 37.

52 Ulrich of Liechtenstein, *Frauendienst,* v. 25,5, ed. Reinhold Bechstein (Leipzig, 1888).

cious gardens. The display of material wealth through such gardens raised the envy of those lesser aristocrats whose scarce financial endowments kept them confined to the old-fashioned hilltop castles. In their view, the new villas and palaces with their gardens were places where the human-made and physical environments were fully integrated.[53]

In conclusion, the history of smell perception displays a remarkable continuity among the peasant farming population from the early Middle Ages to the eighteenth century. But changes of smell perception did occur among the inhabitants of towns and cities. In the course of the sixteenth century, these groups developed a new standard of smell perception according to which persons were given the task of making their own efforts to control the emission of bad smell. In response to this new standard of perception, urban artisans and the peasant farming population became identified as uneducated folk because they displayed little willingness and saw no necessity to control smell emission. It is difficult to classify the changes of the standard of smell perception in the qualitative terms of amplification and intensification. Instead, what is possible is the association of changes in smell perception with the emergence of new ethical codes and educational standards. From the sixteenth century, the insistence that human actors should make their own efforts to control smell emission triggered an activism that was targeted at suppressing evil smells and transmitting good scents.

Enlarging the space around the body: the history of touch perception

Unlike the sense of smell, the sense of touch has attracted little interest among historians even though the sense of touch relates to the skin as the largest organ of the human body.[54] Of the several aspects of touch perception this chapter deals solely with touching among persons through the use of the hands. In this limited sense, person-to-person touching has been regulated throughout European history, although the types of rule have varied according to groups, areas and periods. Moreover, touching has received varying responses depending upon whether it was carried out purposefully or without intention.

The strictest prohibitions of purposeful person-to-person touching date from the eighth-century version of the Frankish *Lex Salica*. These prohibitions were legal in kind and concerned primarily the higher ranks of 'free' persons, that is, people not subjected to ties of servitude. They were intended to protect women against four kinds of purposeful touches: the touching of the finger or the head of an *ingenua* (a 'free' woman) by an *ingenuus* (a 'free' man); the touching of an arm under the same condition; the placing of a hand

---

53 Ulrich von Hutten [Letter to Willibald Pirckheimer, 25 October 1518], in Hutten, *Schriften*, vol. 1, ed. Eduard Böcking (Leipzig, 1859), pp. 201–3.
54 Conrad of Megenberg, *Buch*, lib. I, cap. 29 (see note 6), pp. 23–4, described the skin without proposing that the skin should be recognised as an organ.

of an *ingenuus* on an elbow of an *ingenua*; and the touching of the woman's breasts.[55]

Punishments for these crimes were severe. In the first case, the penalty was 15 shillings, equivalent to half of the fine for the forced abduction of a woman; in the second case, 30 shillings were due, the exact equivalent of the fine for the forced abduction of a woman; in the third case, the fine was 35 shillings, the equivalent of the fine for the intended mutilation of the finger used for shooting arrows; and, in the fourth case, the fine was 45 shillings, equivalent of what had to be paid for rape or illegal sexual intercourse with a married *ingenua*.

The severity of these punishments suggests that the specified illegal touching of parts of a woman's body was categorised as types of attempted attack on the person, with insinuated intentions of abduction, injury and sexual abuse. Other contemporary legal sanctions, such as corresponding articles in the *Lex Baiwariorum* and the *Lex Alamannorum*, were less casuistic and more focused on the prevention of sexual abuse.[56] In any case, the person-to-person touches that were legally banned in the early Middle Ages were regarded as purposeful actions and as potential or manifest acts of aggression against protected members of kin groups.

Yet, purposeful person-to-person touching was performed without legal restrictions to the end of transferring energies, when higher-ranking persons touched lower-ranking persons. In this respect, touching was a normative element of the Christian liturgy where it was used as a blessing gesture. Likewise, touching could be part of the royal ceremonial, such as in the coronation ceremony, where the unction and the placing of a crown on the head of the newly elected rulers involved touching (Figure 18).[57]

Moreover, most notably in the English and French royal rituals, touching was used for the purpose of healing certain diseases subsumed under the term scrofula.[58] These practices support the contention that touching was more than a symbol visualising some metaphysical energy transfer but could be

---

[55] *Lex Salica*, 100 Titel Text, cap. 26, 1–4, ed. Karl August Eckhardt (Weimar, 1953), p. 142 [= *Pactus legis Salicae*, cap. 20].

[56] *Lex Baiwariorum*, cap. VIII/3–VIII/8 (see note 9), pp. 355–7. *Lex Alamannorum*, version A, cap. LVI, ed. Karl Lehmann, 2nd edn by Karl August Eckhardt, MGH, LL nat. Germ. V,1 (Hanover, 1966), p. 115. Similar rules are in *Cáin Adamnáin*, ed. Kuno Meyer, Anecdota Oxoniensia, Ser. IV, Mediaeval and Modern Series I, vol. 12 (Oxford, 1905), p. 33. *Laws of Alfred*, cap. 11, 18, ed. Felix Liebermann, *Die Gesetze der Angelsachsen*, vol. 1 (Halle, 1903), pp. 56, 58. Wybren Jan Buma, *Das Emsiger Recht* (Göttingen, 1967), pp. 72–5, 121, 185. Buma and Wilhelm Ebel, *Das Hunsingoer Recht* (Göttingen, 1969), p. 52.

[57] The texts have been edited by Percy Ernst Schramm, *Kaiser, Könige und Päpste*, vol. 2 (Stuttgart, 1968), pp. 208–41, and by Reinhard Elze, ed., *Die Ordines für die Weihe und Krönung des Kaisers und der Kaiserin*, MGH Font. IX (Hanover, 1960).

[58] For a study, see Marc Léopold Benjamin Bloch, *The Royal Touch* (London, 1973) [new edn (New York, 1989); first published, Publications de la Faculté des Letters de l'Université de Strasbourg. XIX (Strasbourg, 1924)].

Fig. 18 Henry the Lion and his wife Mathilda, crowned by the hand of God.
c. 1170, from the gospel book of Henry the Lion. Wolfenbüttel,
Herzog-August-Bibliothek Cod. Guelph. 105, Noviss. 2°, fol. 171v.

considered materially as a process provoking an energy flow from a powerful
to a powerless or from a healthy to an ill person.

The effects of touching were thus regarded as ambivalent and could be
judged as either evil or benign. Nevertheless, whether they prohibited or
desired, touches were associated with power and the facilitation of energy
transfer. Yet the severe punishments against evil purposeful touches and the

Fig. 19 Master E. S., A loving couple. c. 1460. Vienna, Albertina, Inv. DG1926/784. Another version is in Munich, Staatliche Graphische Sammlung.

strong desire for benign purposeful touches were both informed by the common expectation that purposeful touches ought to have strong consequences and were thus not a small matter. By the same standard, unintended touches did not form part of the normative frameworks enforced in the contexts of laws and rulers' ritual.

Only late in the Middle Ages did purposeful touching of specific parts of the body, notably a woman's breasts, lose its power-transmitting capability and come to be recorded as a mere topos for the depiction of loving couples in privacy (Figure 19). From this time touching became a technique for the expression of such emotions as love.

Moral restrictions against unintended touching emerged only in the thirteenth century together with regulations about gestures. These regulations were first formulated within the aristocracy and some groups of inhabitants of towns and cities and were laid down in poetical texts with an educational purpose.[59] In these late medieval literary texts, numerous moral codes propa-

---

[59] *Early English Meals and Manners. The Babees Book etc.*, ed. Frederick James Furnival, EETS OS XXXII (London, 1868). Robert de Blois, *Le chastoiement des dames*, vv. 91–8, in Blois, *Sämtliche Werke*, vol. 3, ed. Jacob Ulrich (Berlin, 1895). Friedrich Dedekind, *Grobianus*, ed. Kaspar Scheidt, Neudrucke deutscher Literaturwerke des XVI. und XVII. Jahrhunderts. XXXIV/XXXV (Halle, 1882), p. 41 [repr. (Tübingen, 1966); another repr. (Berlin, 1995)].

Fig. 20a & 20b opposite Flyleaf *Ein kurtzweiliger Bawren-Dantz*. Second half
of the seventeenth century. Berlin, Staatsbibliothek zu Berlin Preussischer
Kulturbesitz, YA 3720 m 1. Printed in D. Alexander and Walter Strauss, ed., *The
German Single-Leaf Woodcut 1600–1700*, vol. 1 (New York, 1977), p. 60.

gated regulations the goals of which were to restrict gesticulating, to reduce
the likelihood of unintended touching and to control physical movements.
Likewise, the thirteenth-, fourteenth- and fifteenth-century literature on educational theory abounds with the advice that the children of aristocrats and
urban patriciates should be scrupulously taught to control their movements.[60]

Peasant farmers were denounced as incapable of controlling their movements adequately, with the consequence that they were frequently displayed
performing disorderly movements and bumping into people.[61] Although,
even in the countryside, purposeful touching remained restricted to certain
ceremonial occasions, mainly dancing parties, moralists living in the cities

---

60 Aegidius Romanus, *De regimine principum libri III* (Rome, 1607), pp. 328–30 [repr.
(Aalen, 1967)]. Aeneas Sylvius Piccolomini [Pope Pius II], [Letter to King Ladislaus of
Hungary], ed. Rudolf Wolkan, Piccolomini, *Der Briefwechsel*, Fontes rerum
Austriacarum, ser. II, vol. 67 (Vienna, 1912), no. 40, pp. 103–58.

61 Neidhart of Reuenthal, *Die Lieder Neidharts*, Winterlieder 3/V, 24/III, 31/VII, ed. Moritz
Haupt and Edmund Wiessner (Leipzig, 1923), pp. 39, 74, 90 [repr. (Stuttgart, 1986)].
Guillaume Perraud, *Summa viciorum* (Basle, 1474), fols 36v–37v, connoted touch with
promiscuity and advised women to avoid touches.

heavily criticised these dances and positioned them in an atmosphere of voluptuousness. Thus, in 1494, for example, Sebastian Brant lamented the custom that dancers 'jump and throw each other about so that one sees their naked legs'.[62] Early modern flyleaves, such as that shown in Figure 20, depicted such movements as characteristic of peasant behaviour.

By contrast, in the high aristocratic world of court life during the sixteenth, seventeenth and most of the eighteenth centuries, courtiers became subjected to rigorous, detailed and stiff ceremonials, the main purpose of which was to maintain proper distance, control movements and prevent unforeseeable actions including unintended touches. Dancing masters were employed to train courtiers in the art of avoiding unintended touching while dancing.[63] Violations of such regulations were characteristically termed *faux pas* (wrong

---

[62] Sebastian Brant, *Narrenschiff* [1494], no. 61, ed. Friedrich Zarncke (Leipzig, 1854), pp. 60–1 [repr. (Hildesheim, 1961)]. For later explicit criticisms of irregular dances with excessive touching, see Johann Boschenstayn, *Wunscht allen Tanntzern und Tenzerin ain schnell umbwenden am Rayen*, 2nd edn (Augsburg, 1537) [first published (Augsburg, 1533)]. Florian Daul, *Der Tanzteuffel* (Frankfurt, 1569), pp. 6–23 [repr., ed. Kurt Petermann (Leipzig, 1978)]. Johann Münster, *Ein gotseliger Tractat von dem ungotseligen Tanz* (Frankfurt, 1594), p. 81.

[63] Humphrey Gilbert, *Queene Elizabeth's Achademy* [London, British Library, MS Lansdowne 98, fol. 2; 1562], ed. Frederick James Furnivall, EETS ES VIII (Oxford, 1869), p. 7.

Fig. 21 John Playford, *The Dancing Master* (London, 1719), title page. London, British Library, a.4.b. By permission from the British Library.

movements) and could entail severe punishments, such as isolation within or expulsion from the courts.[64]

Dancing masters produced voluminous handbooks containing norms of proper movements and touching behaviour. In one of these handbooks, the following rule for avoiding touches was expressed:

> It is a terrible custom if someone keeps his body and his limbs obliquely and untidily on bent knees for negligence or pure idleness. Such a person has neither proportion and shape nor appeal, but behaves like a ninety-nine-year-old peasant woman. He also has the disadvantage that the proper conduct of his body is impeded if he overextends the measures and distances between his limbs, does not keep them in equilibrium and shifts the weight more to the one than to the other side.[65]

This rule demanded efforts to keep a straight, upright and balanced comportment, to measure steps carefully and to avoid all bodily bends that were not necessary to execute steps. Stiffness of comportment was a positive value as it helped visualise the capability and willingness to control movements. Needless to say, these aristocratic patterns of controlled behaviour became the source for drilling rules that rulers and their army commanders were keen to enforce upon the well-trained common soldiers throughout Europe in the course of the seventeenth and eighteenth centuries.

The clearest ceremonial expression for this intention of minimising the likelihood of touching in dancing was the minuet. Figure 21 displays the well-ordered arrangement of a dancing couple moving in a relatively wide space and executing their movements according to strict choreographical rules by which the likelihood of touching was greatly reduced.

---

64 Julius Bernhard von Rohr, *Einleitung zur Ceremoniel-Wissenschaft der Privat-Personen* (Berlin, 1728), pp. 197–8 [repr., ed. Gotthardt Frühsorge (Weinheim, 1990)].

65 Gottfried Taubert, *Rechtschaffener Tanzmeister* (Leipzig 1717), p. 418 [repr., ed. Kurt Petermann, Documenta choreologica XXXII (Leipzig, 1976)].

In a long process from the fourteenth to the eighteenth centuries, touch avoidance thus emerged as the dominant goal of touch perception, replacing the previous conviction that touches could transfer energy. These initially aristocratic standards of touch perception were generalised into societal norms in the later eighteenth century. They became part of the general moral education of school children, and were advocated, among others, by Johann Heinrich Pestalozzi.[66] Pestalozzi urged his pupils to control their movements and avoid purposeful as well as unintended touches.

Hence a general overview of the history of touch perception reveals a change of relevant legal norms into moral norms during the late Middle Ages. From that time, the number and significance of legal norms declined, although some kinds of touching has continued to be judged as a severe crime. The declining significance of legal norms for touch perception found its expression in the waning willingness of persons to associate purposeful touches with the transfer of external energies. In lieu of the expectation that touches should transfer energy, the demand arose to prominence as a moral norm that persons should make efforts to control their movements and avoid unintended touching. In doing so the new standard of perception anticipated the later demand that persons should make efforts to control smell emission. From the seventeenth century, this new standard of touch perception widened the space around high ranking persons where touching was expected not to occur. It was closely intertwined with contemporary demands for the rigorous self-control of bodily movements.

Creating a social order: the history of taste perception

Taste is a form of touch, said Aristotle, and St Thomas Aquinas was convinced that Aristotle was right.[67] Both theorists ranked taste as a sensation that passes through the mouth. Other medieval theorists concurred.[68] It is only in this limited sense that this section discusses taste perception primarily at the level of attitudes towards the social organisation of meals, while it excludes the history of tastes in the wider modern sense of the history of value preferences given to customs, dress, literature, music or art.[69]

---

[66] Johann Heinrich Pestalozzi, 'Brief an einen Freund', in Pestalozzi, *Kleine Schriften zur Volkserziehung und Menschenbildung*, 5th edn (Bad Heilbrunn, 1983), p. 28.

[67] Aristotle, *De anima*, 441a. Thomas Aquinas, *Commentaria in Aristotelem et alios*, in *S. Thomae Aquinatis Opera Omnia*, ed. Roberto Busa, SJ, vol. 4 (Stuttgart, 1980), p. 370. Albert the Great concurred in his description of the sense of taste without reference to organs in the mouth. See Albertus, *Summa*, lib. II, cap. 32, pars 3 (see note 5), pp. 278–9.

[68] See, among others, Vincent, *Speculum* (see note 5), lib. XXV, cap. 70, col. 1819.

[69] Historians of philosophy have usually assumed that the history of taste perception in Europe began in the sixteenth and seventeenth centuries because theoretical reflections on taste are not extant from earlier periods. See Francisco Sanchez-Blanco, 'Die Anfänge der Ästhetik des Geschmacks in der spanischen Renaissance', in *Archiv für Begriffsgeschichte* 23 (1978), pp. 202–14. Friedrich Schümmer, 'Die Entwicklung des Geschmacksbegrffs in der Philosophie des 17. und 18. Jahrhunderts', in *Archiv für*

The meal has most commonly been considered as the scene of peace enforced among people who are willing to subject their bodily desires to more or less strictly regulated habits of food consumption. The enforcement of peace during meals has worked in two opposite ways. On the one side, guests have been asked to subject themselves to certain rules of conduct, whereas, on the other side, hosts have been obliged to establish and maintain an atmosphere in which peaceful conduct among guests could be secured during the meal. These two opposite, yet complementary obligations have not always been fulfilled. On the one hand, meals could be used as opportunities for the making of friendship contracts and the forging of alliances, as Tacitus had observed. In the early Middle Ages, similar notices were entered into annalistic records.[70] On the other hand, meals could be violent and were used for various kinds of plots, including assassination attempts.[71] That such crimes were common can be judged from laws enforcing peace while meals were going on and imposed fines upon breaches of certain rules of conduct. Thus the late seventh-century laws of King Hlothere and King Eadric, joint rulers of Kent, contained clauses that prohibited the display of weapons during the meals and regulated a certain drinking order.[72] Meals and feasts also provided ferment for and could result in other sorts of violence, mainly through the activities of autonomously acting contractual guilds. To prevent such activities, legal prohibitions were enacted in the eighth and ninth centuries.[73] In addition, the Church began to exert its own influence on rulers as lawgivers. Following the ecclesiastical food restrictions, the early eighth-century laws of King Wihtred of Kent banned the consumption of meat on fasting days.[74]

An aristocratic setting for meals is well recorded in the epic of *Beowulf* in which the poet describes the scene of a formal feast in a royal hall. According

Begriffsgeschichte 1 (1956), pp. 120–41. Karlheinz Stierle, H. Klein and Friedrich Schümmer, 'Geschmack', in Joachim Ritter, ed., *Historisches Wörterbuch der Philosophie*, 2nd edn, vol. 3 (Stuttgart and Basle, 1974), cols 444–56. However, taste perception can have existed even if it did not become the subject of reflections laid down in writing.

70 Cornelius Tacitus, *Die Germania des Tacitus*, cap. 22, ed. Rudolf Much, Herbert Jankuhn and Wolfgang Lange, 3rd edn (Heidelberg, 1967), p. 305. *Annales Fuldenses*, s. a. 847, ed. Friedrich Kurze, MGH, SS rer. Germ. VII (Hanover, 1891), p. 36, and *Annales Bertiniani*, s. a. 841, ed. Georg Waitz, MGH, SS rer. Germ. V (Hanover, 1883), p. 25 [recording the belief that a friendship alliance between the Carolingian rulers Lothair and Louis may have been concluded on the occasion of a meal]; Regino of Prüm, *Chronicon cum continuatione Treverensi*, s. a. 931, ed. Friedrich Kurze, MGH, SS rer. Germ. L (Hanover, 1890), p. 159, and Widukind of Corvey, *Rerum gestarum Saxonicarum libri III*, cap. II/15, ed. Paul Hirsch and Hans-Eberhard Lohmann, MGH, SS rer. Germ. LX (Hanover, 1935), pp. 79–80.

71 Gregory of Tours, *Libri Historiarum X*, cap. III/7, ed. Bruno Krusch and Wilhelm Levison, MGH, SS rer. Merov. I (Hanover, 1951), p. 105.

72 Ed. Liebermann, *Gesetze* (see note 56), p. 11.

73 *Capitulary of Heristal*, cap. 16, ed. Alfred Boretius, MGH Cap., vol. 1 (Hanover, 1883), p. 51; *Diedenhofen capitulary*, cap. 10, ibid., p. 124; *Capitulare missorum*, cap. 7, ibid., p. 301.

74 Ed. Liebermann, *Gesetze* (see note 56), p. 13.

to the description, the king and queen entertained and fed a number of retainers around their hearth. Recitals of oral traditions accompanied the meal. The setting was highly formalised, each participant being seated according to his rank around one and the same table.[75] As in most early and high medieval poetic records of meals and feasts, the *Beowulf* poet mentioned the drinking of ale but refrained from describing in detail the ingredients of the food that was being served. Evidently, what was more attractive for the poet and the audience than the kind and taste of the food was the unfolding of the interactions among the group members in the course of the feast in the royal compound.

According to the *Beowulf* poet, the feast thus provided an occasion during which the group remained undisturbed by interferences from the environment. Only after the feast ended did the group become subject to the death-dealing evil forces represented by Grendel and Grendel's mother. When the group members were asleep Grendel and, later, Grendel's mother sneaked into the hall, snatched a number of retainers and devoured them. The poet made it explicitly clear that the encroachment was the monsters' revenge for the human efforts to exclude them from the meal.

The epic of *Beowulf* does not stand alone as a record of carefully orchestrated feasts. In the second half of the tenth century, Bishop Liutprand of Cremona, who was proud of his Langobardian ancestry and was sent on a mission to Byzantium by Emperor Otto I, complained about the rudeness of the Roman emperor in Byzantium who, on the occasion of a feast, seated Liutprand, his honoured guest, at the far end of the table and would not allow his entourage to accompany him.[76] There was obviously a fundamental difference between Byzantine and Occidental table manners at the time. Unaware of the difference, the bishop expected to be treated in Byzantium in accordance with the traditional habits at home. That these habits were similar to those described in the epic of *Beowulf* becomes clear from a further incident. Early in the eleventh century Bishop Thietmar of Merseburg criticised Emperor Otto III for having neglected his duties towards his retainers when the emperor tried to introduce a new feasting order by which he and his retainers would eat at separate tables. The reform was inspired by Byzantine court rules. According to Thietmar, Otto was determined to quit the company of his retainers and sit at a separate table. Otto's table was to be placed at a higher level than that of his retainers in the same room so that the emperor could mark the difference in rank between himself and the ordinary aristocrats in his entourage. In Thietmar's view, the emperor tried to change the seating order because he claimed a special rank for himself as an anointed ruler who owed his position to divine grace and not to consent from the

---

[75] *Beowulf*, vv. 860–1093, 1279–95, ed. Frederick Klaeber, 3rd edn (Lexington, MA, 1950), pp. 4–8, 48–9.

[76] See Liutprand of Cremona, *Relatio de legatione Constantinopolitana*, cap. XI, ed. Joseph Becker, *Die Werke Liudprands*, MGH, SS rer. Germ. XLI (Hanover and Leipzig, 1915), pp. 181–82.

Fig. 22 Early medieval feast. Eleventh century, from the Bayeux Tapestry.

ruled. Although Otto's design was less radical than the Byzantine model and did not ban the retainers from the feasting rooms, the emperor met with storming protest from his retainers who demanded recognition of the fact that the emperor would be unable to rule without their consent and support.[77] The traditionally minded retainers shared Liutprand's and Thietmar's view that it was mandatory for a ruler to adhere to the established ceremonial and remain integrated in the group of supporting retainers while feasting. In their view, adherence to the traditional feasting ceremony was the expression of legitimacy cast in practical action.

The story reflects Otto's attempt to reconstruct the Occidental imperial feasting ceremonial after the Byzantine model. In the new context, ceremonial action continued to be of significance, but its significance was different from that of the old. Otto's choice of the new feasting arrangements did not focus on communication and the maintenance of social bonds and ties between

[77] Thietmar of Merseburg, *Chronicon*, lib. IV, cap. 47, ed. Robert Holtzmann, MGH, SS rer. Germ. N. S. IX (Berlin, 1935), pp. 185–6.

himself and his retainers. Instead, he chose to emphasise the uniqueness of his position as a ruler by divine grace. Claiming legitimacy by divine grace, Otto tried to restructure interaction with his entourage, whose members were no longer on an equal footing with him and would no longer share the same table. Instead, a hierarchical relationship was to emerge that spatially separated the emperor from his retainers. The attempt failed in Otto's time. But, already before the middle of the eleventh century, King Conrad II actually implemented the Ottonian design.[78] In the middle of the tenth century, Bishop Liutprand took for granted that maintaining communication between the lord and his retainers during the feast was the lord's essential duty. It was congruent with this tradition that he broke off negotiations with the Byzantine court. Two generations later, however, there were no marked differences between the feasting rules of the Byzantine and Occidental imperial courts.

What mattered in the early Middle Ages was group action, the establishment and maintenance of social order in the context of meals and fests. By contrast, the action of eating was secondary and, consequently, the food and its taste were of minor significance, as long as sufficient quantity of food was available. Thus, early medieval taste perception was centred on the participants of the meal but not on the food served. The quantity of the food that the lord could offer was seen as an indicator of his personal power. Hosting guests, holding feasts and providing food were thus instruments for demonstrating power within a group. In his *capitulare de villis* of the early ninth century, Charlemagne, King of the Franks, ruled that foodstuffs for the travelling royal entourage must be provided from the stocks of the manors and monasteries that had to play host to the king.[79] Hence, itinerant rulers took care to have sufficient quantities of food ready for themselves and their guests at places they and their entourage intended to visit.

Maintaining communication within groups through feasts ceased to be a major concern in the eleventh century, even though quantity continued to overwhelm quality in the high Middle Ages. Instead, the lavishness of food consumption together with increasing efforts to develop well-ordered table arrangements signified the power of two social groups, namely the aristocracy and the urban patriciates, over other groups. This can be inferred from the increasing frequency of ecclesiastical prohibitions against the *gula* or gluttony, as one of the deadly sins. From during the thirteenth century, the ecclesiastical prohibition against the *gula* began to be popularised in vernacular sermons

---

[78] Wipo, *Gesta Cuonradi*, cap. 39, ed. Harry Bresslau, *Die Werke Wipos*, MGH, SS rer. Germ. LXI (Hanover, 1915), p. 59. For the background of the relationship between rulers and the members of the higher aristocracy in the early eleventh-century Empire, see Dorothea von Kessler, *Der Eheprozess Ottos und Irmingards von Hammerstein,* Historische Studien. CLVII (Berlin, 1923) [repr. (Vaduz, 1965)].

[79] *Capitulare de villis*, cap. 62, 70, ed. Carlrichard Brühl, *Capitulare de villis. Cod. Guelf. 254, Helmstedt, der Herzog-August-Bibliothek Wolfenbüttel* (Stuttgart, 1971), Facsimileband, fols 15r–v, 16v, Textband, pp. 61–3.

strongly reminding those succumbing to this deadly sin of their lack of concern for others:

> You guzzlers, you drinkers; if you cannot even be prevented from such sin by God, you should at least abstain from it because you are the world's evil and foes, because you swallow and devour all that you have and of which also your children and your wife should live. . . . Well, licker, suck and pour into you whatever you like, and you will suffer the best repent for it in hell.[80]

Berthold of Ratisbon, from whose sermon this warning is taken, was a powerful preacher who attracted large audiences. He attacked persons for wishing to demonstrate that they could consume more food than others. From the thirteenth century, this was a common habit in the aristocracy against which not only the Church but also secular rulers enforced prohibitions, even though without much success.[81] There is an instructive pictorial record of the lavishness of aristocratic feasting in the frontispiece to the *Book of Hours* of the Duke of Berry of 1400.[82] As only wealthy persons could afford such demonstrations of power, they emphasised the distinctness of their rank and sought to make it understood that the lack of lavish food consumption should be considered an indicator of poverty. Thus aristocrats and the members of the urban patriciates, who followed the lead of the aristocracy, used lavish food consumption as a means to articulate their contempt of peasant farmers and urban artisans.

These demonstrations of contempt, however, continued to trigger resentment and protest among the people at whom they were targeted. During the English Rebellion of 1381, for example, angry peasants in county of Huntingdonshire, who were servants of the abbot of Ramsey, were reported to have demanded

> victuals to comfort and refresh them. The abbot accordingly sent them bread, wine, ale and other victuals in large quantities. For he dared not do otherwise.

80 Berthold of Ratisbon, *Vollständige Ausgabe seiner Predigten*, no. 27, vol. 1, ed. Franz Pfeiffer (Vienna, 1862), pp. 430–2, 437–40 [repr., ed. Kurt Ruh (Berlin, 1965)]. Likewise: Guilelmus Peraldus, *Summa* (see note 61), fols 14v–22r. Brant, *Narrenschiff*, cap. 16 (see note 62), pp. 18–19. Jakob Geiler von Kaysersberg [Sermon against Gluttony], 'Der XVI. Narr. Von Praßnarren, Füllnarren, Fässelnarren, Weinschleuchen, Büß den Wein, Weingänßlen', ed. Johann Scheible, *Das Kloster*, vol. 1 (Stuttgart, 1845), pp. 306–16 [who used Brant's work for his series of sermons]. All are based on Augustine, *Confessiones*, lib. X, cap. 31 (see note 8), pp. 136–7.

81 [Edict of King Philip III of France, 1279], ed. Henri Duplès-Agier, 'Ordonnance somptuaire inédite de Philippe le Hardi', in *Bibliothèque de l'Ecole des Chartes*, 3e sér., vol. 5 (1854), pp. 177–8. For a record of well-ordered lavish arrangements for feasts, mainly at courts, from the thirteenth century see Bartholomaeus Anglicus, *De proprietatibus*, lib. VI, cap. 23 (see note 38), pp. 265–6. For a verbal description of a thirteenth-century lavish courtly meal held by King Louis IX of France for his brother Alfonsus of Poitiers, see Jean de Joinville, *Histoire de Saint Louis*, ed. Natalis de Wailly (Paris, 1868), pp. 34–6.

82 See *Les très riches heures du Duc de Berry*, facsimile edn (Lucerne, 1984), frontispiece.

The rebels ate and drank to satiety, and afterwards slept late into the morning, to their own confusion.[83]

The abbot knew no way of counteracting the demand peacefully and had the rebels disarmed while they were asleep. The author of the chronicle report took the abbot's side in ascribing inappropriate behaviour to the peasant farming population. Hunger was not the problem.[84] Neither the angry peasants of Huntingdonshire nor rebellious peasant farmers elsewhere were starving.[85] Instead, they strove to abolish the distinctions of rank portrayed through the different food consumption patterns and wanted to demonstrate their equality with their lord in terms of food consumption. Hence it is safe to conclude that the standard of taste perception during the later Middle Ages and the sixteenth century was the maintenance or rejection of distinctions among social groups.

The conceptual relationship between taste perception and social order has thus varied significantly. During the early Middle Ages, the orientation of taste perception was towards the expression of power within groups. Under these conditions, observing table manners and arranging tables for feasts needed no particular concern; no significant attention was given to them in written and pictorial sources. However, from the eleventh century, the desire to mark differences between social groups began to dominate and entailed efforts to establish meals and feasts as representations of the well-ordered world of courts and urban patriciates with the observation of strict rules of conduct and in contradistinction to the seemingly unorganised style of food consumption in the countryside. Thus, didactical literature with instructions on table manners for aristocratic courtiers and members of the urban patriciates loomed large, and feasting tables in courts could carry sophisticated arrangements of dishes and plates (Figure 23).[86]

Church-stipulated prohibitions of certain dishes continued to be in force during specified days of the week. Some of these rules prescribed the consumption of fish instead of meat on Fridays, and they were usually respected and followed with great care, although not under all circumstances. Disregard for these rules could have painful consequences. For example, in his early

83 *Anonimale Chronicle*, ed. Vivian Hunter Galbraith (Manchester, 1927), pp. 150–1.

84 Heinrich Wittenwiler, *Der Ring*, vv. 5541–6178, ed. Horst Brunner (Stuttgart, 1991), pp. 322–58, has a sarcastic literary rendering of a peasant marriage feast with reports of extravagantly lavish food consumption. For studies on archival records on peasant food consumption, see Christopher Dyer, *Standards of Living in the Later Middle Ages*, rev. edn (Cambridge, 1998), pp. 151–87 [first published (Cambridge, 1989)]. Dyer, *Everyday Life in Medieval England* (London and New York, 2000), pp. 77–99 [first published (London and New York, 1994)].

85 For the German Peasants' War of the early sixteenth century, see *An die Versammlung gemayner Bawerschafft* [early 1525], in *Dokumente aus dem Bauernkrieg*, ed. Werner Lenk (Frankfurt, 1983), pp. 183–4.

86 For editions of normative texts on table manners, see Thomas Perry Thornton, ed., *Höfische Tischzuchtsitten*, Texte des späten Mittelalters IV (Berlin, 1957). Thornton, ed., *Grobianische Tischzuchtsitten*, Texte des späten Mittelalters V (Berlin, 1957).

Fig. 23 Early sixteenth-century feasting scene, from Maximilian I, *Weisskunig* (Vienna, 1775), plate 24. Albertina, Vienna.

sixteenth-century autobiography, Johannes Butzbach, humanist and citizen of Frankfurt, recollected the pain of an incident, in which, as a boy, he had forgotten the rule that prohibited the consumption of meat on Fridays. As a child, he thoroughly disliked going to school, although his parents encouraged him to do so. Thus he had to leave his home on school days pretending to attend school. But, instead of going there, he often hid himself in an abandoned punt on the river Main. This solution helped him to find two excuses at the same time: to his mother, he could say that he had been at school, while to his teacher, he could pretend that he had not been able to attend school because his parents had not let him go. These excuses worked until, one Friday, he had been at school, but claimed not having been able to attend school on the previous Thursday with a clumsy argument. The argument was that his parents had not let him go because they had wanted him to prepare the meat for the following day. Immediately, Johannes was exposed as a liar because he could not possibly have been asked to prepare meat on a Thursday for the following day. The consequences were dreadful: poor Johannes was severely beaten by the school's clerk, and his previous habit of ducking away in the old punt was disclosed. After that, he had to attend school regularly.[87] The story is significant because Johannes Butzbach still remembered it as a youthful sin when he was old. In addition to displaying the regularity of formal school education among children in the urban communities of towns and cities around 1500, the story shows that infringements of regulations regarding prohibitions of food were carefully controlled at that time.

Yet, already during the fourteenth and fifteenth centuries, dishes were becoming more variegated and quality was added to quantity of food consumption. While lavish food consumption remained the sign of aristocratic and urban wealth, princely courts and the high-ranking affluent households in towns and cities emerged as centres whose residents learned to appreciate the equally lavish use of rare and expensive spices from remote areas and of complicated, time-consuming cooking procedures. The new focus on exotic ingredients required wealth, and elaborate cooking procedures demanded the availability of specialised cooks and servants who could provide the labour that was necessary for preparing complicated meals with choreographies for many courses. These complicated meals could hardly be prepared without the existence of written recipes that orchestrated the various successive stages of cooking, listing the necessary materials and prescribing their proper mixture and arrangement. Thus the combination of quantity with quality of foodstuffs widened taste perception beyond the demonstration and maintenance of differences among social groups and generated the stereotype of aristocrats and members of the urban patriciates as food connoisseurs. Recipes grew out of attempts to provide the choreographies for and avoid extemporisation during the meals. Meals were organised as ever increasing sequences of courses (Figure 24).

Variety of courses together with quality of foodstuffs remained characteristic of refined taste well into the seventeenth century although, from the sixteenth century, critics insisted that overconsumption of food was detrimental to health. Thus García de Loaysa, father confessor to Emperor Charles V, recommended that the ruler should avoid eating fish, where it was difficult to provide, and should be mindful that his life belonged to everyone. Loaysa added that the emperor should remember that if he destroyed his own life he

---

[87] Johannes Butzbach, *[Hodoeporicon] Chronika eines fahrenden Schülers*, cap. III, ed. Damian Joseph Becker (Regensburg, 1869) [new edn (Graz, 1984), repr. (Graz, 1988), pp. 171–2; another edn by Andreas Beriger (Zurich, 1991), pp. 26–7]. The relevant passage has also been edited by Klaus Arnold, *Kind und Gesellschaft in Mittelalter und Renaissance* (Paderborn, 1980), p. 168.

Fig. 24 A sixteenth-century table arrangement for an aristocratic marriage ceremony. 1587, from Dietrich Graminaeus, *Fürstliche Hochzeit so . . . Wilhelm Hertzog zu Gülich Cleve und Berg . . . und der . . . Jacobae gebornen Markgräfinn zu Baden . . . in Düsseldorf gehaltenn Anno Domini 1585 am 16. Junij* (Düsseldorf, 1587).

might destroy the lives of many other people as well.[88] Even as late as at the turn of the eighteenth century, the moralist Abraham a Sancta Clara could lament the mannerism of consumption of food and drinks from distant areas and at uncommon seasons; specifically, he deplored the habit of drinking Italian wines in Germany, as well as the eating of oysters in October and of radish in February.[89] Despite these criticisms, meals consisting of more than a hundred courses were considered a common phenomenon at princely courts.[90] In fact, the French word *gourmand* (later *gourmet*) originally

---

[88] Georg Heine, ed., *Briefe an Kaiser Karl V, geschrieben von seinem Beichtvater in den Jahren 1530–1532,* nr XXX: Letter of 20 December 1530 (Berlin, 1848), p. 405. For an account of dishes served at the court of Charles V, see Alfred de Ridder, *La cour de Charles-Quint,* Mémoire. Société de littérature de l'Université Catholique de Louvain XIV (Bruges, 1889). For a further pictorial display of elaborate table settings see John Michael Writ, *Ragguaglio della solenne comparsa fatta in Roma gli otto di genaio MCCLXXXVII dall' illustrissimo conte di Castelmaine, ambassadore straordinario della sagra real Maestà di Giacomo secondo rè d'Inghliterra . . . alla Santa Sede Apostolica* (Rome, 1687), folded plate, following p. 62.

[89] Abraham a Sancta Clara, *Centi-folium stultorum in quarto. Oder Hundert Ausbündige Narren* (Nuremberg, 1709), pp. 81–4 [repr. (Dortmund, 1978)].

[90] Julius Bernhard von Rohr, *Einleitung zur Ceremoniel-Wissenschaft der Grossen Herren* (Berlin, 1733), p. 99 [repr., ed. Monika Schlechte (Weinheim, 1990)].

denoted gluttony, but came into use throughout Europe as a label for the food connoisseur.

In summary, in the high Middle Ages standards of taste perception changed. The early medieval focus of taste perception on the maintenance of social order in groups was given up in the eleventh century and gave way to the late medieval orientation to the expression and maintenance of social distance. Among aristocrats and urban patriciates, the new standard stimulated the lavish consumption of food as well as the search for extensive variety, in terms of ingredients and cooking procedures. As a result, food consumption began to be distinguished in terms of quantity and quality.

Conclusion

The perceptions of smell, touch and taste demonstrate conceptual histories that differ much in detail, but show some overlap. Dates of the major changes converge around the high Middle Ages. Up to the eleventh century, acting for the purpose of the maintenance of groups and social order was considered more important than regulating details of the perception of smell, touch and taste. From then on, new standards of the perception of smell, touch and taste emerged that marked social distance. From the thirteenth century the aristocracy and the upper echelons of the urban population developed standards of smell perception that focused on the capability and willingness of individuals to manipulate their smell emission; established standards of touch perception under the goal of the prevention of unintended touching among persons; and created standards of taste perception that appreciated high quality together with large quantity of food, elaborated strategies for cooking and table arrangements. The peasant farming population was largely excluded from these changes and became stigmatised as uneducated folk. In no case has the conceptual history of the perceptions of smell, touch and taste confirmed arguments that an alleged and overall qualitative trend towards increasing affect control has ever existed or that, materially, perception intensified or decreased.

The following chapter shifts emphasis from perception to action. The overall question is whether the changes in standards of perception described in this and the previous chapters were paralleled by similar changes in concepts of action. A standard of perception by which persons could take for granted that perception would translate into action in a divinely willed world order must be based on a concept of action different from that underlying a standard of perception according to which persons were given the task to reflect on their perceptions before beginning to act. Hence persons could anticipate that their actions would accomplish goals that the actors had set in advance. If they did so, they faced the demand that they should plan their actions strategically and measure the success of goal-attainment. If they wanted to meet this demand persons had to be ready to perceive themselves as capable of imposing their own will upon their physical and social environments. But persons could also anticipate that their actions proceeded from external factors, which other people or superhuman agents appeared to have set for them. Furthermore, they could expect that process of action mattered more than goal-attainment as a measure of success. If they did so, demand arose that persons should act in fulfilment of externally set goals and follow what was recognised as long and well-established processes of action. If they wanted to meet this demand persons had to be ready to subject themselves to impacts from, and to ascribe to themselves only limited capability to impose their will upon, their physical and social environments. The next chapter scrutinises sources relevant to the concept of action and juxtaposes the variety of medieval records against modern theories of action.

IV

Impacts on the Environment:
The Rationality of Action*

Qui facit veritatem venit ad lucem**
Augustine of Hippo

Introduction

Modern sociologists have commonly defined action as a purposeful process towards the attainment of goals. These theorists derive purposes of action from certain motives that actors were held to have or receive in order to attain their desired goals.[1] The measure of success then was the degree by which the actor accomplishes the goal or goals through the application of appropriate means. As long as actions take place in a social context, they are believed to be rational if and as long as the degree of success in the choice of appropriate ways and means to attain the set goal or goals can be measured independent of the actors' beliefs. Max Weber promoted the use of the term 'end-rationality' (*Zweckrationalität*) for this notion of action.[2] In these cases, actors are believed or expected to make decisions in situations where they must choose appropriate processes to accomplish the goals of their actions in future situations. Consequently, the measurement of success in the attain-

---

* I would like to thank Professor Yoshiki Morimoto of Kurume University for his insightful comments on an earlier version of this chapter.

** Whoever establishes the truth goes to the light.

[1] Talcott Parsons and Edward A. Shils, *A General Theory of Action* (Cambridge, MA, 1951), pp. 53–69.

[2] Max Weber, *Wirtschaft und Gesellschaft*, book I, para. 1, sections 1–2, 5th edn Studienausgabe, ed. Johannes Winckelmann (Tübingen, 1980), pp. 1–2. Cf. later versions of the theory, which placed more emphasis than Weber on the interconnectedness of goal-making and goal-attainment: Vilfredo Pareto, *Trattado di sociologia generale*, vol. 1 (Florence, 1916), pp. 63–71. From the point of view of ethics, the equation of rational action with end-rational action follows from Immanuel Kant's insistence that action is 'completely indistinguishable from the process of nature according to the law of causality' [Kant, *Kritik der reinen Vernunft* (Riga, 1781), in Kant, *Werke in zwölf Bänden*, ed. Wilhelm Weischedel, vol. 4 (Frankfurt, 1968), p. 493]. If rational action results from causes, then it must have effects and, consequently, be directed to an end.

ment of the goals of actions demands situations in which not only the actors but also other persons can observe the actions in progress and can thus make judgements about the degree of goal-attainment. The situations thus have to be ones in which communication between the actors and observing persons is possible. Were actions not connected with communicative situations, such as thinking, dreaming or wandering about in deserted areas, no communication between the actors and their social environment would be possible and, hence, no one would be able to pass judgement on whether the actions took place at all or whether the goal or goals associated with them were accomplished.

Whatever the value of these theories may be they have been characterised by their lack of historicity; that is, their proponents have been inclined to assume that their theories define general principles of the conduct of actions with purportedly universal validity across cultures and periods.[3] However, this assumption is far from obvious or self-evident. This is so not only because cognitive anthropologists have called into question the possibility of establishing universally valid rationality criteria but also, and more fundamentally, because there is no prima facie justification for the matter-of-fact association of the rationality of action with goal-attainment. The association has sparked a number of intriguing questions. Why does the rationality of an action have to be determined in relation to the degree of successful accomplishment of one or several predetermined goals? Or, historically speaking, since when and under what conditions did the assumption receive support and credibility that all rational actions must be end-rational actions?

In the following chapter, I intend to outline the conditions under which these questions may be answered. My attempt to historicise the concept of rational action is meant to be a contribution to the history of ethics. From the point of view of the history of action, I define ethics broadly as the field of inquiry into the interconnectedness of action with values, norms and rules. I shall argue that rational action was beginning to be transformed from a mainly process-related concept to a mainly goal-oriented concept during the ninth and tenth centuries. I shall adduce supportive evidence from exegeses of the Book of Genesis as well as from late Carolingian polyptychs, and I shall correlate evidence from these sources with findings from other early medieval normative and narrative sources, among them ecclesiastical canons, and a variety of historiographical writings.

---

3 Most radically Arthur Coleman Danto, *Analytical Philosophy of Action* (Cambridge, 1973). There is also little awareness among historians of the historicity of the concept of action. For one, Robin George Collingwood, *The Idea of History*, ed. by Thomas Malcolm Knox (Oxford, 1946), pp. 213–16, treated action as a constant feature of history. Similarly, Richard van Dülmen, in his introductory survey *Historische Anthropologie*, 2nd edn (Cologne, 2001) [first published (Cologne, 2000)], categorises the human being as an actor in history but does not consider the history of action.

Preliminary examination: standards of communication, social organisation, modes of behaviour and the concept of action in the early Middle Ages

Modern theories of action have been strongly correlated with a particular standard of communication. By standards of communication, I understand complexes of norms and rules according to which communicating persons exchange messages. In other words, standards of communication are the normative frameworks that actors follow in situations when they make or become the object of authoritative and irrevocable decisions. There are basically two standards of communication, namely literacy and orality. The dichotomy does not imply that actors must always choose between communicating either through writing or by speech. But it does suggest that they will choose the one or the other standard in critical situations or formal settings, such as at court. Although not all actions are communicative, and even under the prevalence of literacy as the standard of communication not all communication takes place by means of writing, written communication as a category of action is more closely linked than orality to the demand that the degree of the goal-attainment of action should be regarded as the essential criterion for the measurement of success. This is so because authoring and sending written messages are actions occurring at a place and time that differ from the place and time at which the messages reach their recipient or recipients. As the recipients of written messages are not considered to be present at the place and the time when the messages had been written, on principle neither can the number of recipients of the messages be determined nor can the place and time be precisely predicted at which the recipient or recipients will obtain the messages. Put differently, where the measurement of the success of the goal-attainment of actions is crucial, literacy is the standard of communication, and setting the goal of a communicative action, namely the provision of information to one or several recipients, may and can be expected to occur in spatial, temporal and, consequently, also social contexts that are distinct from the process of authoring and sending the messages. The difference of space, time and social setting can alter the contents and the significance of the information provided through written messages and can thus transform the goal or goals of the action. As authors of written messages are normally aware of this potential, they try to establish probability calculations about changes of context conditioned by the difference between their own spatial, temporal and social setting and those of the expected or intended recipients. For example, most senders of written messages commonly make assumptions about the length of time usually needed for transmission and reception, they will choose the paths of transmission that are most likely to meet their demands, and they will make provisions for the eventuality that such demands cannot be met.

In the European context, literacy emerged as a standard of communication late in the early Middle Ages and has been dominant since then. However, up until the ninth and tenth centuries, not only was most communication oral but orality was a concurrent standard of communication. The practice of oral communication then implied that the communicating actors had to be present at the same spot at the same time. Therefore, the goals could not be separated from the processes of communicative action. Consequently, modern theories of action that ignore changes of standards of communication cannot deal appropriately with actions taking place in social contexts in which actors do not assume that they should themselves determine the goals for their actions, scale down the significance of the goals of their actions and, instead, turn their attention to processes. If actors in orally communicating groups have less incentive to focus their actions on accomplishing set goals, it becomes difficult to hypothesise that purposeful goal-setting is generally a mandatory part of actions. Instead, it must be admitted that actors can believe that they are accomplishing goals that others have set for them or they can take the view that goal-attainment is a marginal or irrelevant aspect of their actions. In these cases, of which there were many in early medieval Europe, process-orientation overwhelmed goal-attainment in conceptualising actions. If process-orientation could have been considered more important than goal-attainment, it is inappropriate for theorists of action to demand or expect that the success of such actions should be measured solely in terms of the degree of goal-attainment. Process-oriented actions have frequently been referred to under the label of magical beliefs.

In short, there were empirical cases of situations in which the rationality of actions did not have to be determined merely through judgements of the success of goal-attainment but mainly through observations of the continuity and consistency of the processes of actions. These situations dominated in orally communicating groups. Hence, contrary to the assumptions of modern theorists of action, the social contexts of action do not have to be shaped by literacy as the standard of communication within and across groups. Instead, in groups where orality was the standard of communication, the situational contexts of actions were different from those in groups with literacy as the standard of communication. One core difference is that oral communication requires the communicating persons to be present simultaneously at the same place and, in these situations, it impossible to isolate spoken words from other communicative signs or signals that communicating actors transmit, namely so-called non-verbal signs and signals, gestures, rituals, bodily bearing, posture and movement. In orally communicating groups, these signs and signals, together with verbal messages, constitute integrated processes of communicative action in which the processes of action necessarily receive a larger share of attention than the accomplishment of set goals. Likewise, the hazard that the messages may not reach the recipients and the potential for manipulating messages through false intentions are minimal as there is no or little time-gap between the sending and the reception of the messages. Although purposeful misunderstandings are obviously possible as integrated processes of communicative action can be faked, it is more difficult to fake an integrated process of communicative action in its entirety than it is to make purposefully false statements in written documents.

Another feature of modern theories of action relates to the criteria for measuring success. Modern theorists of action maintained that success can only be measured if two conditions are met: first, that the actors set one or several goals before the beginning of an action; second, that the actors are motivated to use their own physical and intellectual energies to accomplish the set goal or goals.[4] Motivation in this context meant the self-controlled mobilisation of physical and intellectual energies by actors, even if exogenous factors were frequently assumed to instill motivation. Hence, modern theorists of action assumed that action is successful when actors can be perceived as willing and capable of mobilising and effectively using their physical and intellectual energies and to do so for the purpose of impacting on their physical and social environments.[5] Goal-orientation includes criteria for measuring the success of action and gives priority to actors' readiness to *impact on* their physical and social environments over their readiness to receive *impacts from* their physical and social environments. Goal-orientation is thus at the very root of individualistic attitudes that place persons in competition with others. Individuals adhering to this mode of behaviour anticipate the likelihood of conflicts of interests and power struggles between themselves and the groups of which they happen to be members, and they demand that, in these conflicts and struggles, the interests and desires of individuals should be given priority over the demands of groups.

The modern concept of society was closely connected with the concept of goal-oriented action. Societies were understood as hierarchically stratified and territorially demarcated types of group claiming exclusive membership in a legal sense.[6] This notion of society came into existence only towards the end of the eighteenth century[7] and thus cannot be taken for granted for previous periods. Up until the end of the eighth century, the Latin word *societas* as well as its derivatives and variants in the vernacular languages carried a wide variety of meanings during the European Middle Ages but did not usually denote societies in the understanding of modern theories of action.[8] Indeed, a generic term for smaller or larger assemblies of people did not exist before the word 'group' came into use in the high Middle Ages, when it suddenly

---

4   Weber (see note 2), cap. 1, para. 1, section 4, p. 3.
5   Alfred Schutz, 'Choosing among Projects of Action', in Schutz, *Collected Papers*, vol. 1: The Problem of Social Reality, ed. by Maurice Natanson (The Hague, 1973), p. 73 [first published in *Philosophy and Phenomenological Research* 12 (1951)]. Mancur Olson, *The Logic of Collective Action*, Harvard Economic Studies CXXIV (Cambridge, MA, 1965), pp. 1–2.
6   Theoretically argued by Parsons/Shils, 'The Social System', in *General Theory* (see note 1), pp. 192–6.
7   Best documented in Johann Gottlieb Fichte, *Der geschloßne Handelsstaat* (Tübingen, 1800). New edn in Fichte, *Werke 1800–1801*, in Fichte. Gesamtausgabe. I, 7, eds Reinhard Lauth and Hans Gliwitzky (Stuttgart, 1988), pp. 1–141. John Stuart Mill, *Considerations on Representative Government* (London, 1861), pp. 146–7 [repr. (Buffalo, 1991)].
8   For sources, see Harald Kleinschmidt, *Understanding the Middle Ages* (Woodbridge, 2000), p. 91.

appeared from unknown origins.[9] Instead, in the early medieval Occident, smaller or larger assemblies of people were usually neither stratified nor territorially demarcated, as modern societies appear to be, but coordinated as more or less autonomous units in their own right. Moreover, these assemblies of people often overlapped in terms of membership through the admission of multiple loyalties.

In the early medieval Occident, kin groups, neighbourhood groups, groups established by contracts, political groups established by adherence to beliefs in common traditions as well as social groups as groups established and maintained by legal codes were the most prominent types of loyalty-commanding and identity-conveying assemblies of people during the Middle Ages. Others, such as age groups or totem groups, appear to have been of marginal significance.[10] The competition among these types of group allowed persons a higher amount of membership choices than modern sociologists would admit.[11] The implication is that the belief that actions must be purposefully directed at either confirming or contesting social hierarchies is applicable only under the premise that societies as a specific and, for that matter, recent type of social group exist. This premise ruled out situations where several types of group can compete for membership and loyalties. In situations of the latter type, the processes and goals of someone's actions had to be focused on the group of which the actor was a member or else had to switch group membership. Orality as a standard of communication and coordination rather than subordination as a principle of social organisation were thus compatible as far as the conceptualisation of action as a primarily process-oriented behaviour was concerned. Yet in this capacity, orality and coordination were incompatible with the key assumptions about hierarchical social organisation on which modern theories of action were built.

This is so because in coordinated types of group in which orality was the standard of communication, the concept of goal-oriented action did not necessarily provide the most important criterias for measuring success. If various types of group competed over their members' partial loyalties, actors were induced to seek integration into groups, as long as the institutional structure of the groups continued, rather than pursuing their own goal or goals. Consequently, the bonds and ties among group members were stronger in coordinated types of group than they are in hierarchically organised societies that demand exclusive membership and subordinate their members to the control of central institutions. Moreover, group members who were dissatisfied with the conditions of their lives in one type of group could easily switch to another type of group and did not have to manifest their own interests and

---

9   Connected with such words as English crop and German *Krippe*. See Niels Kranemann, 'Über den Gebrauch des Wortes Krippe im Sachbereich der Uferbefestigung', Ph.D. diss. (University of Munster, 1958), pp. 107–12.

10 Kleinschmidt, *Understanding the Middle Ages* (see note 8), p. 90.

11 Explicitly in Niklas Luhmann, *Soziale Systeme* (Frankfurt, 1987), pp. 268–9 [first published (Frankfurt, 1984)].

desires against those of the group. Consequently, in coordinated groups, the mutual dependence of the group members on support from their group as well as of the group on support from its members formed the basis for attitudes and expectations that were irreconcilable with the goal-orientation of action. These attitudes and expectations demanded that the measure of the success of actions should consist in the degree to which actors were able and willing to avail themselves of the supportive physical and intellectual energies provided by other group members rather than on the energies contained in their own bodies. Likewise, actors as members in coordinated types of group were ready to assume that their chances for acting successfully increased to the extent that they were able and willing to avail themselves of these exogenous supportive energies. Consequently, they would even expect that the goals for their actions might more frequently be determined by other group members or be regarded as givens than result from their own free will. In other words, they focused more on the processes than on the goals of actions.[12] The process-orientation of action required elaborate communication for the purpose of maintaining group structures, and actors expected that they should give a high degree of attention to the processes of actions and measured the success of their actions primarily in terms of their ability and willingness to utilise external physical and intellectual energies.[13] Doing so, they acted rationally.

The concept of process-oriented action was appropriate at a time when, as in late Antiquity and the early Middle Ages, migration loomed large. Under these conditions, actors did not only perceive their physical and social environments as hostile,[14] but also chose to rely on support from other group members or even divine and other superhuman agents and seek favourable conditions for their actions, rather than prioritising the use of their own physical and intellectual energies. This preference was advantageous at times of long-distance migrations because solitary migrants were more directly exposed to the hazards that were perceived or imagined to emanate from the physical and social environments. As a consequence, solitary migration was exceedingly rare. Indeed, some late antique and early medieval group migrations lasted for several generations and thus continued beyond the lifetime of

---

[12] Cf. Charles Radding, 'The Evolution of Medieval Mentalities', in *American Historical Review* 83 (1978), pp. 577–97, who argued that what he referred to as 'early medieval mentality' was characterised by the lack of significance that actors afforded to the intentions of their actions.

[13] In Aristotle, *Nicomachean Ethics*, 1139a–b, there is a plea to conceptualise action as the triad of planning, decision and pursuit. Included in this plea was the demand that action should be understood as the integrated process of preparing and executing what persons intended to do. In articulating this demand, Aristotle allocated a higher significance to process than to goal-orientation than the theory of action would admit. However, some late twentieth-century theorists of action have taken a position similar to Aristotle's but contrary to Weber's. See Jürgen Habermas, *Theorie des kommunikativen Handens*, vol. 1, 4th edn (Frankfurt, 1987), pp. 33–44 [first published (Frankfurt, 1981)].

[14] Kleinschmidt, *Understanding the Middle Ages* (see note 8), pp. 36–46.

a person. These perceptions or imaginations induced most migrants to seek shelter in groups. A large number of place-names in the northern and western parts of the Roman Empire record settlements at which these groups of migrants eventually remained. Many of these names, like Birmingham, fossilised structures of autonomously acting groups. These groups were tied together by some kind of contractual agreement about membership conditions, the purpose, if any, of the migration and the expected rewards for the members. Other place-names, like Beaverington (Sussex), Meeching (Sussex) and Sissinghurst (Kent), record groups constituted by neighbourhood relations, beliefs in common descent among the migrants and adherence to common traditions of some political significance.[15] These place-names are frequent in Britain, Swabia, Bavaria and the Rhine valley. It is therefore possible to conclude that the social organisation of these groups had its share in shaping the actions of people on the move. After migrants converted into settlers, the names of many of their settlements continued to provide a record of the social structures of the migrant groups.

As these settlements were mostly agricultural in kind, the concept of process-oriented action could also enhance the willingness of group members to subject themselves to the natural rhythms of growth and decay for the purpose of making optimal use of nature's bounties. Up until the eighth century, many settlements in western, northern and eastern Europe can be classed as residences of clusters of kin and neighbourhood groups among whom production was mainly, though not exclusively, undertaken for local consumption.[16] Under these conditions, farming consisted mainly of undertaking agriculture under the constraints of the vagaries of nature. Farmers' work was embedded in the divinely willed order of the world and followed predetermined rules. In the early Middle Ages, many of these rules will have been transmitted orally within kin and neighbourhood groups, although they could be reflected in penitentials when they touched upon ecclesiastical matters. Farmers could thus interpret the harvesting of crops as a predetermined feature of the divinely willed world, not as the result of human-made plans.[17] Hence, they took it as their main tasks to make appropriate choice of

---

15 I have reviewed the evidence in Kleinschmidt, 'The Name England', in *Archives* 26 (2001), pp. 97–111.

16 For a discussion of some archaeological evidence, see Christopher J. Arnold, 'Territories and Leadership', in Stephen Taffe Driscoll and Margaret R. Nieke, ed., *Power and Politics in Early Medieval Britain and Ireland* (Edinburgh, 1988), pp. 111–27.

17 On farming as a divinely willed work, see Haymo of Halberstadt, *De varietate librorum*, lib. II, cap. 50–1, in *PL* vol. 118, cols 917–18. For a study of the concept of process-orientated action in penitentials, see Hubertus Lutterbach, 'Intentions- oder Tathaftung? Zum Bussverständnis in den frühmittelalterlichen Bussbüchern', in *Frühmittelalterliche Studien* 29 (1995), pp. 120–43. Lutterbach maintains that in the early medieval Irish penitentials, a concept of penitence becomes explicit that associates sin with the process of an evil action in conjunction with an evil intention whereas the ancient Christian penitential literature defined sin solely in terms of action with evil intentions.

production processes and observe the local environmental conditions and seasonal rhythms.

That is to say, settled groups of agriculturalists preferred to organise their lives in accordance with the seasonal rhythms that they could not determine. It was the prime goal of settlers to accommodate themselves with, and adapt to, the local conditions of life as much as possible and produce most of the necessary victuals and other commodities locally. While the economic significance of trade for the provision of essential commodities remained low,[18] trade continued to be part of agricultural economies throughout the early Middle Ages because settlements were not naturally affluent,[19] and the merchandising of surplus products was a common though not necessarily regular practice. Hence, there is ample archaeological evidence from the fifth, sixth and seventh centuries that road traffic declined,[20] that the supply of goods of remote origin became less frequent[21] and that Roman professional traders became less prominent in areas on the fringes or beyond the boundaries of the Roman Empire of Antiquity. Increased need for agricultural fields may have been the reason behind the reassessment, in some sub-Roman cities of Gaul, of the value of landed property on which Bishop Gregory of Tours reported late in the sixth century.[22] In addition, written sources confirm that

---

[18] Kleinschmidt, *Understanding the Middle Ages* (see note 8), pp. 146–52. This is obviously neither to say that trade was insignificant nor that traders were inactive at this time. Sufficient evidence exists proving that this view, articulated, among others, by Henri Pirenne, is untenable. But, despite the existence of urban centres in the Frankish kingdom and its dependencies already from the seventh century, trade focused on the provision of specialised or luxury goods, sometimes of remote origin, and some needs were provided for by migrant producers rather than trading products. For records on the availability of long-distance trading goods, such as spicies of Indian origin, in markets in Western Europe, see Georg Jacob, *Arabische Berichte von Gesandten an germanische Fürstenhöfe aus dem 9. und 10. Jahrhundert*, Quellen zur deutschen Volkskunde I (Berlin, 1927).

[19] For this term, see Marshall David Sahlins, *Stone Age Economics* (Chicago, 1972), pp. 1–39.

[20] Brian Hugh St John O'Neill, 'Grim's Bank, Padworth, Berkshire', in *Antiquity* 27 (1943), pp. 188–95. William I. Robertson IV, *Romano-British Pottery*, British Archaeological Reports. British Series CVI (Oxford, 1982). T. R. Slater, ed., *Towns in Decline. AD 100–1600* (Aldershot, 2000). Hayo Vierck, 'Trachtenkunde und Trachtengeschichte in der Sachsen-Forschung', in Claus Ahrens, ed., *Sachsen und Angelsachsen*, Veröffentlichungen des Helms-Museums XXIII (Hamburg, 1978), pp. 231–70.

[21] See Heiko Steuer et al., 'Handel', in *Reallexikon der Germanischen Altertumskunde*, 2nd edn (Berlin and New York, 1999), pp. 542–4.

[22] Gregory of Tours, *Libri Historiarum X*, lib. IX, cap. 30, ed. Bruno Krusch and Wilhelm Levison, MGH, SS rer. Merov. 1, 1 (Hanover, 1951), pp. 448–9. On the reassessment, see Jean Durliat, *Les finances publiques de Dioclétien aux Carolingiens (285–889)*, Beihefte zur Francis XXI (Sigmaringen, 1990), pp. 310–14. For studies on the decline of trade under the control of Roman merchants in the early medieval Occident, see Dietrich Claude, *Der Handel im westlichen Mittelmeer während des Frühmittelalters*, Abhandlungen der Akademie der Wissenschaften in Göttingen, Philol.-Hist. Kl. 3. F. CXLIV = Untersuchungen zu Handel und Verkehr der vor- und frühgeschichtlichen Zeit in Mittel- und Nordeuropa, Part II (Göttingen, 1985). Jürgen Kunow, *Negotiator et vectura. Händler und Transport im Freien Germanien*, Kleine Schriften des

rulers or local lords managed much of the trade.[23] Therefore, much as trade was common during the fifth, sixth and seventh centuries, it was not essential. Instead of pursuing the goal of maintaining distribution networks with much of their own energy, early medieval actors could expect to be more successful if they were able to adapt their production processes to environmental factors when they tried to accomplish predetermined goals.

Exegeses of the *Book of Genesis* as a source on the medieval theory of action

Against this background, the question is which sources are available to provide evidence on the process-orientation of action in early and high medieval Europe. There are on principle two categories of sources. One category reflects the general theory of action, the other concerns the practicalities of action. One interesting early eleventh-century statement relevant to the general theory of action refers to the meaning of the word *facere*. Around 1100, St Anselm of Canterbury observed that this verb could be used to replace virtually any other verb, and he concluded that *facere* was the most general expression for doing. He thus seems to have imagined action as primarily process-oriented. By contrast, Conrad of Hirsau, a contemporary of Anselm, demanded that readers should take notice of the intentions pursued by the authors of texts before them, and that for authors, the *finalis causa* (final purpose) of their work should consist of contributing to the benefits of their readers. Conrad seems to have categorised action as primarily goal-oriented.[24] Moreover, in the context of his thirteenth-century theory of ethics, Albert the Great remarked that time and space were conditions without which

Vorgeschichtlichen Seminars Marburg VI (Marburg, 1980). Kunow, 'Zum Handel mit römischen Importen in der Germania libera', in Klaus Düwel, Herbert Jankuhn, Harald Siems and Dieter Timpe, ed., *Untersuchungen zu Handel und Verkehr in vor- und frühgeschichtlicher Zeit in Mittel- und Nordeuropa*, Part I, Abhandlungen der Akademie der Wissenschaften in Göttingen, Philol.-Hist. Kl. 3. F. CXLIII (Göttingen 1985), pp. 430–59.

23 For pieces of evidence, see the charter in the names of King Alfred of Wessex and Æthelred, under-king of the Mercians to Bishop Wærfrith of Worcester, AD 889, ed. Walter de Gray Birch, *Cartularium Saxonicum*, vol. 2, no. 561 (London, 1887) [repr. (New York, 1964)], and. the charter by Emperor Otto II, dated 26 June 975, on Magdeburg traders, ed. Theodor Sickel, *Die Urkunden Otto des II*, MGH DD. 2,1 (Berlin, 1888), no. 112. Occasionally, the polyptychs contain references to merchants. For example, see the Saint-Germain-des-Prés polyptych, lib. V, cap. 110, fol. 101v, ed. Dieter Hägermann, *Das Polyptychon von Saint-Germain-des-Prés* (Cologne, Weimar and Vienna, 1993), p. 38. On managed trade in the Levant and North Africa, see Olivia Remie Constable, *Housing the Stranger in the Mediterranean World* (Cambridge, 2003).

24 Anselm made his observation in a fragment that was left among his papers in Lambeth Palace and was published only in 1936. See Franciscus Salesius Schmitt, *Ein neues unvollendetes Werk des Hl. Anselm von Canterbury*, Beiträge zur Geschichte der Philosophie und Theologie des Mittelalters, vol. XXXIII, no. 2 (Munster, 1936), pp. 25–35. Conrad of Hirsau, *Accessus ad auctores*, ed. and transl. Alistair J. Minnis and

actions could not take place. The remark seems to suggest that Albert understood actions as finite processes that needed to occur at a given place and
within a given period of time. Thus Conrad's and Albert's concept of action
appears to have been less process-oriented than Anselm's.[25] But these inciden-
tal remarks neither form a coherent corpus of text exclusively relevant for the
theory of action nor do they allow the specification of theory changes. Therefore, the various aspects of the medieval theory of action have to be reconstructed on the basis of sources concerned with practical action.

One type of source on practical action is represented in the commentaries
on the creation myth recorded in the *Book of Genesis*. Within a Christian
context, the earliest substantial[26] commentary on *Genesis* is found in the work
of St Augustine. In *De Genesi ad litteram*, Augustine reflected on the Vulgate
version of the creation myth, specifically the phrase *Dixitque Deus fiat lux*
(And God said: Let there be light). In the opening passage of the *Book of
Genesis*, the phrase follows a descriptive statement that the divinity created
heaven and earth as vacant places. Augustine focused on the meaning of the
verb *dixit* (he said). He linked this word to a communicative situation in
which the message, to which the word refers, should go from the divinity to a
recipient. Yet, according to the myth, there was no one to whom the divinity
could have sent a message, let alone given an order to do something. Hence,
there was no one who could have carried out the order of the divinity to
create light. The problem Augustine raised was twofold: how could the divinity speak without there being a recipient of the message; and how could the
divinity act by giving an order if there was no one to carry it out?[27] Augustine's answers followed from his theology of the divine word. He assumed that
the divine word was simultaneously divine and human and in no need of the
differentiation between form and substance.[28] Therefore, according to Augustine, the divine word, unlike the human word, did not have to leave the
speaker in order to go into the world but the divinity could be the undivided
sender and recipient of a message. Augustine thus concluded that the divinity
needed no one to be the recipient of its command. Creation was possible as a
self-contained action that had to be understood as an intellectual process
rather than a physical generation. Whereas, in Augustine's exegesis, human
action required that actors should differentiate between form and substance,
between *physis* and intellect, and, consequently, between process and goals,
Augustine held the view that divine action was comprehensive with no distinction between process and goals.[29] Augustine thus did not deny the

Alexander Brian Scott, *Medieval Literary Theory and Criticism* (Oxford, 1988), p. 46
[first ed. Robert Burchard Constantyne Huygens, *Accessus ad auctores* (Leiden, 1970)].

25 Albertus Magnus, *De nature boni*, lib. II, cap. 1, 2, in Albertus Magnus, *Opera omnia*
XXV, 1, ed. Ephrem Filthaut (Munster, 1974), p. 12.

26 A brief commentary was previously written by Ambrose, *Hexaemeron*, lib. I, cap. 3, in
PL vol. 14, cols 137–8.

27 Augustine, *De Genesi ad litteram*, lib. I, cap. 2–5, in *PL* vol. 34, cols 248–50.

28 Augustine, *Tractatus in Johannem Evangelium*, in *PL* vol. 35, cols 1379–84.

29 Augustine, *De Genesi ad litteram*, lib. I, cap. 3 (see note 27), col. 249.

goal-orientation of action but allocated this type of action to the human world. In his view, it was the divinely willed imperfection of human nature that required the specification of goals and the motivation to accomplish them. By contrast, the process-orientation of action belonged to the perfect divine world.[30]

Between the sixth and the eleventh centuries, the textual genre of commentaries on the *Book of Genesis* was poorly recorded, although variants of Augustine's exegesis can be found in general surveys of the world. For one, Raban Maur insisted that the divinity did not have the goal of creating the world and, consequently, there was no need for the divinity to have the will to accomplish any goals.[31] In the thirteenth century, however, the biblical creation myth received renewed exegetical interest. St Thomas Aquinas devoted a chapter of his *Summa theologiae* to the question of whether the divinity must be believed to have had the will to create the world. Before providing what he considered the only appropriate answer to the question, Thomas referred to a position that he rejected as inadequate. He let unidentified protagonists of this position believe that the divinity, being perfect and eternal, could not have a will and thus could not be assumed to have been motivated to pursue goals of action. According to Thomas, this view classed the creation of the world was merely a process without motive and goal.[32] This is the view that Raban Maur had argued before.[33] In the second step, Thomas defended this view with two seemingly supportive arguments. The first argument followed from the definition of the actors' will as the endeavour to obtain something that they did not have. If this definition was accepted, the divinity could not have had a will because the divinity was perfect and there was, consequently, nothing that the divinity could possibly want. For the second argument Thomas drew on Aristotle, who had written in *De anima* that the will was motivation to move.[34] Thomas concluded that the divinity could not have wanted to move because, following Aristotle, he categorised the divinity as the immovable prime mover.

In the third step, then, Thomas rejected the view that the divinity could not have had a will and based his rejection on an exegesis of *Romans* 12. In this letter, the Apostle Paul demanded that believers should probe the will of the divinity.[35] If that demand was to be fulfilled, the divinity had to be credited with a free will. Thus Thomas called on the authority of the Bible to help reject ancient Greek ethics.[36] He gave preference to the Apostle Paul over Aristotle because the Apostle seemed to suggest that the divinity had a will. Thomas defended his position through the following deduction: he construed

---

30 Ibid., lib. I, cap. 4, col. 249.

31 Raban Maur, *De universo libri XXII*, lib. I, cap. 1, in *PL* vol. 111, cols 13–19.

32 Thomas Aquinas, *Summa theologiae* I, qu. 19, ar. 1, in *S. Thomae Aquinatis Opera omnia*, ed. Roberto Busa, SJ, vol. 2 (Stuttgart, 1980), p. 215.

33 Raban Maur, *De universo* (see note 31), col. 16.

34 Aristotle, *De anima*, lib. III, cap. 10, 433a–b.

35 *Romans* 12, 2.

36 Thomas, *Summa theologiae* (see note 32), p. 215.

the will as equivalent to what he termed the 'appetite of brutes'. He then argued that the appetite of brutes was triggered by the senses. Accordingly, he further assumed that will existed wherever there was insight and believed that insight should spark willingness to act. As no one could deny that the divinity had insight, Thomas concluded that the divinity ought to be credited with the will to create the world.[37] His result was that the divinity, even though perfect and eternal, could very well have had a will and that, consequently, the divinity could have had motives for creating the world and could also have acted in pursuit of goals. Thomas then specified the motives and goals, which, in his view, the divinity could have had. In his view, there was no alternative to the belief that the divinity acted because of its love of the world and the human beings therein and that it would not pursue goals that were irreconcilable with its love of the world.[38] For Aquinas, then, divine action and human action were tied together by the common principle of goal-orientation. Thus goal-orientation gained in significance as an ethical principle during the Middle Ages.

Thomas elaborated the minority position that Peter Abelard and others had taken before. In the twelfth century, Abelard proposed an ethics based on human free will and conscience.[39] In turn, Abelard's position that human beings should be credited with free will had previously been argued by John Scotus Eriugena in the ninth century and further back in the fifth-century work of Pseudo-Dionysius the Areopagite.[40] In crediting the divinity with free will, Thomas extended this minority position to the superhuman realm and applied it to divine action itself. According to his view, the divinity had created the world according to its free will. It might as well have decided not to create the world. Because the divinity had manifestly made the decision to create the world, Thomas felt compelled to add eleven distinctions, with affirmative answers to the following questions: whether the divinity had a will that reached beyond itself; whether the divinity wanted whatever it wanted out of some necessity; whether the divine will was the cause for everything; whether the divine will could determine other factors; whether the divine will had to be carried out; whether the divine will was unchangeable; whether the divine will needed to be imposed upon what had already been willed by the divinity; whether it could be believed that the divine will did not include the pursuit of evil; whether the divinity had the capability of free decision (*liberum arbitrium*); whether the divine will was recognisable to mortals; and whether

---

37 Ibid., I, qu. 19 ar. 2–12, pp. 215–18.
38 Ibid., I, qu. 20, pp. 218–19.
39 Peter Abelard, *Liber dictus scito te ipsum*, cap. III, in *PL* vol. 178, col. 636. New edition s. t.: *Ethical Writings. Know Yourself* (Indianapolis, 1995).
40 Pseudo-Dionysius the Areopagite. *De divinis nominibus*, lib. IV, cap. 11, in *PG*, vol. 3, cols 770–1. See also Dionysius, *De divina hierarchia / de divinis nominibus*, 2 vols, ed. Philippe Chevalier (Paris, 1937). Dionysius, *The Divine Names and Mystical Theology*, ed. John D. Jones, (Milwaukee, 1980). For the ninth-century version of the doctrine, see John Scotus Eriugena, *Versio operum S. Dionysii*, cap. IV, in *PL* vol. 122, cols 1140–41, 1145.

the signs of the divine will remained recognisable against a variety of obstacles. Thomas concluded by professing his conviction that the divinity would use its will to act for human benefit because he ascribed to the divinity love, justice and clemency as primordial motives.[41]

St Thomas Aquinas's exegesis of the biblical creation myth thus reflected an approach to action that differed in many respects from that favoured by Augustine and most early medieval theorists. Thomas's distinctions were informed by a general concept of action comprising the divine and the human worlds as well as by his assumption that divine and human action were goal-oriented. Actions as mere processes were taken to be neutral and were thought to acquire meaning through the specification of motives and goals. Contrary to the theologians of late Antiquity and the early Middle Ages, Thomas supported the doctrine that actions had to be recognised as goal-oriented doings under all circumstances. The theory of action changed its focus dramatically from the prioritisation of process-orientation to the preference for goal-orientation of action. Evidence for this change emerges from a comparison between the concepts of action by Augustine on the one hand and Thomas Aquinas on the other.

Sources for the translation of medieval theory of action into practice

The differences between early and late medieval concepts of action must now be correlated with what can be ascertained from sources describing manifest actions. Among these sources, land charters, narrative texts and, last but not least, polyptychs can be scrutinised.

Early medieval charters[42] present several specific features of formulary containing written statements about actions. As a rule, charters were carefully designed and executed written documents whose production was expensive and time-consuming. It has been estimated that the making of a charter could take several years, could require the cooperation and consent of a substantial number of persons and could involve a considerable number of specialists in various fields. Thus making a charter had a value in itself and carried at least the same importance as the preservation of the charter as a record. At the end of the process of making a charter, the act of handing it over to the recipient could be a legal act in its own right. Therefore, the processes of making and handing over the charter were more than just means for the accomplishment of a goal. For example, as late as in 966 Æthelwold, Bishop of Winchester, received a charter written in the name of King Edgar of England and listing the privileges of the recently refounded Benedictine monastery of New

---

41 Thomas Aquinas, *Summa theologiae* (see note 32), I, qu. 19 ar. 2–12, pp. 215–18.

42 Groundbreaking and still valuable for the terminology of insular diplomatics are the Sandars Lectures in Bibliography delivered by the Oxford philologist William Henry Stevenson at Cambridge in 1898. The unpublished manuscript of the lectures is preserved among the Stevenson Papers in St John's College, Oxford.

Minster at Winchester. The charter documented the royal support for the reform of Benedictine monasteries. The reform had been launched in 963 when the bishop expelled lay clergy from the monasteries under his control. Simultaneously, Æthelwold authorised the compilation of a revised rule for monks and the making of several lavish liturgical books for his and other dioceses.[43] The charter was written and decorated in the monastic scriptorium at Winchester in which the liturgical books were also made out. It is extant in its original version. The text is carefully written in a book minuscule and begins with a dedication picture as its frontispiece showing King Edgar presenting the book charter to Christ in a *mandorla*.[44] In this case, then, making the charter was part of the monastic reform and may have covered most of the three years between the beginning of the movement and the date of the promulgation of the charter. In summary, the making of charters shed light on the preference for processes of action. Whereas, obviously, the goal of establishing a legal record mattered, the processes considered necessary for the accomplishment of goals were not merely subsidiary means. Rather, they could be constitutive parts of legal actions. As written documents charters were equivalent to the final point of processes of action in which oral communication, rituals and the making of written texts were inextricably intertwined.

A further conspicuous feature is a stereotyped motivation for the issue of charters that is found in the *arenga* as part of the protocol of the more elaborate early medieval charters of land grants. This stereotyped motivation appeared in the formula *pro remedio animae meae* (for the rescue of my soul) contained a number of ninth- and tenth-century land charters for ecclesiastical recipients. The formula indicated that donors intended their grants made or recorded in the charters for the *post mortem* care of their souls. That means that grants could be connected with the cult of the dead.[45] The donors appear to have expected that the ecclesiastical recipients of their grants would shoulder the task of saying *post mortem* prayers for the donors' souls as part of their

---

[43] *Regularis Concordia*, ed. Thomas Symons (London, 1962). *The Benedictional of Aethelwold*, ed. George Frederic Warner and Henry Austin Wilson (Oxford, 1910). Facsimile edn by Andrew Prescott, *The Benedictional of Aethelwold* (Toronto, 2002). *King Edgar's Establishment of Monasteries*, ed. Dorothy Whitelock, Martin Brett and Christopher Brooke, *Councils and Synods with Other Documents Relating to the English Church*, vol. 1 (Oxford, 1981), pp. 148–9.

[44] The text of the charter is in Birch, *Cartularium* (see note 23), vol. 3, no. 1190. For a print of the dedication picture, see Janet Backhouse, Derek Howard Turner and Leslie Webster, ed., *The Golden Age of Anglo-Saxon Art* (London, 1984), Pl. IV [from London, British Library, MS Cotton Vespasian A VIII].

[45] For details, see Arnold Angenendt, Thomas Braucks, Rolf Busch, Thomas Lentes and Hubertus Lutterbach, 'Gezählte Frömmigkeit', in *Frühmittelalterliche Studien* 29 (1995), pp. 26–30, 36–8. Michael Borgolte, 'Gedenkstiftungen in St. Galler Urkunden', in Karl Schmid and Joachim Wollasch, ed., *Memoria*, Münsterische Mittelalter-Schriften XLVIII (Munich, 1984), pp. 578–602. However, Angenendt et al. position the contracts between donors and recipients in the context of penitence rather than of the cult of the dead.

regular liturgical duties. That many Christian believers in the early medieval West shared such expectations appears from extant monastic registers or memory books (*libri memoriales*). These sources mainly listed the names of persons for whom prayers were to be said by monks and nuns,[46] but they occasionally also included the formulary of a contract specifying the duties that monks and nuns were expected to fulfil in return for donations to their monasteries. In a number of cases, the entries suggest that clusters of names written in the same hand were presumably entered consecutively within a short period of time. In these cases, the entries may represent groups of persons related to each other by kin or neighbourhood ties or that entries were made in return for donations for specific purposes such as the defence of the Church and the people. While donations by persons seeking to involve the monastic clergy in the care of their souls did not only have to consist of land grants, this particular form of donation perhaps obliged the recipient monastic communities to perform their liturgical duties more strongly than other kinds of donation. This may have been so because charters were preserved in the recipient monasteries' archives, thereby serving as a lasting piece of evidence for both the will of the donor and the obligations of the recipients. The *pro remedio animae meae* formula thus served as a motivation for concluding contracts of which the donations were part.[47] On the side of the donors, the

46 Some of the more elaborate *libri memoriales* are available in the following editions: Johanne Autenrieth, Dieter Geuenich and Karl Schmid, ed., *Das Verbrüderungsbuch der Abtei Reichenau*, MGH, Libri Mem. N. S. I (Hanover, 1979). Walter de Gray Birch, ed., *Liber Vitae. Register and Martyrology of New Minster, Winchester* (London, 1892). Jan Gerchow, *Die Gedenküberlieferung der Angelsachsen*, Arbeiten zur Frühmittelalterforschung XX (Berlin and New York, 1988). Eduard Hlawitschka, Karl Schmid and Gerd Tellenbach, ed., *Liber memorialis von Rémiremont*, MGH, Libri Mem. I (Munich, 1970). Sigismund Herzberg-Frankel, ed., *Monumenta necrologia monasterii s. Petri Salisburgensis. Liber confraternitatum vetustior*, MGH Necr. II (Berlin, 1904). Karl Schmid, ed., *Die Klostergemeinschaft von Fulda im früheren Mittelalter*, vol. 1 (Munich, 1978). Schmid and Joachim Wollasch, ed., *Der Liber Vitae der Abtei Corvey*, Veröffentlichungen der Historischen Kommission des Provinzialinstituts für westfälische Landes- und Volkskunde, Series XL, vol. 2 (Wiesbaden, 1983). Schmid, Dieter Geuenich and Roland Rappmann, 'Die Verbrüderungsbücher', in Michael Borgolte, Dieter Geuenich and Karl Schmid, ed., *Subsidia Sangallensia*, vol. 1, St Galler Kultur und Geschichte XVI (St Gallen, 1986), pp. 13–283. The opening page of the *liber memorialis* of the nunnery at Rémiremont, p. 1, contains a contract formulary, which specifies the duty of the monastic recipients to say mass once per day for the donors. Similar entries are in the Salzburg *liber memorialis*, pp. 6, 42.

47 E.g. Birch, ed. *Cartularium* (see note 23), vol. 1, no. 45, vol. 2, no. 701. These are charters written in the name of King Hlothere of Kent, dated 679, for Abbot Berhtwald granting land in Thanet, and for St Mary Worcester written in the name of King Athelstan [7 June 934?]. The latter is preserved in a copy written probably late in the eleventh century on the basis of the lost original. A large number of further charters containing the same formula are preserved in the archive of the monastery of St Gall. See Hermann Wartmann, ed., *Urkundenbuch der Abtei Sanct Gallen*, vol. 1, nos 37 (10 Oct. 762), 47 (25 Febr. 765), 238 (24 Oct. 818), 241 (6 Apr. 819), 242 (8 Apr. 819), 244 (16 June 819), 251 (12 May 820), 252 (15 May 820) (Zurich, 1863), pp. 39, 48, 230, 233, 235, 241, vol. 2, nos 502 (10 Aug. 864), 507 (11 March 865), 508 (16 March 865), 509 (11 June 865), 510

contract specified the size of the land and the rights to be transferred into the recipient's ownership. On the side of the recipients, the contract stipulated the *memoria* as a liturgical duty to be performed on principle up until Judgement Day. In some cases, variants of the formula *pro remedio animae meae* were used in polyptychs, that is, in texts without a charter formulary.[48]

Memoria as the liturgical duty of monks and nuns is further recorded in a number of Bible manuscripts opening with pictures of rulers or other persons of high status as the donors of the manuscripts. These books were usually kept in monasteries as well as episcopal churches and served as evidence that the donors had made their grants hoping that the monastic recipients of the gifts would perform the liturgical duties of the *memoria*. That this was the overall purpose of such book donations emerges from a poem added to a ninth-century Gospel Book now in the possession of the Bibliothèque nationale de France, to which reference has been made in Chapter I. The book, which was kept in the monastery of St Martin in Tours during the Middle Ages, opens with a dedication picture showing Emperor Lothair I.[49] The poem explains that the dedication picture was included in the book in order to remind its monastic readers of their duty to say prayers for the emperor.[50]

At first sight, these arrangements appear to give priority to a clearly specified goal of actions. It thus appears that the goal was the conclusion of contracts between the donors and ecclesiastical institutions for mutual benefit. However, the sets of obligations into which the contracting parties entered were unequal. Donations of private or kin property to ecclesiastical institutions were finite and irrevocable processes of property transactions. Hence, while the ecclesiastical recipients controlled the transfer of property into their ownership, the donors had no possibility of supervising the proper execution of the liturgical duties demanded by the *memoria*. That is to say, the legal process of the transfer of property rights on the one side was compensated on the other side by no more than the pledge of *memoria* for the donors' souls. While it may have been the case that surviving kin members would execute some degree of control over these duties for a while, they obviously were unable to do so forever.

This was so because generation change would sooner or later reduce the interest in and knowledge of the more remote ancestors, even where descendants continued to live in the vicinity of the recipient monasteries. That the willingness to transmit memories of the dead orally was declining in the tenth century becomes clear from a decree passed by the Synod of Ingelheim in 948.

(11 June 865), 728 (2 Nov. 903), 729 (12 Dec. 903), 747 (13 Aug. 905) (Zurich, 1866), pp. 116, 121–3, 331, and others [repr. (Frankfurt, 1981)].

[48] See Rudolf Kötzschke, ed., *Urbar A*, in Kötzschke, ed., *Die Urbare der Abtei Werden an der Ruhr*, Publikationen der Gesellschaft für Rheinische Geschichtskunde V (Bonn, 1906), pp. 32–3, 44.

[49] Ms Paris, Bibliothèque nationale de France, Fonds Lat. 266, printed, among others, in Hermann Fillitz, *Das Mittelalter*, vol. 1 (Berlin, 1990), Pl. IX.

[50] Ed. Ernst Dümmler, MGH Poet., vol. 2 (Hanover, 1884), p. 671, vv. 23–7.

The decree ruled that kin members should keep written genealogies in order not to forget their ancestries.[51] The decree was probably made for reasons other than facilitating the control of *memoria*, namely observing the Church ban on marriages between closely related kin members. But in any event, it made sense only under the assumption that there had been many cases where kin members were becoming unable or unwilling to record their genealogies with exactitude through oral transmission. Thus, the traditional mechanism of transmitting genealogical knowledge was becoming obsolete in the course of the tenth century, and this process must have had its own impact on the memory culture. Therefore, the belief in divine omniscience remained as the sole basis for trust.

Yet, a more significant aspect of the inequality between the two mutually intertwined sets of obligations resulted from the fact that the donation as a finite process was equated with the *memoria* as a process that was to be continued up until Judgement Day. Thus, the larger the number of donations for church institutions became, the longer became the lists of persons for whom prayers were to be said, year in and year out. It is therefore difficult to make more manifest the preference for the process-orientation of action than through contractual agreements about *memoria*. If, in cases of land donations processes mattered, in cases of *memoria* they did so even more. Therefore, process-oriented actions must have been considered as rational actions in the early Middle Ages.

At the turn of the eleventh century, the formulary of the solemn land charters underwent an important change. Many of the formulae, which had previously filled charter protocols, were given up in a new type of charter, appropriately termed *breve* or writ.[52] These simplified charters focused on the disposition of the legal matter, and many of them were hastily scribbled down as mere written records of legal acts. Among the deleted or substantively reduced parts was the *arenga* with its *pro remedio animae meae* formula. Although solemn charters continued to be issued, mainly in the names of high-ranking rulers, their share in the estimated total of completed charters declined. The more businesslike writs had the advantage of being cheaper to produce and required fewer people as well as less time to issue. They also reflected a new attitude towards the concept of action, for the drafters and makers of the writs showed less willingness to appreciate the circumstantial formulae and ceremonies that focused more on processes than motives for and goals of actions. The changing charter formulary thus supports the conclusion that goal-attainment gained priority over process-orientation in conceptualising action during the eleventh century.

This conclusion can be confirmed from a review of selected narrative sources. Among early medieval descriptions of human action, reports about

51 *Synod of Ingelheim* [7 June 948], ed. Ernst-Dieter Hehl, *Die Konzilien Deutschlands und Reichsitaliens. 916–1001*, MGH Conc., vol. VI, part 1 (Hanover, 1987), p. 162.
52 Florence Elizabeth Harmer, ed., *Anglo-Saxon Writs* (Manchester, 1952) [repr. (Stamford, 1989)].

embassies dispatched between rulers convey the impression that they were sent out to maintain communication processes rather than to accomplish the goals of a particular action.[53] These reports contain ample record of lengthy proceedings and time-consuming rituals that attached significance to processes of action in their own right, thus relativising the importance of goal-attainment. That is to say, the sending of embassies mattered for its own sake, even if the results were meagre or non-existent.[54] Embassies could fail in consequence of disagreement over procedural issues. The tenth-century account (to which reference has been made in the previous chapter) by Bishop Liutprand of Cremona of the embassy he undertook to Byzantium at the request of Emperor Otto I in 968 provides ample evidence to this effect. The bishop blamed his failure on the Byzantine side, which he accused of having selected inappropriate and unacceptable negotiation procedures.

In addition, the ninth-century Frankish polyptychs represent a category of source that specifies the concept of action in the context of relations between rulers and ruled, mainly in the rural countryside.[55] Monasteries made and kept polyptychs as records of the specific production obligations and other types of service of the farmers to their monastic lords. According to these sources, the relations between monastic lords and their dependant farmers were no longer displayed exclusively in terms of personal bonds and ties, but rather of control over people as cultivators of land. The institutional framework was that of the *seigneurité* or *Grundherrschaft* through which kin and neighbourhood groups of peasant farmers were subjected to the control of personal or institutional lords. These polyptychs were not systematic records in the sense that descriptions of every holding and the conditions of service of all residents were entered. Yet major efforts were made to record production and service obligations at least partly through the medium of writing. For example, in order to prepare the first version of the Prüm polyptych at the end of the ninth century, specially appointed commissioners travelled to the widely dispersed holdings of the monastery, made inquiries and collected data. At Prüm and in other monasteries,[56] the polyptychs were records whose

[53] Nithard, *Historiarum libri IIII*, lib. II, cap. 2, ed. Ernst Müller, MGH, SS rer. Germ. XLIV (Hanover, 1907), p. 14. John of Metz, *De vita Joannis Abbatis Gorziensis*, cap. 115, in *PL* vol. 137, col. 298.

[54] *Die Werke Liudprands von Cremona*, ed. Joseph Becker, MGH, SS rer. Germ. XLI (Hanover, 1915).

[55] For editions of major polyptychs, see Claus-Dieter Droste, ed., *Das Polyptychon von Montierender* (Trier, 1988). Ingo Schwab, ed., *Das Prümer Urbar*, Publikationen der Gesellschaft für Rheinische Geschichtskunde XX (Düsseldorf, 1983). François-Louis Ganshof, ed., *Le Polyptyque de l'abbaye de Saint-Bertin* (Paris, 1975). Jean-Pierre Devroey, ed., *Le polyptyque et les listes de cens de l'abbaye de Saint-Remi de Reims (IX–XIe siècle. Edition critique*, Travaux de l'Académie nationale de Reims CLXIII (Reims, 1984). Hägermann, ed., *Polyptychon* (see note 23). Dieter Hägermann and Andreas Hedwig, ed., *Das Polyptychon und die notitia de areis von Saint-Maur-des Fossés. Analyse und kritische Edition* (Sigmaringen, 1990). Kötzschke (see note 48).

[56] The texts consulted for this chapter are the polyptychs of Montierender, Prüm, Reims, Saint-Germain-des-Prés and Saint-Maur-des-Fossés, quoted in note 55.

medium of transmission unwillingly made explicit a new conceptualisation of action. The novelty of this concept becomes clear when compared with patterns that had informed agricultural production in the previous centuries of the early Middle Ages.

As has been shown earlier in this chapter, agricultural production followed a concept of action up to the eighth century, according to which the choice of process was considered to be crucial, rather than the setting of goals. However, at the turn of the ninth century, Charlemagne inserted stipulations into his *capitulare de villis*[57] to the effect that constant stocks of food should be kept in the royal vills and at other places where itinerant rulers might stop over. Here then, goals for action were set in writing and Charlemagne expected that the farmers to implement the stipulations of his capitulary. This was a rare case in which a ruler set a goal for agricultural production and thereby added to the divinely willed order of the world.

Neither Charlemagne nor the ninth- and tenth-century polyptychs broke entirely with these older patterns. But they added two important aspects to the conceptualisation of action. One was writing as the means of production control. The other was the centralisation of rule. The combination of both aspects added to the significance of goal-attainment and promoted changes in agricultural work ethics. In itself, laying down records of agricultural production in writing was an ambivalent procedure. This was so because the texts, as the scribes of the Prüm polyptych occasionally admitted, reproduced incomplete data on crop yield, output of manufactured goods and provision of manual service. They also recorded deviations from the productions norms that were not met because exemptions had been granted.[58] The holdings of the monasteries continued to be widely dispersed and were inhabited by a substantial variety of types of group for whose members specific norms were in effect. The polyptychs contain evidence that the administrators frequently paid respect to the various special legal statuses of their peasant servants to which reference was made through the formula *secundum ordinem suum* (according to his / her status).[59] The formula served as a means to recognise the empirical fact that the conditions of service were usually defined in terms of specific personal bonds and ties rather than general legislation. Thus the norms had little effect because their general application upon the several different types of group was difficult to engineer. Nevertheless, the compilers of the data as well as the monastic administrators used the production norms to measure the output of crops, manufactured agricultural products and service and then insisted that the peasant farmers under their control should abide by

---

57 *Capitulare de villis*, cap. 70, ed. Carlrichard Brühl, *Capitulare de villis. Cod. Guelf. 254, Helmstedt, der Herzog-August-Bibliothek Wolfenbüttel* (Stuttgart, 1971), Facsimile-Band, fol. 16r, Textband, p. 63. For the context see chapter 3, note 79.

58 See for cases of exemptions from norms in the Prüm polyptych, among others, fols 7v, 8v, 9r, 12r (ed. Schwab, see note 55, pp. 164, 169, 170, 177). For a summary list of holdings with unspecified service obligations, see, among others, the polyptych of Saint-Germain, breve III, cap. 61, ed. Hägermann (see note 23), p. 23.

59 Prüm polyptych, among others, fols 12r, 13v (ed. Schwab, see note 55, p. 176, 180, 181).

these norms. They took for granted that these norms should be met continuously throughout the year, irrespective of the vagaries of nature and the physical condition of the working people. Hence, like Charlemagne, the ninth- and tenth-century compilers of the data for the polyptychs and monastic administrators displayed their willingness to focus agricultural production on the attainment of goals that had not been predetermined by the divinity at the time of the creation of the world but were human-made and implemented under divine as well as human control.[60] Moreover, archaeological finds provide indirect evidence for trade in mass, bulk and expensive goods, such as wood, pottery, millstones, glass, weapons, jewels and textiles. These activities, like the attempts to enforce production norms, could only be successfully conducted if goal-attainment was given priority. This was so because the trading goods were now daily commodities. Therefore, trade was interconnecting supply and demand crowds and, from the eighth century, established distribution networks that could cover long distances.[61] The partners in the trading networks became mutually dependent on the regularity of demand and supply that had to operate irrespective of the vagaries of nature and the capability of the traders.

Even if the vagaries of nature could not be circumvented and exemptions had to be granted, the written norms of crop yield, output of agricultural products and manual service provided lasting standards by which success or failure of production could be measured. The Prüm polyptych provides evidence for the care with which these norms were maintained. Whereas the production of the solemn charters of the previous centuries of the early Middle Ages had equated the finite actions of donations with indefinite obligations of liturgical service, the detailed information on the names and duties of dependant farmers, which the polyptychs contained, defined human-made goals of action. Thus the making of the polyptychs in its own right already testified to the willingness of the monastic administrators to set goals for themselves and their farmers and control the implementation of these goals. At least in one case, the implementation process was abundantly successful: when the original late ninth-century manuscript of the Prüm polyptych was edited in the thirteenth century, few changes had to be made in the edited version.[62]

Similarly, the centralisation of control set new demands for the regularisation of production. The monastic institutions as major landholders not only

---

[60] Note in the Prüm polyptych, fol. 9r (ed. Schwab, see note 55, p. 170). The note included the warning that persons intending to act against the norms should know that they were offending the omniscient divinity even if their lack of loyalty remained undiscovered by the monastic lords.

[61] For the record of a merchant (*mercator*) in a polyptych, see Hägermann, ed. *Polyptychon*, breve V, cap. 110 (see note 23), p. 38.

[62] Caesarius, the thirteenth-century editor of the Prüm polyptych, fol. 51r (ed. Schwab, see note 55, p. 259), remarked that 329 years after the completion of the original manuscript, woodlands had disappeared, new villages had been founded, mills had been built and new lands had been prepared for cultivation.

depended on the supply of food from the peasant farmers under their control but also needed to maintain agricultural production as well as manufacturing levels in a variety of sectors that were not connected with food production. Most important in this context were the religious services of the monasteries that required the provision of certain organic materials at regular intervals, such as wax and animal skin, used for liturgical purposes and the production of charters. It was thus mandatory to oblige peasant farmers to deliver the demanded produce at regular intervals. Again, the degree of goal-attainment became measurable against the norms recorded in the polyptychs and other normative texts.[63] Once more, the concept of goal-oriented action was essential if the monasteries wanted to fulfil their liturgical and administrative duties. The goals of harvesting crops and manufacturing agricultural products obtained priority over efforts to adjust production processes to local climatic conditions, seasonal rhythms and the vagaries of nature.

It is difficult to determine with precision which measures were taken to advance the degree of goal-attainment of agricultural production in the monastic holdings. But there are a number of indicators showing that the yield ratio and the output of agricultural products increased during the ninth and tenth centuries. Thus the yield ratio of key crops such as rye went up. Although this outcome may also have been due to the improving climatic conditions at the time, other sources confirm that it resulted from a new work ethic that emphasised the consistency of fieldwork and the necessity of supervision and control.[64]

Moreover, the polyptychs were not unique in their own time. In contexts other than the agricultural economy, normative as well as descriptive sources exist from the late ninth and early tenth centuries showing that rulers were willing to establish norms and sought to enforce them among the people under their control. Some of these sources record aspects of the defence policy of the kings of Wessex and Saxony, who appear to have been determined to erect defence systems against armed immigrants from Scandinavia (the so-called Vikings) and east central Europe (the Magyars).[65] Defensive earth-

---

63 For sources, see above, note 59. For a normative text spelling out the concept of goal-oriented action in the context of farming see: *Gerefa*, ed. Felix Liebermann, *Die Gesetze der Angelsachsen*, vol. 1 (Halle, 1903), pp. 453–5. For a study of the liturgical needs of monasteries, see Paul Fouracre, 'Eternal Light and Earthly Needs. Practical Aspects of the Development of Frankish Immunities', in Wendy Davies and Paul Fouracre, ed., *Property and Power in Early Medieval Europe* (Cambridge, 1995), pp. 53–81.

64 Atto of Vercelli, *Polypticum*, cap. 9, in *PL* vol. 134, col. 869. *Rectitudines singularum personarum*, ed. Liebermann, *Gesetze* (see note 64), pp. 444–53.

65 The most convenient edn of the *Burghal Hidage* is by Agnes Jane Robertson, ed., *Anglo-Saxon Charters* (Cambridge, 1939), pp. 246–9 [2nd edn (Cambridge, 1957)]. The text has been re-edited with critical comments by Alexander R. Rumble, 'An edition and translation of the Burghal Hidage, together with Recension C of the Tribal Hidage', in David Hill and Alexander R. Rumble, ed., *The Defence of Wessex* (Manchester and New York, 1996), pp. 24–31. On Saxony, see Widukind of Corvey, *Rerum gestarum Saxonicarum libri III*, lib. I, cap. 35, ed. Paul Hirsch and Hans-Eberhard Lohmann,

works were built, manned and controlled under central commands in both kingdoms. Reports on the building activities placed the kings of Wessex and Saxony as rulers over land and people in charge of the supervision of building, guarding and maintaining defensive fortresses.[66] Mobile units supplemented these defence works. They could easily be dispatched to places where highly mobile immigrant armies appeared. The joint command of the mobile forces and the fortresses made defence coordination efforts possible and effectively constrained the range of activity of the armed immigrants. Thus the goal of defending wide stretches of land and variegated types of population group against armed immigrants assumed priority over the processes of organising armed forces and constructing defence systems, which were now reduced to mere instruments for the accomplishment of the set goal.

This, of course, is not to say that early medieval warfare up to the turn of the tenth century was conducted without strategy and that war aims were not defined in advance of military action. Indeed, war aims are on record from the early period but, contrary to the goal pursued by the defence systems in Wessex and Saxony at the turn of the tenth century, the previous types of war aims appear to have been focused mainly on increasing, maintaining or resisting the change of the social status of rulers and combatants[67] rather than on defending or conquering territories.[68] Aiming at success in the indefinite processes of controversies about acquiring or keeping status or avoiding its decline was more favourable to the process-orientation of action than the territorial defence systems, which were organised in pursuit of predetermined goals. The defence systems that came into existence from the turn of the tenth century were not built for permanent use but mainly for the purpose of fending off or repelling a specific enemy force. It was thus assumed (though not always correctly) that a tactical defensive action was completed with the accomplishment of the strategic goal that had been set for it. Nevertheless, the degree of success of keeping enemy forces at bay could be measured more easily than the accomplishment of the previous aims of promoting or preventing changes in the status of rulers and combatants. Therefore, the actions leading to the late ninth- and early tenth-century defence systems carried with them a higher degree of goal-orientation than previous military actions. Only about a century later, the new paradigm of goal-orientation began to evolve into the model for high and late medieval ethics. Rulers and their aris-

MGH, SS rer. Germ. LX (Hanover, 1935), pp. 48–9. Janet M. Bately, ed., *The Anglo-Saxon Chronicle*, vol. 3: MS A, s. a. 893 (Cambridge, 1986), pp. 55–6.

[66] Explicitly so in the *Anglo-Saxon Chronicle*, s. a. 893 (see note 65), p. 56.

[67] For evidence see *Anglo-Saxon Chronicle* (note 65), s. a. 755, pp. 36–7. Gregory of Tours, *Libri Historiarum*, lib. III, cap. 3 (see note 22), p. 99.

[68] Early medieval conquerors, with the exception of Charlemagne who was noteworthy for defeating Saxons and subjecting them to continuous Frankish rule through an intensive campaign of altogether thirty-three years, hardly used military victories for the purpose of establishing bureaucratic control over population groups that they subjected to their rule. See Einhard, *Vita Caroli*, cap. 8–9, 15, ed. Oswald Holder-Egger, MGH, SS. Rer. Germ. [25] (Hanover, 1911), pp. 11–13, 17–18.

tocratic seigneurial lords made increasing efforts to place themselves at the highest possible rank in elaborate and rigid hierarchies. Aristocratic occupants of lesser ranks were classed as servants to those occupying the higher ranks. While many occupants of lower ranks acted in pursuit of the goal of aggrandising their power and upgrading their rank, the hierarchy of power-holders itself emerged as fixed and was taken for granted as an element of the divinely willed world order. In the reflection of the courtly literature of the high Middle Ages, the ideal knight, which minstrels like Ulrich von Liechtenstein sought to portray, served a lady but would not ask why he was doing so.[69]

Moreover, the newly cherished goal-orientation of action became the main feature of the socio-economic organisation of towns and cities from the eleventh century. Obviously, neither trade nor the manufacturing of market goods were inventions of the urban communities of this and the subsequent centuries. However, during the early Middle Ages up until the eighth century, production and distribution had to satisfy local demand rather than local or product markets. This relationship was reversed through the increasing significance applied to goal-orientation from the eleventh century. Urban traders and producers began to act with the goal of supplying interconnected product markets that could span the entire old world of the tri-continental *ecumene.*[70]

Conclusion

In summary, it has been shown that modern sociologists were not justified in assuming that action could be defined without respect for conceptual change. Instead, the historicity of the concept of action has emerged as a consequence of the changes from process-orientation to goal-orientation. Much of the early medieval period was governed by a concept of action that was focused on processes. That is to say, the specification of motives and the reflection on intentions received less attention and the measurement of the degree of goal-attainment carried with it less significance than structuring and maintaining processes of action. The rationality of actions was thus determined in ways that differed from those admitted by modern sociologists. They have taken for granted that rational actions were classed as social actions, were conducted towards goals set by the actors themselves and under circumstances where observers could measure the success or failure of actions in terms of the degree of goal-attainment. However, in the early Middle Ages, actors considered their doings rational if actions were compatible with the conditions of the physical and social environments and served the attainment of goals that

---

69 Ulrich of Liechtenstein, *Lieder*, no III/3, 1–4, ed. Carl von Kraus, *Deutsche Liederdichter des 13. Jahrhunderts*, vol. 1 (Tübingen, 1952), p. 430 [2nd edn (Tübingen, 1978)].

70 For a survey, see Janet Lippman Abu-Lughod, *Before European Hegemony* (Oxford and New York, 1989).

were believed to have been set by the divinity rather than by human actors themselves. Oral communication featured first and foremost in many processes during the early Middle Ages and served the purposes of fostering social bonds and ties among members of kin, neighbourhood and contractual groups. As actors could be members of various types of group simultaneously, they could expect to receive assistance from various group members. Only then could they hope to succeed in their attempts to conduct processes of action in accordance with the local conditions of life and the natural rhythms of growth as well as decay and to use the bounties of nature while being exposed to its vagaries. This attitude towards action was suitable in a social and physical environment in which the largest part of the early medieval population consisted of farmers and was engaged in the production of crops, agricultural products (largely for local consumption) and providing mandatory service to their lords. The attitude was also appropriate in a world in which, up to the seventh century, long-distance migration across several generations loomed large. Under these circumstances, integrating persons into groups was vital and demanded the subordination of personal interests, wishes and desires to the demands of the groups.

With the end of the long-distance migrations and their gradual replacement by movements of internal colonisation in nearby woodland areas from the seventh century, action had to be reconceptualised. While process-orientation continued to have highest significance down to the eleventh century, the desire to accomplish goals set by the actors themselves increased as agriculture became more intensive and was extended to less favourable soils in highland locations. The decision, through which Emperor Otto III tried to transform the traditional setting of meals according to the Byzantine model and to which reference was made in the previous chapter, emerged as an early and somewhat premature attempt to shift the focus of the ceremonial from the task of maintaining integrated processes of communicative action between the rulers and their retainers to the display of the rulers' elevated rank and their rule by divine grace. The new structure of the ceremonial reduced the importance of the processes of actions because social bonds and ties were no longer maintained through communication and gift-giving. Instead, what mattered more than the maintenance of ritualised process was the goal of marking difference between rulers and ruled. Likewise, the transformation of village communities into settlements of dependant peasant farmers and the emergence of landholder classes consisting of secular aristocrats and church institutions enforced a division of labour between producers and consumers of crops and agricultural products. Specifically, church institutions were in need of a steady supply of products from their dependant peasants whom they expected to provide food as well as certain goods necessary for the performance of religious duties. The late ninth-century polyptychs together with contemporary normative and narrative sources recorded the injection of more goal-oriented action into agricultural production and central control over land and people.

The injection of a higher degree of goal-oriented action in the ninth century sparked the emergence of a new agricultural work ethic, an agricultural revolution, which in turn contributed to an increase in yield ratios and the enlargement of local markets for agricultural products. Up until the tenth century, trade remained mainly managed trade while it did become increasingly supply-oriented. From the eleventh century, ever more producers and traders gathered in autonomous settlements categorised as towns and cities. There they could often act without interference from external rulers, make efforts to control the physical and social environments and thus reconceptualise action as goal-oriented. Some late medieval theorists of action who refocus theorising from process-oriented to goal-oriented action worked in urban settings or wrote for essentially urban audiences. They ascribed only to urban actors the readiness to orientate actions towards self-imposed goals and reduce the role of processes to instruments of goal-attainment and thereby widened the urban–rural divide. It was against this background that early twelfth-century scholars working in cities could begin to articulate the demand that persons should first reflect on their motives and intentions before acting in pursuit of their goals.

The evidence discussed in this chapter discloses the parallelism of changes in standards of perception and concepts of action. As new standards of perception evolved that demanded actors' self-reliance and the separation of perception from action, the concept of action moved from emphasising process-orientation to demanding goal-orientation. The last chapter revisits the separation of perception from action in the light of the history of aesthetic and ethical theory.

V

Aesthetics and Ethics:
Their Separation as Concepts

> One eye witnesse is better to be belyved
> than a thousand eare witnesses besydes
>
> Philip Stubbes

Introduction

The Middle Ages have long been accused of lacking systematic and formalised aesthetic and ethical theories, despite a variety of scattered statements that can be related to aesthetics and ethics. Most historians of philosophical theories about aesthetics and ethics have devoted virtually no attention to the early Middle Ages[1] and have subjected to closer scrutiny only a few prolific authors from the later Middle Ages, among them Peter Abelard, St Thomas Aquinas, William Ockham and John Duns Scotus. As far as aesthetics is concerned, the most persuasive justification for this approach has been drawn from the history of the word aesthetics. Indeed, the word *aesthetica* was invented only in the middle of the eighteenth century when it served as a term for the academic study of perception in general.[2] Some historians of aesthetics have drawn attention to the fact that, before the word *aesthetica* was derived from Ancient Greek in Germany, seventeenth- and early eighteenth-century British sensualists had already laid down the principles of the philosophical inquiry into perception.[3] Aesthetics did not become generally applied as a

---

[1] An exception is the work of John Scotus Eriugena, the ninth-century theologian whose views on aesthetics and ethics have received some reappraisal.

[2] The earliest use of the word *aesthetica* in mid-eighteenth-century German philosophy still carried with it the meaning of the ancient Greek original αισθά νομαι and was equated with *cognitio sensitiva*, that is, perception. See Alexander Gottlieb Baumgarten, *Theoretische Ästhetik*, ed. Hans Rudolf Schweizer (Hamburg, 1983), pp. 10–12 [newly and partly ed. from Baumgarten, *Aesthetica*, vol. 1, pars I, cap. 7, §7 (Frankfurt, 1750); repr. (Hildesheim, 1961); 3rd edn of the repr. (Hildesheim, New York, 1986)]. Cf.: Baumgarten, ibid., vol. 1, pars I, cap. 1, §17. Baumgarten, *Texte zur Grundlegung der Ästhetik*, ed. Hans Rudolf Schweizer (Hamburg, 1983), p. 81.

[3] Karlheinz Barck, ' "Ästhetik". Wandel ihres Begriffs im Kontext verschiedener Disziplinen und unterschiedlicher Wissenschaftskulturen', and Martin Fontius,

term for a philosophical discipline until the nineteenth century, when the eighteenth-century wider meaning[4] was narrowed down to the study of the means to determine the criteria for judgements of beauty, in the context either of art alone or jointly of nature and art.[5] Yet it can hardly be denied that aesthetic thought existed during the Middle Ages, even without necessarily being recorded in writing.[6]

Without using the word aesthetics, medieval aestheticians studied perception in general and established connections with ontology and with ethics. There were many controversies. One long-term controversial issue was the ontological relationship between the perceivers and the objects perceived. In the words of St Augustine: 'If I were to ask first whether things are beautiful

---

'Kommentar', in Gunter Scholtz, ed., *Die Interdisziplinarität der Begriffsgeschichte*, Archiv für Begriffsgeschichte Sonderheft 2000 (Hamburg, 2000), pp. 55–65. Peter Kivy, *The Seventh Sense. A Study of Francis Hutcheson's Aesthetics and Its Influence in Eighteenth-Century Britain* (New York, 1976), pp. 124–5.

4   Kant used the word aesthetics in its wider meaning and became well known for his rejection of the notion of aesthetics as a philosophical discipline. See Immanuel Kant, *Vorlesungen über Logik. Logik Philippi* [1772], ed. Preußische Akademie der Wissenschaften, Kant, *Gesammelte Werke*, vol. 24, part 1 (Berlin, 1966), p. 359. Instead, he subsumed the general discussion of the notions of space and time under the term 'transcendental aesthetics' which he equated with the theory of perception: Kant, *Kritik der reinen Vernunft* [Riga, 1781], in Kant, *Werke in zwölf Bänden*, ed. Wilhelm Weischedel, vol. 3 (Frankfurt, 1968), pp. 69–86.

5   Jean Paul [*Vorschule der Ästhetik*, Preface to the 2nd edn [1812], ed. Norbert Miller and Wolfhart Henckmann (Hamburg, 1990), p. 22] famously observed that 'our time is teeming with aestheticians', which made a certain cynicism explicit about the field of inquiry. Similarly 'Revision der Ästhetik in den letzten Dezennien des verflossenen Jahrhunderts', in *Hallesche Allgemeine Literaturzeitung* (1805/06). Friedrich Theodor Vischer, *Aesthetik oder Wissenschaft des Schönen*, vol. 1 (Reutlingen and Leipzig, 1846), pp. 1–2 [2nd edn by Robert Vischer (Munich, 1922); repr. (Hildesheim and New York, 1996)]. Vischer, *Das Schöne und die Kunst. Zur Einführung in die Aesthetik*, 2nd edn (Stuttgart, 1898), pp. 24–5, first published (1898); 3rd edn (Stuttgart, 1907)], was even more explicit in criticising Baumgarten for his seemingly mechanistic Cartesian approach to the beautiful. In the meantime, Hegel set the precedent for the narrow definition of aesthetics as the theory of the beautiful in art. See Georg Wilhelm Friedrich Hegel, *Ästhetik*, ed. Georg Lukács (Berlin, 1955), p. 49. The lectures were first edited from student transcripts by Heinrich Gustav Hotho in 1835 and presented again in a revised edition in 1842. The opposite view that aesthetics was the philosophical discipline concerned with beauty in nature and art was adopted, among others, by Moritz Carrière, *Aesthetik. Die Idee des Schönen und ihre Verwirklichung im Leben und in der Kunst*, vol. 1, 3rd edn (Leipzig, 1885), pp. V–X. Avary W. Holmes Forbes, *The Science of Beauty. An Analytical Inquiry into the Laws of Aethetics* (London, 1881). Pierre Guastalla, *Esthétique* (Paris, 1925), p. 5. Karl Köstlin, *Aesthetik* (Tübingen, 1869), pp. 1–4. Theodor Lipps, *Grundlegung des Ästhetik*, vol. 1 (Hamburg and Leipzig, 1903), p. 1. George Santayana, *The Sense of Beauty. Being the Outline of Aesthetic Theory* (New York, 1896), pp. 1–13. Vischer, *Aesthetik*, vol. 1 (as above), p. 1. Yet Baumgarten's wide definition was still defended by Johannes Volkelt, *System der Ästhetik*, vol. 1 (Leipzig, 1905), pp. 4–5.

6   See Götz Pochat, *Geschichte der Ästhetik und Kunsttheorie* (Cologne, 1987), p. 11. Władysław Tatarkiewicz, *The History of Aesthetics*, ed. Cyril Barrett, SJ, vol. 2 (The Hague, Paris and Warsaw, 1970) [first published (Warsaw, 1962)], pp. 285–6.

because they give pleasure, or give pleasure because they are beautiful, I have no doubt that I will be given the answer that they give pleasure because they are beautiful.' Augustine recorded an objectivist doctrine that dominated in his own time and connected perception and being. What constituted beauty according to this doctrine was the quality of the objects perceived, not some activity of the perceiving person. In the fifth century, Pseudo-Dionysius the Areopagite used Augustinian objectivism to establish his doctrine that perceivers were neither obliged nor considered to be capable of passing aesthetic judgements.[7] In accordance with this doctrine, John Scotus Eriugena argued in the ninth century that the only capability of perceivers lay with the more or less appropriate apprehension of the quality of the perceived objects.[8] Nevertheless, perception was not merely a passive absorption of impressions through the senses but a process considered to be convertible into predetermined action. For John this was so because the beautiful and the good were inseparable manifestations of divine will and, consequently, apprehending the beautiful meant striving to act in favour of the good.[9] The objectivism passed down to the Middle Ages through the works of Augustine and Pseudo-Dionysius the Areopagite and remained the dominant attitude towards perception up until the second half of the thirteenth century when, if Eco's interpretation is correct,[10] St Thomas Aquinas introduced into philosophical theory the knowledgeable person as a perceiver with an innate 'cognitive power'.[11] At the same time, the sense organs began to receive greater attention not only as objects of scientific inquiry but also as media in the interaction between the object perceived and the perceiving person.[12] That aesthetics had to be conceptualised as a comprehensive theory of perception was self-evident under these premises.

Likewise ethics, although the word was in use already in Greek Antiquity, was not considered to be a field of study of its own in the Middle Ages. This was so because ethics at the time remained embedded in the intellectual

---

[7] Pseudo-Dionysius the Areopagite, *De divinis nominibus,* lib. IV, cap. 11, in *PG* vol. 3, col. 770. Other editions are: Dionysius, *De divina hierarchia / de divinis nominibus,* ed. Philippe Chevalier, 2 vols (Paris, 1937). Dionysius, *The Divine Names and Mystical Theology,* ed. John D. Jones (Milwaukee, 1980).

[8] John Scotus Eriugena, *Expositiones in ierarchiam coelestem,* lib. I, cap. 3, ed. J. Barbet, CCCM XXXI (Turnhout, 1975), p. 15.

[9] John Scotus Eriugena, *Versio operum S. Dionysii,* cap. IV, in *PL* vol. 122, col. 1132.

[10] In the first half of the twelfth century, Hugh of St Victor still commented on Pseudo-Dionysius the Areopagite along the lines of John Scotus Eriugena. See Hugh of St Victor, *Commentariorum in Hierarchiam Coelestam secundum interpretationem Joannis Scoti libri X,* in *PL* vol. 175, cols 923–1154. On the dating see Umberto Eco, *The Aesthetics of Thomas Aquinas* (Cambridge, MA, 1988), p. 119 [first published Milan, 1970]].

[11] Thomas Aquinas, *Summa theologiae,* Secunda secundae, qu. 132, ar. 1, in *S. Thomae Opera omnia,* ed. Roberto Busa, SJ, vol. 2 (Stuttgart, 1980), p. 688.

[12] See Roger Bacon, *Perspectiva,* Distinctio III, cap. 1, ed. David Charles Lindberg, *Roger Bacon and the Origins of* Perspectiva *in the Middle Ages. A Critical Edition and English Translation of Bacon's Perspectiva with Introduction and Notes* (Oxford, 1996), pp. 320–4.

efforts of making and maintaining the Christian theological doctrine of moral action as acting in accordance with the divine will. Early medieval theologians positioned discourses on moral action in the context of the onto-logical question about the origins of evil. The starting point of these dis-courses was the axiom that the divinity was the perfect good and had created the world according to its own image. Following this axiom, there were two possible answers to the question about the origin of evil. The first was that evil had been divinely willed as part of the creation of the world. If so, the cre-ation of evil in the world was to be considered as an instrument to demon-strate the goodness of the good vis-à-vis the very opposite of the good.[13] The alternative answer was that evil was the result of human actions against divine will. If so, evil did not exist as part of the divinely willed creation but was in the world as the denial of what had come into being through divine cre-ation.[14] Whichever answer was given, the common platform for both argu-ments was the view that evil had come into the world not through human intention or conscience but through divine will or the lack of orientation towards the divinely willed good. It was only Peter Abelard who, early in the twelfth century, introduced the notion of conscience into ethical theory. He did so by arguing that actions themselves were neither good nor evil but could be evaluated as good or evil through the human intentions leading to them. To Abelard, conscience was the medium through which human actors could be induced to commit evil actions. Abelard demanded that persons should become conscious of their own intentions and that they should avoid com-mitting evil actions after having recognised the evilness of their intentions. In Abelard's view, then, actions were evil that actors were determined to pursue consciously and with an evil intention.[15] As evilness of intention was different in scope and extent in different contexts, the tripartite Aristotelian scheme resurfaced,[16] according to which human action was to be evaluated differently, depending on whether it affected personal conduct, grew out of the duty to preserve the integrity of the household or the kin group, or resulted from

---

[13] Ambrose, *De officiis ministrorum*, lib. I, cap. 4, in *PL* vol. 16, col. 31. Augustine, *De natura boni*, cap. 4–5, in *PL* vol. 42, cols 553–4.

[14] John Scotus Eriugena, *Versio*, cap. IV (see note 9), cols 1140–1.

[15] Peter Abelard, *Liber dictus scito te ipsum*, cap. III, in *PL* vol. 178, col. 636. New edn s. t. *Ethical Writings. Know Yourself* (Indianapolis, 1995).

[16] Anicius Manlius Torquatus Severinus Boethius, *In Porphyrium Dialogi*, in *PL* vol. 64, cols 11–12. Cassiodore, *De artibus*, cap. 3, in *PL* vol. 70, cols 1167–8. Hugh of St Victor, *De studio legendi*, lib. II, cap. 20, in *PL* vol. 176, col. 759. Another edn is Hugh, *Didascalion*, ed. Charles H. Buttimer (Washington, DC, 1939), p. 39. John Duns Scotus, *Utrum potestas peccandi sit a Deo* [Ordinatio II, dist. 44], ed. Allan Bernard Wolter, *Duns Scotus on the Will and Morality* (Washington, DC, 1986), pp. 31–123. Josef Lechner, 'Johann von Rodington, OFM, und sein Quodlibet de conscientia', in Albert Lang, Josef Lechner and Michael Schmaus, ed., *Aus der Geisteswelt des Mittelalters. Studien und Texte. Martin Grabmann zur Vollendung des 60. Lebensjahres*, Beiträge zur Geschichte der Philosophie und Theologie des Mittelalters. Supplementbd III,2 (Munster, 1935), pp. 1125–68 [at p. 1149, Lechner prints a passage from the Bruges City Library MS of the *Quodlibet*, fol. 14b, about the necessity to recognise human free will].

obligations towards the polity. That ethics was to be categorised as a general theory of moral action was self-evident under these premises.

Only after Justus Lipsius cautiously attempted to secularise ethics and tried to construe humankind rationalistically as a metaphysical source of moral norms at the end of the sixteenth century did ethics emerge as a branch of practical philosophy or practical theology.[17] It has since been regarded as a discipline by means of which its practitioners have been able to define the criteria for determining the nature of the good and devise a theory of justice and moral action. In the Middle Ages, however, aesthetics and ethics were closely associated with each other. This can easily be recognised as many authors simultaneously addressed both subjects. At the theoretical level, John Scotus Eriugena reflected on the interconnectedness of perception and action by ranking the beautiful together with the good as the most precious of the divine names.[18] He described the divinity as supreme light and the most plentiful beauty penetrating into almost everything in the divinely created world.[19] Likewise, Pseudo-Dionysius the Areopagite regarded the divinity as the sole source of the good in the world.[20] Therefore, in the name of the divinity the beautiful was indistinguishable from the good. If perception was believed and expected to be convertible into action, any theory of perception would have to include statements about action. Consequently, any aesthetic theory would have to be an ethical theory combining, at the same time, statements about beauty with statements about morally defensible action. Moreover, theoretical discourses focusing on aesthetic and ethical judgements had to rest on the assumption that these judgements could be made by persons with the capability and willingness to do so in a responsible way. However, such discourses required recognising the concept of persons as autonomous actors in their own right, distinct from the rights and the status obligations that were conveyed upon members of various types of group. But this requirement ran contrary to the early medieval integrated processes of communicative action that tied persons into networks of groups. The group-bound rights and status obligations also demanded that perceivers should adequately translate their perceptions into predetermined action in accordance with group-specific norms rather than their own aesthetic judgements. In other words, aesthetic as well as ethical judgements remained an element of the practicalities of actions within particularistic groups while

---

17 Justus Lipsius, *Two Bookes of Constancie*, transl. John Stradling [London, 1584], ed. R. Kirk and C. M. Hall (New Brunswick, 1939), pp. 77–9, 95–6 [first published (Antwerp, 1584)]. Lipsius, *Six Bookes of Politickes or Civil Doctrine* [Antwerp, 1589], transl. William Jones (London, 1594) [repr. The English Experience. 2CCLXXXVII (Amsterdam and New York, 1970), p. 128].

18 John Scotus Eriugena, *Versio* (see note 9), col. 1132.

19 For a reflection of this theory in hagiography, see the vision of King Oswald of Northumbria before a battle, referred to in the Introduction. Adomnán, *Life of Columba*, lib. I, cap. 1, ed. Alan Orr Anderson and Marjorie Ogilvie Anderson (Edinburgh and London, 1961), pp. 14–16 [new edn (Oxford, 1991)].

20 Dionysius, *De divinis nominibus* (see note 7), cap. XI, col. 770.

they did not require theoretical abstractions in universalistic terms. The abstractions that were nevertheless on record from the early Middle Ages were not focused on specific parts of the perceptible world, such as pieces of art or natural objects, but were, as Curtius has shown,[21] concerned with the metaphysics of beauty. The metaphysics of beauty appealed to all senses equally, as John Scotus Eriugena insisted, and directed contemplative perceivers' attention away from earthly things to imaginations through which the divinity appeared to allow human minds to catch a glimpse of its own pure though invisible beauty.[22] Despite differences in details, the professionalisation of aesthetics and ethics was a comparatively late process. Professionalisation meant narrowing the focus. In consequence of this professionalisation, the fuzziness that had been characteristic of medieval aesthetics and ethics has become discredited, and investigations into the interconnectedness of aesthetics and ethics have met with substantial and increasing scepticism.

In this chapter, I relate the post-medieval emergence of philosophical theories of aesthetics (as theories of judgements about the beautiful) and ethics (as theories of judgements about the good) to changes in standards of perception and concepts of action in the course of the Middle Ages. I first describe perception in the early Middle Ages when aesthetics was the means to juxtapose or intermediate between various group-specific standards of perception. I then examine the transformation of standards of perception during the thirteenth century, whence aesthetics was turned into a means to philosophically reflect on perception in general and beauty in particular. Thereafter, I move on to ethics and relate early medieval ethical theory to a concept of action that was focused on process rather than on goal-attainment. And I trace the transformation of ethics from a means to resolve conflicts among groups with different legal norms and political institutions into a theory of judgements about moral action in general and the good in particular during the twelfth century. It was at the same time that persons received the duties to make themselves knowledgeable about their intentions and to make efforts to direct their

---

21 Ernst Robert Curtius, *Europäische Literatur und lateinisches Mittelalter*, 2nd edn (Bern, 1954), p. 231, note 1 [first published (1948); English version (London, 1953), at p. 224, note 20].

22 John Scotus Eriugena, *Expositiones*, lib. I, cap. 3 (see note 7), p. 15. Cf. Augustine, *De trinitate libri XV*, lib. VIII, cap. 3, in *PL* 42, cols 949–50. Augustine, *De libero arbitrio*, lib. II, cap. 3, in *PL* 32, col. 1244. However, Augustine described the eye as the most important of all sense organs (ibid., lib. XI, cap. 1, col. 985). Similarly, the ninth-century silver Fuller Brooch shows an image of the five senses but places vision in its centre. Augustine differentiated three types of vision: that through the eyes, that through the mind and that through the intellect [*De Genesi ad litteram*, lib. XII, cap. 4, in *PL* 34, cols 458–9]. For a similar position in recent aesthetic theory, see Theodor Wiesengrund Adorno, *Ästhetische Theorie* (Frankfurt, 1970), pp. 336, 371. For references to the belief that aural perception received a higher appreciation than visual perception in late Antiquity and the early Middle Ages, see Donat de Chapeaurouge, '*Das Auge ist ein Herr, das Ohr sein Kecht*'. *Der Weg von der mittelalterlichen zur abstrakten Malerei* (Wiesbaden, 1983), pp. 1–14.

actions towards self-conceived and morally defensible goals. The final part of the chapter deals with the problem of the changing patterns of interconnectedness between aesthetics and ethics.

Coordinating standards of perception in the early Middle Ages

In orally communicating groups, the various signs and signals through which persons sent and received messages remained part of an integrated process of communicative action. As the communicating persons had to be present in one spot, communication involved all senses, and the spoken word could not be isolated from gestures and other motions of the body. But this did not imply that standards of perception were not controversial. At the latest from the end of the eighth century, controversies arose in consequence of the Catholic mission, as the Catholic Church began to impose its standard of perception first upon the clergy and, subsequently, upon the laity at large. This standard of perception was enshrined in the universalistic biblical record of all perceptible objects in the divinely willed world. According to St Augustine, the Bible was the sole universal source of standards of perception.[23] Consequently, the Bible had to be accepted as the sole source of those norms and rules through which persons should regulate perception. Along the same lines, Raban Maur pleaded in favour of using the work of non-Christian authors only to the extent that their writings were compatible with Christian aesthetics. The Church made efforts to suppress the pre-Christian communicative standards and habits practised in kin and other types of group. But these efforts entailed resistance among monks and nuns who remained connected with kin groups of high rank and insisted that group-bound traditions should continue to be accepted as sources of standards of perception.[24]

At the end of the eighth century, the clash between particularistic and universalistic standards of perception eclipsed in an otherwise cryptic exclamation by Alcuin, Abbot of the monastery of St Martin in Tours. Alcuin occupied a central role in the educational and liturgical reform movements launched under Charlemagne. In a letter addressed to an unidentified bishop in England, he criticised the use of non-Christian group-bound oral traditions in monasteries, asking: 'What does Ingeld have to do with Christ?' He demanded that Ingeld be removed from the musical repertoire of the monks and nuns in England.[25] The phrase refers to the monastic practice of singing lay songs featuring a secular hero named Ingeld who was popular in English and Scandinavian legend. Moreover, the phrase juxtaposed two aesthetic pref-

---

[23] Augustine, *De vera religione*, cap. 17, in *PL* 34, cols 136–7. See also Raban Maur, *De clericorum institutione*, cap. 18, in *PL* 107, col. 396.

[24] See above, chapter I, note 40, for the case of a nun in the Merovingian convent of St Radegundis. In her younger days before entering the monastery, the nun had composed lay songs. To her embarrassment, she heard one of these songs being sung in proximity to the convent and was thus reminded of her youthful sins.

[25] Alcuin, *Ep.*, no. 124, ed. Ernst Dümmler, MGH Epp., vol. 2 (Hanover, 1892), p. 183.

erences, namely for songs based on the Bible and represented by the name of Christ on the one hand, and, on the other, for songs drawn on oral traditions about deceased group members and represented by the name of Ingeld.[26] Alcuin's juxtaposition of Ingeld to Christ disclosed that standards of perception regulated the transmission of oral traditions and were not merely confined to vision but were related to the integrated processes of communicative action maintained within or among the particularistic groups of the time. Alcuin's question thus confirms the tenacity of recitals of oral traditions in English monasteries and, simultaneously, certifies the determination of the Church authorities to suppress such practices.[27] Instead of accepting the dualism of standards of perception derived from biblical sources on the one hand and from group-specific oral traditions on the other, the Church took the view that the authority of the Bible should dominate standards of perception. Thus, early medieval aesthetics was conceivable solely as a pragmatic means to differentiate either between various particularistic group-specific standards of perception or to enforce one single universalistic standard of perception.

Constructing aesthetics as a theory of perception

From the tenth century, the waning size and significance of particularistic groups reduced the gains that persons could expect to derive from continuing to transmit oral traditions. By the middle of this century, Church authorities believed that kin groups were too weak to be able to transmit genealogical traditions orally, as has been shown in the previous chapter. Therefore, the Church requested that genealogies should be laid down in writing. In the eleventh and twelfth centuries, oral traditions could travel freely beyond specific kin groups, and they attracted the interest of gifted poets who began to use them in their written works. Thus, the integrated process of communicative action fragmented. The fragmentation had the consequence that the universalistic standards of the Church could be enforced for perception and communication. Likewise, neighbourhood groups, such as the early elev-

---

26 For a recent discussion of Alcuin's letter, see Whitney French Bolton, *Alcuin and 'Beowulf'* (New Brunswick, 1979), pp. 102–3. Donald A. Bullough, 'What Does Ingeld Have to Do with Lindisfarne?', in *Anglo-Saxon England* 22 (1993), pp. 93–125. Neither author, however, treated aesthetics.

27 Katherine O'Brien O'Keeffe, *Visible Song* (Cambridge, 1990). pp. 8–14, has re-emphasised the importance of murmuring or loud reading written texts throughout the early and high Middle Ages and has categorised Old English poetic manuscripts as living texts under the control of their scribes. She has produced evidence that oral communication continued to be of significance even within groups whose members would be trained to communicate habitually through the medium of writing. Strangely, Christoph Wulf, 'Ohr', in Wulf, ed., *Vom Menschen. Handbuch Historische Anthropologie* (Weinheim and. Basle, 1997), p. 461, completely ignores the orality of medieval culture and dates the beginning of the 'dominance of the eye' to the age of Plato.

enth-century village community at Kölbigk, proved to be too weak to control the behaviour of their members and to impose appropriate sanctions against the infringement of rules.

The universalistic Church-enforced standard of perception awarded increasing practical significance to visual perception. Around 1200, the English monastic chronicler William of Newburgh recorded a series of spectacular events that had happened in the vicinity of the priory of St Mary at Newburgh in Yorkshire in 1196. William was worried by the frequent reports about various vampires and similar ghosts that had been seen by a number of eyewitnesses. He wondered how reasonable and otherwise clear-minded persons could claim, apparently independent of each other and with perfect seriousness, that they had seen dead bodies rising from their graves and inflicting fatal wounds on the living before returning to their burial places. Yet William dared not doubt the reports because they were too many and they were recorded by otherwise trustworthy witnesses. William gave the following record of one of the reports:

> Some years ago, the chaplain of a noble lady died, and he was buried in Melrose abbey church. The clergyman had dedicated himself to the vain passion of hunting so much that many gave him the contemptuous nickname 'dog's priest'. After his death, his sin was revealed. At nights, he would leave his grave, but he did not harass the monastery because of the merits of its sacred inhabitants; so he could not molest or frighten anyone there. Instead, he wandered outside the monastery and, with much noise and terrible groans, he terrified the sleeping chamber of his former lady in the immediate neighbourhood. After this had happened several times, the lady entrusted her fright to a monk, asking him to help her in the danger in which she lived. The monk sought advice from his subprior. Together with three trustworthy and brave clergymen, he went to the graveyard at night, where the chaplain had been buried, and stayed on guard. When half of the night had passed, the monster had not yet appeared. Then the three assistants to the monk withdrew in order to make a fire because they felt cold. Now the devil believed that his time had come, and he set life into the human body that had remained calm longer than usual. When the monk saw the dead body, he stood as if petrified. But soon he regained his courage because there was no hope for escaping. He resisted the terrible groaning of the monster and struck him with a double-edged axe in his hand. Having received wounds, the monster cried, turned around and retreated, but more slowly than he had come. Puzzled, the monk pursued the monster and chased him towards his grave. The grave opened itself, grabbed its host from his pursuer and closed itself. The assistants rushed towards the grave. Next morning, they dug out the cursed carcass. When they had removed the earth, they saw the dead body with a big wound and found the grave filled with its blood. They carried the carcass away from the graveyard, burnt it and dispersed the ashes.[28]

---

[28] William of Newburgh, *Historia rerum Anglicarum*, lib. V, cap. 24, ed. Richard Howlett, *Chronicles of the Reigns of Stephen, Henry II and Richard I*, vol. 2, RS LXXXII (London, 1885), pp. 474–82 [repr. (New York, 1965)].

What is of interest here among the many remarkable features of the story is that the monk was made to have 'seen' the chaplain-turned-monster, although the monster had been conspicuous and frightening for its noise during its previous visits to the lady's sleeping chamber. That means that the monastic investigation into the lady's report was conducted in such a way that the report was taken to be trustworthy under the condition that the monster was not only audible but also visible. This supposition was not surprising, as hagiographers had the custom of adducing eyewitness reports as proof of evidence from the ninth century, sometimes together with ear witnesses.[29] But these references to *idonei testes* (qualified witnesses) were sketchy and topical compared to the detailed observations reproduced in the high medieval ghost stories. Here, visibility became an instrument of proof ranked higher than perception through the other senses. William's emphasis on vision neatly matches his statement that he had been informed in other cases by 'eyewitnesses', that is, by persons who claimed to have 'seen' monsters, ghosts or other evil spirits wandering about. Seeing monsters, ghosts and other evil spirits rather than perceiving them in other ways thus became characteristic of late twelfth-century church-influenced reports and their subsequent literary renderings. In several ghost stories reported in the miracles of the late twelfth-century cleric Caesarius of Heisterbach, ghosts usually visited people who first became aware of their ghostly visitors by way of 'seeing' their appearances.[30] This implies that by that time, vision acquired prominence over other senses among ecclesiastical authors.

Moreover, reports about monsters, ghosts and other evil spirits were likened to the *visiones*, which were a literary genre of reports about, and simultaneously the practice of, envisioning the other world. Without attempting to suppress *visiones*, the Church articulated reservations about taking them seriously in late Antiquity and the early Middle Ages.[31] Yet from the eleventh century, a variety of *visiones* enjoyed an increasing popularity. They

---

[29] Among others, see *De miraculis quae in ecclesia Fiscanensi contigerunt*, lib. I, cap. 1, ed. Arthur Isak Edvard Lånfoss, Annales Academiae Scientiarum Fennicae Ser. B, vol. 25, part 1 (Helsinki, 1930), p. 6. *Vita S. Odilonis*, in *PL* vol. 142, col. 935.

[30] Caesarius of Heisterbach, *Dialogus miraculorum atque magnum visionum*, Distinctio II, cap. 22, Distinctio V, cap. 6–7, Distinctio V, cap. 39, ed. Joseph Strange, vol. 1 (Cologne, 1851), pp. 91, 286–7, 324 [repr. (Ridgwood, NJ, 1966)]. For other kinds of stories, see Montague Rhodes James, ed., 'Twelve Medieval English Ghost Stories', in *English Historical Review* 37 (1922), pp. 413–22. Andrew Joynes, ed., *Medieval Ghost Stories* (Woodbridge, 2003).

[31] Augustine, *De Genesi*, lib. XII, cap. 2 (see note 22), col. 455, believed that only paradise was truly visible in dreams. Pope Gregory I knew four causes of *visiones*: an illusion, a reflection together with an illusion, a revelation, a reflection together with a revelation. He ascribed the first two causes to experience and the latter two to the Bible. The empirical causes were unacceptable. See Gregory I, *Dialogues*, lib. IV, cap. 50, ed. Adalbert de Vogüé, vol. 3, Sources Chrétiennes CCLXV (Paris, 1980), pp. 172–6. Isidore of Seville articulated a similar scepticism when he denounced *visiones* as nightly disturbances caused by demons: Isidore of Seville, *Sententiarum liber*, lib. III, cap. 6, in *PL* vol. 83, col. 668.

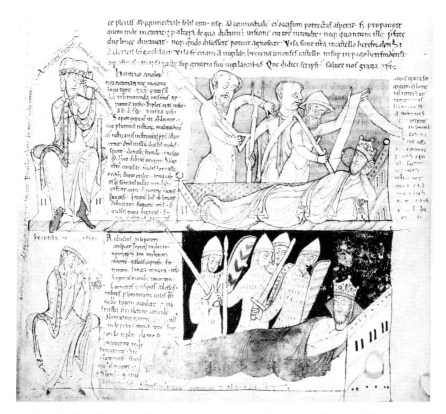

Fig. 25 King Henry I of England, dreaming of a future rebellion, twelfth century. Ms Oxford, Corpus Christi College 157, fol. 382v. By permission of the President and Fellows of Corpus Christi College, Oxford.

represented accounts of visionaries who were primarily made to have 'seen' what was going to happen in the future (Figure 25). Thus the increasing acceptance of the *visiones* confirmed the view that vision began to dominate the other senses at the time.[32] It then seems appropriate to relate the emergence of vision as the most important of the senses to the fragmentation of the integrated process of communicative action. From the twelfth century, the fragmented process of communicative action induced authors to disseminate their knowledge through the medium of writing and thus reflected the elevation of literacy and accounts of what had been 'seen' to the level of high evidential value.

It is therefore small wonder that twelfth-century theorists such as Conrad of Hirsau and Hugh of St Victor emphasised the importance of vision for the acquisition of knowledge and judgements about beauty, even though Hugh

[32] See Lantbert von Deutz, *Miracula Heriberti*, ed. Bernhard Vogel, Lantbert von Deutz, *Vita Heriberti. Miracula Heriberti. Gedichte. Liturgische Texte*, MGH, SS rer. Germ. LXXIII (Hanover, 2001), pp. 203–63.

elsewhere stressed the equal importance of all five senses.[33] Other theorists followed suit, restated the ancient Christian preference for vision over the other senses and gave the eye special significance as the sole organ credited with the capability of emitting as well as absorbing light. It was thus believed that the eye was active as well as passive while the ear was taken to be merely a receptive organ.[34] Moreover, the twelfth, thirteenth and fourteenth centuries witnessed the re-emergence of mnemotechnic strategies that had been common already in the didactical literature of Antiquity.[35] These schemes, of which little use had been made in the early Middle Ages, were even more explicit than their antique models in using images as mnemotechnic devices. Students were to train themselves in associating abstract matters with images of living beings or real-world objects and in recreating the divinely willed order of the world in their minds. In these exercises, vision was the most important sense as reading was the core technique of acquiring knowledge. Consequently, vision was given priority over the other senses. In doing so, high and late medieval theorists followed Cicero who had classed smell, touch and taste as the lower senses.[36] Finally, the increased importance given to visual perception is confirmed by the fact that, from the thirteenth century, physicists as well as physicians took greater care than before to produce technical appliances, made from cut crystal or glass to improve eyesight,[37] although, at the same time, no efforts were made to improve the use of other senses.

From the thirteenth century, aesthetics was no longer a pragmatic instrument by which conflicts among various particularistic group-bound

---

33 Conrad of Hirsau, *Accessus ad auctores*, ed. and trans. Alistair J. Minnis and Alexander Brian Scott, *Medieval Literary Theory and Criticism* (Oxford, 1988), pp. 43–4 [first edn by Robert Burchard Constantyne Huygens, *Accessus ad auctores* (Leiden, 1970)]. Hugh of St Victor, *Soliloquium de arrha animae*, in *PL* vol. 176, col. 953. Hugh, *Studio*, lib. VII, cap. 1, lib. VII, cap. 12 (see note 16), cols 813, 821.

34 See Bacon, *Perspectiva* (see note 12), pp. 326–8. John of Rodington, In libros sententiarum. Ms Biblioteca Apostolica Vaticana lat. 5306, fol. 8ra, ed. Katherine Tachau, *Vision and Certitude in the Age of Ockham. Epistemology and the Foundations of Semantics. 1250–1345* (Leiden, 1988), p. 227. Without reference to Bacon or Rodington, Georg Simmel argued that the ear was receptive whereas the eye was receiving and sending messages and was therefore more important as a sense organ than the ear. See Simmel, 'Soziologie der Sinne', in Simmel, *Aufsätze und Abhandlungen. 1901–1908*, vol. 2, ed. Alessandro Cavalli and Volkhard Krech (Frankfurt, 1993), pp. 286–7 [first published in *Neue Rundschau* 18, 9 (1907)].

35 See Hugh of St Victor, *De tribus maximis circumstantiis gestorum*, ed. William M. Green, in *Speculum* 18 (1943), pp. 484–93. Hugh, *De arca Noe mystica*, ed. Patrice Siccard, CCCM CLXXVI/CLXXVIA (Turnhout, 2001). Thomas Bradwardine, 'De memoria artificali adquirenda', ed. Mary Carruthers, in *Journal of Medieval Latin* 2 (1992), pp. 25–43. For further texts, see *The Medieval Craft of Memory*, ed. Mary Carruthers and Jan M. Ziolkowski (Philadelphia, 2002), pp. 41–70, 205–14.

36 Cicero, *De oratore*, lib. III, cap. 98–9.

37 See Roger Bacon, *Opus majus*, lib. 3, pars 3, distinctio 2, cap. 4, ed. Samuel Jebb (London, 1733), p. 352. Another edn by John Henry Bridges, vol. 2 (Oxford, 1900), p. 157.

standards of perception could be resolved. Instead, aesthetics turned into the philosophical discipline reflecting on the standards of visual perception. Reducing aesthetics to a theory of visual perception opened the door for systematic inquiries into the conditions for the existence of natural beauty and the generation of beauty through the arts. St Thomas Aquinas who, like his teacher Albert the Great, commented on the work of Pseudo-Dionysius the Areopagite, arrived at conclusions that were independent from both his source and his teacher's opinions. He followed his source and his teacher in ascribing the sameness of substance to both the good and the beautiful. Yet he specified that the beautiful was a concept different from that of the good. He maintained that the human mind needed to have a distinct cognitive power in order to be able to sense the beauty of nature or art.[38] Because, according to St Thomas and others, only good things in the divinely willed world could be recognised as beautiful, the beautiful had existence not per se but by virtue of passing through the good. In other words, human beings could perceive something as beautiful not because it was beautiful but because they had some cognitive power to help them recognise the good as beautiful.[39] Thomas and his fellow theorists[40] insisted that, in order to become recognisable as beautiful, the good had to acquire some order. Thus they expected that the beautiful should add order to the good. In the world of human existence the good then became distinguishable from the beautiful, even though both continued to be regarded as indistinguishable within the name of the divinity. The most important sense contributing to the formation of the cognitive power was vision, although Thomas admitted that audition could contribute to the formation of that power to a lesser extent.

Practitioners concurred. In the thirteenth century, the master architect Villard de Honnecourt drew a lion and wrote the phrase, 'how to tame a lion' into his sketchbook. He explained that the picture accompanying the phrase 'was drawn from life' (*al vif*) and insisted that his draughtsman had derived

---

38 Thomas Aquinas, *Summa theologiae*, Prima secundae, qu. 27, ar. 1 ad 3, ed. Busa (see note 11), p. 393. Thomas, *Commentarius de divinis nominibus*, in *S. Thomae Opera omnia*, ed. Roberto Busa, SJ, vol. 4 (Stuttgart, 1980), pp. 555–6. Similarly William of Auvergne, *De bono et malo*, ed. Henri Pouillon, *La beauté, propriété transcendentale, chez les scolastiques. 1220–1270*, Archives d'histoire doctrinale et littéraire du Moyen Age XXI (Paris, 1946), pp. 315–316. The views by Albert the Great on aesthetics and ethics are recorded in Albertus Magnus, *De bono*, ed. Heinrich Kühle, Karl Feckes, Bernhard Geyer and Wilhelm Kübel, *Alberti Magni Opera omnia*, vol. 23 (Munster, 1951), quaestio I–II, pp. 1–36. Albertus, *De pulchro et bono*, ed. Roberto Busa, SJ, *S. Thomae Aquinatis Opera omnia*, vol. 7 (Stuttgart, 1980), pp. 43–7.

39 Thomas, *Summa theologiae*, Prima secundae, qu. 27, ar. 1 ad 3, ed. Busa (see note 11), p. 393.

40 Bonaventure, *Itinerarium*, lib. II, cap. 4–6, in Bonaventure, *Opera omnia*, vol. 5 (Quaracchi, 1892), p. 300 [also in Tatarkiewciz, *History* (see note 6), pp. 237–8]. Witelo, *De Perspectiva*, lib. III, cap. 60, lib. IV, cap. 148, ed. Clemens Baeumker, *Witelo. Ein Philosoph und Naturforscher des XIII. Jahrhunderts*, Beiträge zur Geschichte der Philosophie des Mittelalters, vol. II, part 3 (Munster, 1908), pp. 143, 172–5 [repr. (Munster, 1991)].

the image from the life appearance of the animal. Villard thus saw human cognitive power at work in order to enable him to recreate the divinely created world in appropriate images.[41] Likewise, when the fourteenth-century chronicler Jean de Jandin described the stone sculptures at the royal palace in Paris, he noted that they were so similar to their originals that observers might regard them as living.[42] Similarly, in 1453, Cardinal Nicholas of Cusa argued that there were four pictures in the history of painting, showing figures with lively faces whose eyes followed the observer into every direction.[43] At around 1500, the new role of vision also became explicit in normative writings such as *Book of the Courtier* published by the diplomat Baldassare Castiglione in 1528. In this work the experienced diplomat ranked the messages conveyed through the eyes above messages carried by words, other signs or signals as well as messages communicated through the other senses. Characteristically, Castiglione included his observations on aesthetics in a statement about the ways and means by which persons were enabled to 'see' and even provoke emotions such as genuine love:

> Assuredly there is otherwise a greater affection of love perceived in a sigh, in a respect, in a feare, than in a thousand wordes. Afterwards, to make the eyes the trustie messengers, that may carrie the ambassades of the hart. Because they oftentimes declare with a more force what passion there is, than can the tongue, or letters, or messages. So that they not only disclose the thoughtes, but also manie times kindle love in the hart of the person beloved.[44]

Castiglione thus ranked vision above all other senses and took for granted that aesthetic judgements could be transformed into ethical judgements. Other early sixteenth-century diplomats made efforts to use vision and their analytical skills to uncover the secrets of the mental and physical condition of potential marriage and alliance partners. These partners became frequent targets of investigative efforts when they were ageing or ailing rulers. Thus, Henry VII, King of England, sent out three emissaries to the kingdom of Naples in 1505 to observe a young princess whom he intended to marry. He supplied the crew of investigators with detailed instructions about the specific features of character and physique that he was keen to know details about.[45]

---

41 Villard de Honnecourt, Plate LEO, in *Kritische Gesamtausgabe des Bauhüttenbuches in s. fr. 19093 der Pariser Nationalbibliothek*, fol. 24r, plate 47, ed. Hans R. Hahnloser, 2nd edn (Graz, 1972), pp. 144, 268–72 [first edn (Vienna, 1935)]. Another edn by Theodore Robert Bowie, *The Sketchbook of Villard de Honnecourt* (Bloomington, 1959) [repr. (Westport, CT, 1982)].

42 Jean de Jandin, *Tractatus de laudibus Parisiensis*, ed. Le Roux de Lincy, *Paris et ses historiens au XIVe et XVe siècles* (Paris, 1857), p. 48.

43 Nicholas of Cusa, *De visione Dei sive de icona liber* [1453] (Paris, 1514), fol. 99r.

44 Baldassare Castiglione, *The Book of the Courtier* [(Venice, 1528)]. English version by Thomas Hoby (London, 1561), pp. 246–7 [repr. Tudor Translations. Ser. I, vol. XXIII (New York, 1967)].

45 Henry VII, 'Instruction to Francis Marsin, James Baybrooke, John Stile to Investigate the Old Queen of Naples and her Daughter for the Marriage Project between Himself and the Younger Queen of Naples [June 1505]', ed. William Campbell, *Materials for a*

Similarly, a Venetian diplomat visited Emperor Charles V in 1557, who was then known to be gravely ill of gout, and took notes of the ruler's outward appearances to determine the current physical condition.[46] Vice versa, the late sixteenth-century London professional dancer William Kemp made a conspicuous effort to advance his career through demonstrations of his physical capability and technical skill. To that end, he danced all the way from London to Norwich, then the second largest town in England. Moreover, in a well-publicised written report on his experiences, he displayed his pride in having attracted many bystanders who looked on while he was dancing.[47] Vision for him was the sense that could most easily shape public opinion.

An emerging theory of ethical judgements

As in the case of aesthetics, the ethical was difficult to conceptualise as a category of its own during the Middle Ages. As persons expected in the early Middle Ages that their actions were focused on and influenced by the various types of group to which they might belong, no general theory of moral action could easily overarch the specific principles transmitted within particularistic groups. Under these conditions, ethics was predominantly a pragmatic instrument for resolving conflicts among competing sets of moral and legal norms, much as aesthetics was then a pragmatic means for resolving conflicts among opposing standards of perception. In the case of ethics, such conflicts could arise if persons were placed in situations in which their membership in various types of groups entailed mutually exclusive rights and obligations, or if groups clashed over the validity of their mutually exclusive norms and rules.

In the late sixth century, St Gregory, Bishop of Tours, recorded one case showing that rights following from membership in certain types of group could militate against rights derived from other sources. The city of Tour was then under the rule of the Frankish kings. Gregory described an episode in which a certain Andarchius was involved. He was about to marry a woman whose name remains unknown. The woman's mother accepted him as the bridegroom whereas the woman's father Ursus hesitated to agree. Andarchius did not want to give up marrying the woman and, in order to succeed, he conceived of the following strategy: he deposited armour in a chest and brought the chest to his fiancée's home. Meeting the mother there, he explained to her

History of the Reign of Henry VII, vol. 1, RS LX (London, 1873), pp. 223–39 [repr. (New York, 1965)].

46 Federico Badoardo, 'Report [1557]', ed. Louis Prosper Gachard, *Relations des ambassadeurs vénéciens sur Charles V et Philippe II* (Brussels, 1856), pp. 19–20.

47 William Kemp, *Kempes Nine Daies VVonder. Performed in a Daunce from London to Norwich* (London, 1600) [ed. Alexander Dyce, Camden Society XI (London, 1840), pp. 11, 17]. For evidence of Kemp's literary fame, see the reference to his dancing skills in the satire by John Marston, *The Scourge of Villanoe*, Satyre XI: Humours (London, 1599) [ed. George Bagshawe Harrison (Edinburgh, 1925), p. 301; repr. (New York, 1966)].

that he had put 16,000 gold coins into the chest as his pledge of faithfulness. The mother accepted the chest without opening it. Then Andarchius looked for someone in the town whose name was also Ursus and after he had found such a person, bribed him to sign a written document. In the written document, the second Ursus agreed that he would return 16,000 gold coins to Andarchius in the case that Ursus should refuse to consent to the marriage of his daughter with Andarchius. The second Ursus found no problem signing this document for Andarchius had never pledged to marry the second Ursus's daughter nor had the second Ursus received 16,000 gold coins from Andarchius. Andarchius then took the document to court and demanded that the first Ursus should agree to the marriage or return the 16,000 gold coins. But the first Ursus did neither. The court ruled that because the first Ursus was unwilling to honour Andarchius's demand, he had to forfeit his property to Andarchius. Soon after Andarchius had moved into the first Ursus's house, the divinity intervened, destroyed the building by fire, put Andarchius to death and allowed the first Ursus to retrieve what was left of his property.[48]

As Gregory tells it, the episode is the story of a crime committed with the employment of a written document under the explicit goal of deception. Among others, the story features two significant aspects of the post-Roman, sixth-century city of Tours. The first aspect is that the declining population of Tours could no longer avail itself of institutions for the purpose of authenticating or testing written documents as there had been in the past under Roman imperial rule.[49] Had such institutions been in existence at Gregory's time, the unlucky Ursus would not have been victimised by the fraud, and the tricky Andarchius would have had to conceive a different technique if he wanted to cheat Ursus. Moreover, institutional constraints would have been able to prevent the execution of the fraud, for the first Ursus could have been in a position to prove that he had not signed the charter submitted to the court. Nevertheless, although no authenticating institutions existed, written documents still carried with them the weight of legal validity against which oral protestations were evidently worthless. Hence the first Ursus escaped complete disaster only because, as Gregory put it, the omniscient divinity had Andarchius destroyed by fire.

The second aspect concerns the names of the protagonists. They are of Roman origin and thus indicate that their bearers were Romanes living in the city under Frankish rule. As is known from contemporary legal sources, the Romanes as inhabitants of the Frankish kingdom lived under a kinship rule according to which collateral relatives did not exercise rights or privileges over individual members of households.[50] This rule implied that among Romanes

---

[48] Gregory of Tours, *Libri historiarum X*, lib. IV, cap. 46, ed. Bruno Krusch and Wilhelm Levison, MGH, SS rer. Merov. I,1 (Hanover, 1951), pp. 180–3.

[49] On sixth-century Tours, see Nancy Gautier, Jean-Chrétien Picard, ed., *Topographie chrétienne des cités de la Gaule des origines au milieu du VIIIe siècle*, vol. 5 (Paris, 1987). Luce Pieri, *La ville de Tours du IVe au VIe siècle* (Paris and Turin, 1983).

[50] See Heinrich Brunner, 'Sippe und Wergeld nach niederdeutschen Rechten', in Brunner,

the extended kin group had no principal legal titles in landed property but that these rights rested with individuals or the heads of households. Hence, the lack of group-based rights in landed property was the second factor that made the Andarchius–Ursus episode possible. Andarchius's strategy could only have been successful under the condition that Andarchius addressed his faked charges to the first Ursus alone. Had Ursus's collateral kin had rights in the estate on which Ursus was living, Ursus would not have been forced to forfeit it completely to Andarchius. Instead, members of Ursus's extended kin group would have stepped in as defenders of their rights. Therefore, the Andarchius–Ursus episode was possible solely under the conventions of Roman kinship law, while the institutions enforcing that law had vanished and partly been replaced by other institutions under Frankish rule.

That this argument is not entirely speculative emerges from a rule preserved in the eighth-century *Lex Alamannorum* according to which witnesses to a donation of landed property to a church had to testify in the case that the donor's children might challenge the authenticity of the transaction. It must then have been common for members of non-Roman kin groups to intervene against transactions of landed property through chartered privileges on the grounds that such transactions were alienations of kin group property and involved the consent of the kin group.[51] By contrast, the Andarchius–Ursus episode arose in a social setting where the Roman traditional framework of ethics was no longer compatible with the institutional framework guaranteed by the Frankish rulers. The lack of compatibility between both frameworks opened venues for fraud and other kinds of abuse.

The ninth-century Old High German poem known as *Hildebrandslied* shows a conflict between opposing obligations resulting from membership in different types of group.[52] The poem describes an episode where two protagonists are made to choose between obligations to their kin groups and obligations to the contractual groups of military retainers of which they happened to be the leaders. These two groups were to confront each other in battle. Both protagonists opted for the latter obligations, displaying their willingness to fight. But their option ended in a tragic situation because both leaders discovered that they were father and son. They discovered their kin relationship by introducing themselves by name. The father had left his kin group, perhaps not entirely voluntarily, many years before and had no direct memory of his son's name. But he was knowledgeable in the standard name-giving practice according to which the kin membership of persons was likely to be determined through characteristic particles of the usually dithematic names. The names thus served as identifiers of kinship and linked persons with the traditions of norms and rules transmitted within their kin groups. Therefore,

---

Abhandlungen zur Rechtsgeschichte, ed. Karl Rauch, vol. 1 (Weimar, 1931), pp. 104–208 [repr. (Leipzig, 1965)].

51 *Lex Alamannorum*, lib. II, cap. 1, ed. Karl Lehmann, 2nd edn by Karl August Eckhardt, MGH, LL nat. Germ., vol. 1 (Hanover, 1966), pp. 66–7.

52 Hartmut Brozinski, ed., *Das Hildebrandslied*, vv. 7–19, 2nd edn (Kassel, 1985), s.p.

recognition of kin membership was identical with abiding by the group-specific norms and rules.

In the case of the episode described in the *Hildebrandslied*, however, both protagonists agreed to act against the demand to maintain peace within their kin group because, as leaders of two opposing warrior bands, they were obliged to fight each other. Conflict thus resulted from the mutually exclusive demand to support kin members on the one hand and, on the other, to act in accordance with pledges towards the warrior bands. Both protagonists could agree to act against their kin obligations because the sanctions they faced would have been more severe had they decided to abandon their warrior bands. For the kin groups could, in the worst case, expel their members, whereas the warriors could desert their leaders or even kill them. In the case of mutually exclusive obligations that could result from membership in these types of group, ethics did not come along as a general theory of moral duties but served only as a set of guidelines that actors could use to determine priorities for their actions. Conflicts could also arise when persons failed to abide by the moral norms stipulated by a ruler on the grounds that the norms were wholly or partly incompatible with the obligations towards their own groups. These cases were usually subsumed under the notion of the feud.

Lastly, conflicts could erupt between groups among which disagreement persisted over the validity of mutually incompatible sets of particularistic norms and rules. In these cases, arbitration was often chosen as a means of conflict resolution[53] but the conflicts could also escalate into warfare. A case is described in the early eleventh-century Old English epic *The Battle of Maldon*. Here, a warrior band of apparently Scandinavian origin travelled to eastern England by ship across the North Sea and was challenged upon arrival in 991 by an armed force made up of local farmers. The farmers seem to have been obliged to rally behind a local aristocrat to defend their lands. In the absence of an overarching framework of norms and rules from which the criteria for the condemnation of the invaders as aggressors and the justice of the action of the defenders could have been derived, warfare was the only solution to the conflict. The invaders won the struggle mainly because some defenders regarded their position as hopeless and deserted the field. In this case, the ethics of the invading warrior band was one according to which victory in battle was decisive for their future fate. Hence they were prepared to risk everything, imagining that defeat would entail the loss of their lives. By contrast, the ethics of the defending force was one according to which local farmers would primarily seek to preserve their lives. For them, victory in battle was thus a value of secondary significance compared to the need to preserve their working capability and experience.[54] In short, the only principle of

---

[53] A tenth-century case is recorded in the context of the struggles within the kin group of Emperor Otto I between the emperor and his son Liudolf. See Ruotger, *Vita Brunonis archipiscopi Coloniensis*, cap. 18, ed. Irene Ott, MGH, SS rer. Germ. X (Weimar, 1951), pp. 16–17.

[54] *The Battle of Maldon*, ed. Donald George Scragg (Manchester, 1981).

ethics that was commonly accepted at this time consisted of the agreement that differences among particularistic group-bound norms and rules should be mutually respected as much as possible, even if the decision over which of these norms and rules should receive priority might have to be accomplished through military means.

Such relativism militated against the universalistic fundamentals of the Christian Church. In the early medieval Occident, the Catholic Church gradually intensified its request that believers should act exclusively in accordance with those moral norms that could be derived from prescriptions contained in the Bible and other important Christian texts. Among the universalistic moral norms stipulated by the Bible, the Ten Commandments featured most prominently because they were regarded as divine. Within the ethical theory authorised by the Church, the universal validity of the Ten Commandments was thus taken for granted. But disputes among Christian ethicists focused on the question whether or not human beings ought to be credited with a free will to act morally or immorally, that is, to follow or not to follow the Ten Commandments and other universalistic moral norms. The answers oscillated between the fundamentalist position, which St Augustine took in his later writings, and the pragmatic view that was bequeathed to the Middle Ages from interpretations of the work of Pelagius and his followers. The position Augustine adopted was that, in consequence of the Fall, human beings had no choice other than to sin and that their redemption was possible only through divine grace. Augustine thus postulated that human beings inherited 'eternal sin' from their biblical ancestors and were henceforth bound to lead sinful lives.[55] On the other hand, the writings of Pelagius inaugurated a tradition of ethical thought in the fourth century according to which actions could only be sinful if human actors had the choice not to sin, and thus demanded recognition of human free will to commit evil actions. Although Augustine unsuccessfully tried to condemn Pelagius, the latter received much attention in late Antiquity and throughout the Middle Ages. He insisted that sin could not follow from a divine command because, if this were so, it would itself be part of the divinely created world and, consequently, no longer a sin.[56]

Pseudo-Dionysius the Areopagite elaborated on this position from his

---

55 Augustine, *Contra duas epistolas Pelagianorum*, lib. IV, cap. 3, parts 30–1, in *PL* vol. 44, col. 754. Augustine, *De natura boni*, cap. 9, in *PL* vol. 42, col. 554. Augustine, *De civitate Dei*, lib. XIII, cap. 14, lib. XIV, cap. 13, ed. Bernard Dombart and Alphons Kalb, CCSL. XLVIII,2 (Turnhout, 1955), pp. 395–6, 434–6. In his earlier work, Augustine took the more moderate position that immoral actions are punishable with the implication that human beings can have a choice not to act immorally. See Augustine, *De libero arbitrio* (see note 22), lib. I, cap. 3, cols 1224–5.

56 Pelagius, *Epistola ad Demetrium*, cap. 3, in *PL*, vol, 30, cols 17–18. On Pelagius's writings, see Georges de Plinval, *Pelage. Ses écrits, sa vie et sa réforme* (Lausanne, 1943), pp. 245–51. The importance of the Pelagian position throughout the Middle Ages can be judged from the fact that Lutheran Protestants still felt compelled to denounce it as an erroneous creed in their defence of the doctrine of eternal sin in the Augsburg Confession of 1530. See *Confessio Augustana*, ed. Rudolf Mau, in *Evangelische Bekenntnisse*, vol. 1 (Bielefeld, 1997), pp. 33–97.

objectivism according to which all good was in the divinity. From this point of view, evil did not have existence as part of the divinely created world and, by consequence, could only have been conditioned by human will. Therefore, Dionysius concluded that human beings ought to be credited with the capability to opt for either good or evil. John Scotus Eriugena followed suit, adding that purgatory could only be necessary because human beings had a real choice to sin or not to sin. Moreover, Eriugena went beyond Dionysius in deriving a theory of action from his ontology of good and evil. He defined the good as the divinely willed beginning and end and argued that evil could only result from some accident. The accident was associated with the misperception through which what was actually evil appeared to be good to the human mind.[57] Contrary to the fundamentalist ethics enshrined in Augustine's work, Eriugena's ethical theory supported the conceptualisation of action as process-related rather than goal-oriented. This concept of action was perfectly in line with early medieval patterns of action that can be reconstructed best from the ninth- and tenth-century polyptychs. As has been shown in the previous chapter, the polyptychs contained rules for the accomplishment of predetermined goals of agricultural production in accordance with the most appropriate production processes. Thus, whereas the goal was taken as a given, practical action was focused on its process and the choice of the best techniques of steering the process towards its predetermined end. The Andarchius–Ursus episode, the *Hildebrandslied* and the *Battle of Maldon* present cases that deviated from this pattern. But in the Andarchius–Ursus episode, the social setting was a town and the action was brandmarked as criminal. The *Hildebrandslied* placed the two protagonists in a situation where they had to make a choice between mutually exclusive particularistic obligations, but displayed this situation as a rare conspicuous and tragic dilemma rather than as a daily occurrence. And in *The Battle of Maldon,* the conflict resulted from the contingent appearance of an offensive warrior band in a social setting that appears to have been characterised by orientation towards agricultural production and a lack of war-proneness.

The concept of action reflected in the polyptychs differed from the concept of action that had been dominant in the previous three centuries. In the world of the polyptychs, the monasteries as seigneurial lords attempted to stabilise the output of agricultural production. They continued to respect the differences in status of their dependant farmers and their affiliations with particularistic groups. But the peasant farmers were losing much of their previous autonomous tradition-transmitting and rule-enforcing capability. As has been shown in chapter II, kin groups in rural settlements were shrinking in size and contractual groups were pressured to subject themselves to the control of territorial rulers. One consequence of these processes was that there was less need for an ethics that served as an instrument for the resolution of conflicts among mutually exclusive particularistic sets of group-specific

---

[57] Dionysius, *De divinis nominibus* (see note 7), lib. IV, cap. 11, cols 770–1. John Scotus Eriugena, *Versio* (see note 9), cap. IV, cols 1140–1, 1145.

norms, rules and obligations. Hence, the Church obtained more favourable conditions for its quest to enforce its universalistic notion of ethics as a general theory of judgements about the good. On this basis Abelard developed his demand that human beings should act consciously in pursuit of the good.

As late as in the thirteenth century, St Thomas Aquinas was in line with the Dionysian tradition of positioning the good as the predetermined general goal of all human action. But, contrary to this tradition, Thomas no longer denied existence to evil. He could no longer do so because if he obliged human beings to make conscious decisions to act in favour of good and against evil, evil had to be in the world. He thus refined Abelard's decisionism into the postulate that human beings were reasonable only if they acted in pursuit of morally defensible goals. Accordingly, the divinely willed inclination towards good objectives could be upset or even overturned by human actors who chose to act unreasonably, that is, to direct their actions to evil ends. In his explication of goal-oriented actions as a core aspect of his ethical theory, Thomas explicitly referred to Aristotle's *Nicomachean Ethics* as the source that had explicated the same concept of action.[58] On the basis of this concept of action, ethics evolved from a pragmatic device for conflict resolution into a theory about the generalisability of judgements about the good. This process began in the twelfth century.

Conclusion: Aesthetics and ethics

In this chapter, I have defined aesthetics in the wide and non-technical term of reflections about standards of perception. The wider definition of aesthetics has allowed a description of changes in standards of perception and promoted insight into the impact of these changes on narrowing the concept of aesthetics to a reflection on judgements about beauty. Likewise, in this chapter, I have defined ethics in its wider non-technical sense of the reflection on concepts of action. Again, the wide definition of ethics has made it possible to describe changes in concepts of action and the impact of these changes on the narrowing down of the definition of ethics to a reflection on judgements about the good. In both cases, narrowing the conceptual frameworks of aesthetics and ethics sparked professionalisation. Whereas the reflection on standards of perception and the reflection on concepts of action could be part and parcel of anybody's activities, the reflection on judgements about beauty eventually fell into the competence of theorists of art and reflections on judgements about the good eventually became the business of practical philosophers and practical theologians.

The most significant and consequential changes took place between the eleventh and the thirteenth centuries and restructured the relationship between perception and action. In the early Middle Ages, perception was con-

---

[58] Thomas Aquinas, *Summa theologiae* (see note 38), pp. 479–80.

sidered appropriate if perceivers could apprehend the qualities of objects and persons perceived, and action was recognised as successful if actors chose appropriate processes towards the accomplishment of predetermined goals. The beautiful and the good were regarded as becoming indistinguishable in the name of the divinity. As a practical consequence, persons could expect that aesthetic judgements were convertible into ethical judgements and vice versa.

As late as in the fourteenth century, matters of ethical significance, among them membership of different social groups, incorporation into contractual groups such as artisans' guilds and merchant trading companies, integration into urban communities of towns and cities as well as subjection to territorial legislation of the peasant farming population, were considered part of the divinely willed world. Consequently, these matters were held to be ascribable to features that could be perceived and judged from the outside through aesthetic judgements and were thus not taken to require declaratory acts. Conrad of Megenberg, for one, took not only social status but the total sum of all physical shapes to be emanations of the divinely willed world.[59] Like physical shapes, dress codes were means to display persons' positions in the divinely willed world order. Consequently, dress codes were the subject of rigid sumptuary laws. Such confidence in the purportedly objective recognisability of appropriate moral conduct through the senses informed the demands that physical features of human actors should be studied carefully and that sumptuary laws and other dress codes should be meticulously observed.[60]

However, the recognition of conscience and the cognitive power of persons in twelfth- and thirteenth-century philosophical theory began to widen the gap between aesthetics and ethics. If persons using their individual conscience could err, as Abelard admitted, or if cognitive power could be handled more or less appropriately, as St Thomas Aquinas believed, the justice of deriving aesthetic judgements from ethical ones and vice versa could be called into question. That these doubts did not haunt medieval theorists was solely due to the continuing conviction, shared by aestheticians as well as ethicists, that the beautiful and the good were indistinguishable in the name of the divinity.

---

[59] Conrad of Megenberg, *Das Buch der Natur*, ed. Franz Pfeiffer (Stuttgart, 1861), p. 423 [repr., ed. Gerhard E. Sollbach (Frankfurt, 1990)].

[60] On dress codes, see Ferdinando Bertelli, ed., *Omnivm fere gentivm nostrae aetatis habitvs nvnqvam ante hac aetatis* (Venice, 1563) [repr. (Unterschneidheim, 1969)]. Hans Weigel, ed., *Habitvs praecipvorvm popvlorvm tam virorvm qvam foeminarvm singvlaruis arte depicti. Trachtenbuch. Darin fast allerley vnd der furnehmbsten Nationen / die heutigen tags bekandt sein / Kleidungen / beyde wie es bey Manns vnd Weibspersonen gebreuchlich / mit allem vleiss abgerissen sein* (Nuremberg, 1577) [repr. Zwickauer Facsimiledrucke. XVII (Zwickau, 1913)]. Cesare Vecellio, *De gli habiti antichi et moderni di diversi arti del mondo* (Venice, 1590) [repr. (Bologna, 1982)]. Jean de Glen, ed., *Des habits, moevrs, façons de faire anciennes & modernes du monde* (Liège, 1601). Abraham a Sancta Clara, *Neu-eröffnete Welt-Galleria worinnen sehr curiös und begnügt unter die Augen kommen allerley Aufzug und Kleidungen unterschiedlicher Stände und Nationen* (Nuremberg, 1703) [repr. (Hildesheim, 1969)].

Epilogue

What was different in the medieval world?

In the modern period, most historians' answers to this question have oscillated between scientism and exoticism. One the one side, economic and social historians applied quantitative methods to measure differences in such fields as yield ratios, climate, transport technology, energy supply, the firepower of weapons, demography and kinship. They also developed techniques of qualitative analysis for the investigation of such matters as attitudes towards birth and death, agricultural work ethics, the relationship between orality and literacy as means of communication, the social organisation of kin and other types of groups, and perceptions of the body and movements in war, sports and dance. On the other side, intellectual, cultural and literary historians dissected medieval culture in layered descriptions of its strangeness and thereby emphasised the alterity of the medieval vis-à-vis the modern world. These historians classed as specifically medieval such cultural features as a cyclical experience of time, beliefs in life after death, the power of ghosts and other supernatural agents, the practice of clumsy rituals and the ubiquity of fantastic images of the world.

Both approaches were born out of cultural self-alienation as a European collective experience. Since the Renaissance, Europeans have learned to look back on their past as a succession of distinct periods that have been lumped together into the notion of European culture as an assemblage of heterogeneous pieces. The notion represented European culture as a mental museum that, like its architectural counterpart, houses objects that are simultaneously in and out. They are in because they are accepted as part of the European cultural heritage. They are out because they are no longer in use. As one part of the assemblage, the Middle Ages are experienced as different not merely because of their remoteness in time but mainly because they appear to have little or no practical significance for or are categorised as odd or even 'dark' by people looking back. The very term 'Middle Ages' has resulted from the experience of cultural self-alienation and has made explicit the perception of discontinuity to the present day. Ever since the end of the seventeenth century, the term that had been in occasional use before has served as a label for an intermittent epoch separating what has been identified as Antiquity from what has been named the Modern period. From its creation in the early nineteenth century, the term 'Renaissance' has similarly emphasised the perception of breaks. Both terms are retrospective constructs presupposing a consciousness of separation from Antiquity and, consequently, of epochal divides. Bridging the epochal divide between the 'Middle' and the 'Modern' ages seems then possible only if, on the one hand, medieval attitudes to the physical and social environments are described and analysed by means of purportedly general 'laws' of nature and principles of social organisation, or, on the other hand, if they are classed as odd and exotic. The choice between scientism and exoticism appears to be inescapable.

However, other cultures exhibit different experiences with history. In Japan, for example, the European triad of periods is applied, with the terms Antiquity, Middle Ages and Modern Period represented by the late nineteenth-century loan translations *kodai, chûsei* and *kindai*. But this periodisation competes with indigenous schemes drawing on ruling dynasties or centres of government in combination with the names of a pottery style and an archaeological site. The indigenous schemes define units of historical time that are integrated into the overall history of Japan, which, in turn, is seen as shaped by an unbroken dynastic succession of rulers and a continuing collective identity. Ever since the seventeenth century, critical historical research has done much to call into question the belief in the continuity of institutions of rulership in Japan, but has done little to alter the conviction that the inhabitants of Japan should be seen as a united homogeneous population group. Consequently, the use of the European triad of periods has done nothing to promote cultural self-alienation in Japan.

This book has approached the Middle Ages with due respect to the European experience of cultural self-alienation and yet in an attempt to avoid the fallacies of scientism and exoticism. It has done so by providing answers to the questions of how persons in the Middle Ages acted in and perceived the world and to what extent medieval standards of perception and concepts of action differed from those of the present. Attitudes towards the interaction between persons and their physical and social environments have been scrutinised as a case of the history of perception. The control of modes of behaviour through groups and ruling institutions has been selected as a case for the history of the concept of action.

Perception through the eyes and ears displayed the change of its standard between the tenth and the thirteenth centuries. In the early Middle Ages, persons used eyes and ears expecting that perception could translate directly into action, and they tied the standard of perception to group-bound norms and rules. By contrast, late medieval vision and audition was oriented towards configurations of continuous space and experiences of linear astronomical time. The change of the standard of visual and aural perception corresponded with the transformation of the cognitive significance of aesthetics in the thirteenth century. At this time, the belief that humans were capable of perceiving the beauty of the divinely created world changed into the expectation that humans should be able to pass judgements on the aesthetic quality of persons and objects at their own discretion. Regarding smell, touch and taste perception, the change of the standard is more difficult to determine owing to the scarcity of sources extant from the early and high Middle Ages. Nevertheless, it has been possible to show that touch and taste perception had been connected with group-bound norms and rules in the early period while it was focused on marking spatial and social distance in the later period. This change of the standard of perception corresponded at the level of theory with the change of the definition of aesthetics, which converted from an instrument for resolving conflicts among various group-bound standards of perception into a speculative theory about the nature of the beautiful during the twelfth and thirteenth centuries. Both changes converged in that they loosened the ties between standards of perception and other group-bound norms and rules and can consequently be described as processes impacting on habits of cognition as well as principles of social organisation.

Action changed from the predominance of process-orientation to the predominance of goal-orientation between the tenth and the thirteenth centuries. Process-orientation was an appropriate concept for regulating human behaviour as long as persons continued to adhere to their multiple memberships in various types of groups and to seek protection by group members against hazards from the physical and social environments. This was so because process-oriented action was based on integrated oral processes of communicative action and thus awarded success most easily to actors who were willing and able to contribute to the social cohesion of groups. The change of emphasis towards goal-orientation promoted a concept of action through which success was more easily awarded to actors who were willing to act in pursuit of their own set goals rather than contribute to the fostering of ties among group members. It coincided with the growth of urban communities of towns and cities in the eleventh and twelfth centuries. It laid the foundation for the devaluation and stigmatisation of those peasant farmers in the rural countryside who chose to continue conceiving their actions as process-oriented, and thereby widened the urban–rural divide. Simultaneously with the change of the concept of action, theorists of action began to recognise the human free will to decide about the direction of actions towards good or evil goals. The new theory of action resulted in the redefinition of ethics. In the early Middle Ages, ethics had been a device to smooth conflicts resulting from mutually exclusive group obligations, whereas from the twelfth century, ethics was transformed into a speculative theory about judgements about the good.

What, then, was different in the medieval world? The question has two answers, one for the early Middle Ages, and a different one for the late Middle Ages. The early medieval period was different in that persons then perceived of and acted in their physical and social environments in ways that differed from those of later periods. The late medieval world displayed several features of perception and action that link up with those of later periods. The medieval histories of perception and action and the theory of perception and action emphasise a gradualism of culture change rather than epochal breaks.

Bibliography

Abel, Wilhelm: *Massenarmut und Hungerkrisen im vorindustriellen Europa* (Göttingen, 1974).

Abels, Richard Philip: *Lordship and Military Obligation in Anglo-Saxon England* (Berkeley and Los Angeles, 1988).

Abu-Lughod, Janet Lippman: *Before European Hegemony. The World System A.D. 1250–1350* (New York, Oxford, 1989).

Adler, Hans, and Ulrike Zeuch, ed.: *Synästhesie* (Würzburg, 2002).

Albala, Ken: *Eating Right in the Renaissance* (Berkeley and Los Angeles, 2002).

Alexander, Jonathan J. G.: 'The Benedictional of St. Aethelwold and Anglo-Saxon Illumination of the Reform Period', in David Parsons, ed., *Tenth-Century Studies* (Chichester, 1975), pp. 169–83.

Allen, Grant: 'The Lower Senses', in Allen, *Physiological Aesthetics* (New York, 1877), pp. 58–88.

Altenburg, Detlef, Jörg Jarnut and Hans-Hugo Steinhoff, ed.: *Feste und Feiern im Mittelalter* (Sigmaringen, 1991).

Althoff, Gerd: *Adels- und Königsfamilien im Spiegel ihrer Memorialüberlieferung. Studien zum Totengedenken der Billunger und Ottonen*, Münsterische Mittelalter-Schriften LXVII (Munich, 1984).

Althoff, Gerd: 'Der friedens-, bündnis-: und gemeinschaftsstiftende Charakter des Mahles im früheren Mittelalter', in Irmgard Bitsch, Trude Ehlert and Xenja von Ertzdorff ed., *Essen und Trinken in Mittelalter und Neuzeit* (Sigmaringen, 1990), pp. 13–25.

Althoff, Gerd: *Amicitia und Pacta*, Schriften der Monumenta Germaniae Historica XXXVII (Hanover, 1992), pp. 69–87.

Althoff, Gerd: 'Schranken der Gewalt. Wie gewalttätig war das "finstere Mittelalter"?', in Horst Brunner, ed., *Der Krieg im Mittelalter und in der Frühen Neuzeit*, Imagines medii aevi III (Wiesbaden, 1999), pp. 1–23.

Andersen, Flemming Gotthelf Esther Nyholm, and F. T. Stubkjaer, ed.: *Medieval Iconography and Narrative* (Odense, 1980).

Andersson-Schmitt, M.: 'Mitteilungen zu den Quellen des Großen Seelentrosts', in *Niederdeutsches Jahrbuch* 105 (1982), pp. 38–40.

Andre, Elsbeth: *Ein Königshof auf Reisen. Der Kontinentaufenthalt Edwards III. von England. 1338–1340*, Behihefte zum Archiv für Kulturgeschichte XLI (Cologne, Weimar and Vienna, 1996).

Andreolli, Bruno: 'Tra podere e gineceo. Il lavoro delle donne nelle grandi aziende agrarie dell' Alto Medioevo', in Giuseppina Muzarelli, Paola Galetti and B. Andreolli, ed., *Donne e lavoro nell' Italia medievale* (Turin, 1991), pp. 29–40.

Andresen, Carl: 'Altchristliche Kritik am Tanz. Ein Ausschnitt aus dem Kampf der alten Kirche gegen heidnische Sitte', in *Zeitschrift für Kirchengeschichte* 72 (1961), pp. 217–62.

Angenendt, Arnold: *Geschichte der Religiosität im Mittelalter* (Darmstadt, 1997).

Anglo, Sydney: *Spectacle, Pageantry and Early Tudor Policy* (Oxford, 1969) [2nd edn (Oxford, 1997)].

Anzulewicz, Henryk: *Die theologische Relevanz des Bildbegriffs und des Spiegelbildmodells in den Frühwerken des Albertus Magnus*, Beiträge zur Geschichte der Philosophie und Theologie des Mittelalters. N. F. LIII, no. 2 (Munster, 1999).

Anzulewicz, Henryk: '*Aeternitas – Aevum – Tempus*. The Concept of Time in the System of Albert the Great', in Pasquale Porro, ed., *The Medieval Concept of Time*, Studien und Texte zur Geistesgeschichte des Mittelalters LXXV (Leiden, Boston and Cologne, 2001), pp. 84–6.

Arentzen, Jörn-Geerd *Imago mundi cartographica. Studien zur Bildlichkeit mittelalterlicher Welt- und Ökumenekarten unter besonderer Berücksichtigung des Zusammenwirkens von Text und Bild*, Münsterische Mittelalter-Schriften LIII (Munich, 1984).

Argan, Giulio Carlo: 'The Architecture of Brunelleschi and the Origins of Perspective Theory in the XVth Century', in *Journal of the Warburg and Courtauld Institutes* 9 (1946), pp. 89–101.

Arlt, Wulf: 'Stylistic Layers in eleventh-century Polyphony', in Susan Rankin and David Hiley, ed., *Music in the Medieval English Liturgy* (Oxford, 1993), pp. 101–41.

Arnade, Peter: *Realms of Ritual. Burgundian Ceremony and Civic Life in Late Medieval Ghent* (Ithaca and London, 1996).

Arnade, Peter: 'City, State, and Public Ritual in the Late-Medieval Burgundian Netherlands', in *Comparative Studies in Society and History* 39 (1997), pp. 300–18.

Arnheim, Rudolf: *Art and Visual Perception* (London, 1956) [2nd English edn (London, 1986)].

Arnold, Gottfried: *Unpartheyische Kirchen- und Ketzer-Historie*, Theil I (Frankfurt, 1699), lib. XXIV, cap. 2, §7.

Arnold, Klaus: '*De bono pacis*. Friedensvorstellungen in Mittelalter und Renaissance', in Jürgen Petersohn, ed., *Überlieferung – Frömmigkeit – Bildung als Leitthemen der Geschichtsforschung. Vorträge beim Wissenschaftlichen Kolloquium aus Anlaß des achtzigsten Geburtstages von Otto Meyer* (Wiesbaden, 1987), pp. 133–54.

Arnold, Klaus: *Mittelalterliche Volksbewegungen für den Frieden* (Stuttgart, Berlin and Cologne, 1996).

Assunto, Rosario: *Die Theorie des Schönen im Mittelalter* (Cologne, 1963) [first published (Milan, 1961)].

Baaken, Gerhard, and Roderich Schmidt: *Königtum, Burgen und Königsfreie. Königsumritt und Huldigung in ottonisch-salischer Zeit*, 2nd edn, Vorträge und Forschungen, hrsg. vom Konstanzer Arbeitskreis für mittelalterliche Geschichte VI (Sigmaringen, 1981) [first published (Constance, 1961)].

Backman, Eugène Louis: *Religious Dances in the Christian Church and in Popular Medicine* (London and Westport, CT, 1952) [first published (Stockholm, 1945)].

Baesecke, Georg: 'Der Kölbigker Tanz. Philologisch und literarisch', in *Zeitschrift für deutsches Altertum und deutsche Literatur* 78 (1941), pp. 1–36 [repr. in Baesecke, *Kleine Schriften zur althochdeutschen Sprache und Literatur*, ed. Werner Schröder (Bern, Munich, 1966)].

Baeumler, Alfred: *Das Irrationalitätsproblem in der Ästhetik und Logik des 18. Jahrhunderts bis zur Kritik der Urteilskraft* (Leipzig, 1923) [repr. (Darmstadt, 1967, 1974, 1981)].

Bagliani, Agostino Paravicini, ed.: *I cinque sensi. The Five Senses*, Micrologus X (Florence and Turnhout, 2002).

Bagliani, Agostino Paravicini, and Giorgio Stabile, ed.: *Träume im Mittelalter* (Stuttgart and Zurich, 1989).

Baier, Annette: 'Intention, Practical Knowledge, and Representation', in Nigel Brand,

and Douglas Walton, ed., *Action Theory. Proceedings of the Winnipeg Conference on Human Action. Held at Winnipeg, Manitoba, Canada, 9–11 May 1975* (Dordrecht and Boston, 1976), pp. 27–43.

Baier, Annette: 'Auf der Suche nach Basis-Handlungen', in Georg Meggle, ed., *Analytische Handlungsbeschreibungen*, vol. 1 (Frankfurt, 1977), pp. 137–62.

Bakka, Egil: 'Ein Beschlagfragment mit Tierornamentik von der karolingischen Pfalz in Paderborn. Westeuropäische und nordische Tierornamentik des 8. Jahrhunderts im überregionalen Stil III', in *Studien zur Sachsenforschung* 4 (1982), pp. 1–56.

Balkema, Annette W., Henk Slager, ed.: *The Archive of Development* (Amsterdam and Atlanta, 1998).

Balogh, Joseph: 'Tänze in Kirchen und auf Kirchhöfen', in *Niederdeutsche Zeitschrift für Volkskunde* 6 (1928), pp. 1–14, 126.

Bandmann, Günter: *Mittelalterliche Architektur als Bedeutungsträger* (Berlin, 1951) [10th edn (Berlin, 1994)].

Barlösius, Eva: 'Riechen und Schmecken. Riechendes und Schmeckendes. Ernährungssoziologische Anmerkungen zum Wandel der sinnlichen Wahrnehmung beim Essen, dargestellt an Beispielen der "grande cuisine" Frankreichs und der modernen Aromendastellung', in *Kölner Zeitschrift für Soziologie und Sozialpsychologie* 39 (1987), pp. 367–75.

Barral, Xavier, and Marco Mostert, ed.: *Image, Text and Script. Studies in the Transformation of Visual Literacy* (Leiden, 2002).

Baschet, Jérôme, and Jean-Claude Schmitt, ed.: *L'image. Fonctions et usages des images dans l'occident médiéval. Actes du 6e International Workshop on Medieval Societies, Centro Ettore Majorana, Erice, Sicily, 17–23 October 1992* (Paris, 1996).

Baumgärtner, Wilhelm, Franz-Peter Burkard and Franz Wiedmann, ed.: *Intentionalität*, Brentano-Studien III (Dettelbach, 1991).

Baxandall, Martin: *Painting and Experience in Fifteenth-Century Italy*, 2nd edn (Oxford and New York, 1988) [first published (Oxford, 1972)].

Bayer, Raymond: *Histoire de l'esthétique* (Paris, 1961).

Beardsley, Monroe Curtis, and Elizabeth Lane Beardsley: *Aesthetics. From Classical Greece to the Present* (New York, 1965).

Beaulieu, Michèle: 'Le costume français. Miroir de la sensibilité (1350–1500)', in Michel Pastoureau, ed., *Le vêtement. Histoire, archéologie et symbolique vestimentaires au Moyen Age*, Cahiers du Leopold d'Or 1 (Paris, 1989), pp. 255–86.

Beckwith, Sarah: *Christ's Body. Identity, Culture and Society in Late Medieval Writings* (New York, 1993).

Becmann, Johann Christoph: *Historie des Fürstenthums Anhalt*, part III (Zerbst, 1710), cap. 4.

Behringer, Wolfgang: 'Vergleichende Städteikonographie als Forschungsgegenstand', in *Stadtbilder. Augsburger Ansichten des 16. bis 19. Jahrhunderts* (Augsburg, 1992), pp. 7–14.

Belting, Hans: *Das Bild und sein Publikum im Mittelalter*, 3rd edn (Berlin, 2000) [first published (Berlin, 1981)].

Belting, Hans: *Bild und Kult*, 5th edn (Munich, 2000) [first edn (Munich, 1990)].

Benedictow, Ole J.: *The Black Death. 1346–1353* (Woodbridge, 2004).

Bergdolt, Klaus, ed.: *Die Pest 1348 in Italien. 50 zeitgenössische Quellen* (Heidelberg, 1989).

Bergmann, Ernst: *Die Begründung der deutschen Ästhetik durch Alexander Gottlieb Baumgarten und Georg Friedrich Meier* (Leipzig, 1911).

Bernecker, Roland: 'Handlungstheorie', in Gert Uerding, ed., *Historisches Wörterbuch der Rhetorik*, vol. 3 (Tübingen, 1996), cols 1286–97.

Bernhardt, I. W.: *Itinerant Kingship and Royal Monasteries in Early Medieval Germany* (Cambridge, 1993).

Berns, Jörg Joachim, and Thomas Rahn, ed.: *Zeremoniell als höfische Ästhetik in Spätmittelalter und Früher Neuzeit* (Tübingen, 1995).

Bernward von Hildesheim und das Zeitalter der Ottonen. Katalog zur Ausstellung (Hildesheim, 1993).

Bertling Biaggini, Claudia: *Il Pordenone. Pictor modernus. Zum Umgang mit Bildrhetorik und Perspektive im Werk des Giovanni Antonio de Sacchis*, Studien zur Kunstgeschichte CXXXIII (Hildesheim, 1999).

Berve, Maurus: *Die Armenbibel* (Beuron, 1969 [2nd edn (Beuron, 1989)].

Bessmerny, J.: 'Les structures de la famille paysanne dans les villages de la France au IXe siècle', in *Le Moyen Age* 90 (1984), pp. 165–93.

Bett, Henry: *Johannes Scotus Eriugena* (Cambridge, 1925).

Biddle, Martin, ed.: *Winchester in the Early Middle Ages*, Winchester Studies I (Oxford, 1976).

Bierbrauer, Katharina: *Die Ornamentik frühkarolingischer Handschriften aus Bayern*, Abhandlungen der Bayerischen Akademie der Wissenschaften, Philos.-Hist. Kl. N. F. LXXXIV (Munich, 1979).

Bierbrauer, Katharina: 'Insulares in der kontinentalen Buchmalerei des 8. Jahrhunderts', in Michael Müller-Wille and Lars Olof Larsson, ed., *Tiere – Menschen – Götter. Wikingerzeitliche Kunststile und ihre neuzeitliche Rezeption*, Veröffentlichung der Joachim-Jungius-Gesellschaft des Wissenschaften XC (Göttingen, 2001), pp. 63–87.

Bierbrauer, Volker: 'Kontinentaler und insularer Tierstil im Kunsthandwerk des 8. Jahrhunderts', in Michael Müller-Wille and Lars Olof Larsson, ed., *Tiere – Menschen – Götter. Wikingerzeitliche Kunststile und ihre neuzeitliche Rezeption*, Veröffentlichung der Joachim-Jungius-Gesellschaft des Wissenschaften XC (Göttingen, 2001), pp. 89–130.

Bieroff, Suzannah: *Sight and Embodiment in the Middle Ages* (Basingstoke, 2002).

Binding, Günther: *Der früh- und hochmittelalterliche Bauherr als sapiens architectus*, Veröffentlichungen der Abteilung Architekturgeschichte des Kunsthistorischen Instituts der Universität zu Köln LXI (Cologne, 1996) [repr. (Darmstadt, 1998)].

Biraben, Jean Noël: *Les hommes et la peste en France et dans les pays européens et méditerranées*, 2 vols (Paris and The Hague, 1975–76).

Bitz, Matthias: *Badewesen in Südwestdeutschland. 1550–1840. Zum Wandel von Gesellschaft und Architektur*, Wissenschaftliche Schriften, Series 9, vol. CVIII (Idstein, 1989).

Black, Maggie: *The Medieval Cookbook* (London, 1996).

Bloch, Howard: *Etymologies and Genealogies. A Literary Anthropology of the French Middle Ages* (Chicago and London, 1983).

Bloch, Marc Léopold Benjamin: *The Royal Touch* (London, 1973) [new edn (New York, 1989); first published (Strasbourg, 1924)].

Blumenberg, Hans: *Die Lesbarkeit der Welt* (Frankfurt, 1981).

Boase, Thomas Scherrer Ross: *Death in the Middle Ages* (London, 1972).

Boehm, Gottfried: 'Zu einer Hermeneutik des Bildes', in Boehm and Hans-Georg Gadamer, eds, *Seminar. Die Hermeneutik und die Wissenschaften* (Frankfurt, 1978), pp. 444–71.

Böhme, Franz Magnus: *Geschichte des Tanzes in Deutschland*, vol. 1 (Leipzig, 1886).

Boersch, Charles: *Essai sur la mortalité à Strasbourg* (Strasbourg, 1836), pp. 124–30.

Bologne, Jean-Claude: *Histoire de la pudeur* (Paris, 1987).

Bonnassie, Paul: 'Les sagrères Catalanes', in Michel Fixot and Elisabeth Zadora-Rio, ed., *L'environnement des églises et la topographie religieuse des campagnes médiévales. Actes du IIIe Congrès international d'archéologie médiévale. Aix-en-Provence, 28–30 septembre 1989* Documents d'archéologie française XL (Paris, 1994), pp. 68–79.

Bonnaud-Delamare, Roger: 'Les institutions de paix en Aquitaine au XIe siècle', in *La paix*, Recueils de la Société Jean Bodin XIV (Brussels, 1961), pp. 415–87.

Bonney, Desmond: 'Early Saxon Boundaries in Wessex', in Peter Jon Fowler, ed., *Archaeology and the Landscape. Essays for Leslie Valentine Grinsell* (London, 1972), pp. 168–86.

Bonney, Desmond: 'Early Boundaries and Estates in Southern England', in Peter Hayes Sawyer, ed., *Medieval Settlement* (London, 1976), pp. 72–82.

Borck, Karl-Heinz: 'Der Tanz von Kölbigk', in *Beiträge zur Geschichte der deutschen Sprache und Literatur* (Tübingen) 76 (1955), pp. 241–320.

Borscheid, Peter: *Geschichte des Alters* (Munich, 1989).

Bosanquet, Bernard: *A History of Aesthetics* (London 1904), pp. 120–50 [describes the Middle Ages with an attempt to trace 'the continuity of aesthetic consciousness' from Antiquity and mentions briefly Scotus Eriugena, St Francis and St Thomas Aquinas].

Boshof, Egon: 'Untersuchungen zur Armenfürsorge im fränkischen Reich des 9. Jahrhunderts', in *Archiv für Kulturgeschichte* 58 (1976), pp. 265–339.

Boter, John F.: 'Ockham on Evident Cognition', in *Franciscan Studies* 36 (1978), pp. 85–98.

Bouchard, Constance Brittain: *'Those of My Blood'. Constructing Noble Families in Medieval Francia* (Philadelphia, 2001).

Braet, Herman, and Werner Verbeke, ed.: *Death in the Middle Ages*, Mediaevalia Lovaniensia. ser. 1, vol. IX (Louvain, 1983).

Bredero, Adriaan Hendrik: 'De godvrede der bischoppen', in Bredero and Lukas de Blois, ed., *Kerk en vrede in oudheid en middeleeuwen* (Kampen, 1980), pp. 95–122.

Brentano, Franz: *Psychologie vom empirischen Standpunkte*, vol. 1 (Leipzig, 1925), pp. 124–5 [repr. (Hamburg, 1973)].

Bresslau, Harry: *Handbuch der Urkundenlehre fur Deutschland und Italien*, first edn, vol. 1 (Leipzig, 1889), pp. 711–890, 818–74 [2nd edn (Leipzig, 1912–15; part 2 of vol. 2, ed. Hans-Walter Klewitz (Berlin, 1931); repr. (Berlin, 1958–60)].

Brincken, Anna-Dorothee von den: 'Mappamundi und Chronographia', in *Deutsches Archiv für Erforschung des Mittelalters* 14 (1968), pp. 118–86.

Brincken, Anna-Dorothee von den: 'Weltbild der lateinischen Universalhistoriker und -kartographen', in *Settimane di studio del Central Italiano di Studi sull'Alto Medioevo* 29 (1983), pp. 377–408.

Brincken, Anna-Dorothee von den: *Fines Terrae*, Schriften der Monumenta Germaniae Historica XXXVI (Hanover, 1992).

Britnell, Richard, ed.: *Pragmatic Literacy in East and West. 1200–1330* (Woodbridge, 1997).

Brooks, Nicholas: 'Arms, Status and Warfare in Late Anglo-Saxon England', in David Hill, ed., *Ethelred the Unready*, British Archaeological Reports. British Series LIX (Oxford, 1978), pp. 81–103.

Brown, Andrew: 'Civic Ritual. Bruges and the Counts of Flanders in the Later Middle Ages', in *English Historical Review* 112 (1997), pp. 277–99.

Brown, Jerome: 'Sensation in Henry of Ghent', in *Archiv für Geschichte der Philosophie* 53 (1971), pp. 238–66.

Brown, Jerome: 'Henry of Ghent on Internal Sensation', in *Journal of the History of Philosophy* 10 (1972), pp. 15–28.

Brucker, Gene: *The Civic World of Early Renaissance Florence* (Princeton, 1977), pp. 283–317.

Brunner, Heinrich: 'Carta und Notitia', in Brunner, *Abhandlungen zur Rechtsgeschichte*, ed. Karl Rauch, vol. 1 (Weimar, 1931), pp. 459–86 [repr. (Leipzig, 1965; first published in *Commentationes philologicae in honorem Theodori Mommsen* (Berlin, 1877)].

Bruyne, Edgar de: *Etudes d'esthétique médiévale*, 3 vols (Bruges, 1946).

Bruyne, Edgar de: *L'esthétique du Moyen Age* (Louvain, 1947).

Bruyne, Edgar de: *Geschiedenis van de Aesthetica*, 5 vols (Antwerp, 1951–55).

Bryant, Lawrence McBride: *The King and the City in the Parisian Royal Entry Ceremony* (Geneva, 1986).

Bryant, Lawrence McBride: 'La cérémonie de l'entrée à Paris au Moyen Age', in *Annales ESC* 41 (1986), pp. 514–42.

Bryant, Lawrence McBride: 'The Medieval Entry Ceremony at Paris', in János M. Bak, ed., *Coronations. Medieval and Early Modern Monarchic Ritual* (Berkeley and Los Angeles, 1990), pp. 88–118.

Bryson, Norman: *Vision and Painting. The Logic of the Gaze* (New Haven, 1983).

Bubner, Rüdiger: 'Action and Reason', in *Ethics* 83 (1972/73), pp. 224–36.

Bubner, Rüdiger, ed.: *Handlungstheorie*, Neue Hefte für Philosophie IX (Göttingen, 1976).

Buck, August: 'Die Rangstellung des Menschen in der Renaissance. Dignitas et miseria hominis', in *Archiv für Kulturgeschichte* 42 (1960), pp. 61–75.

Büttner, Frank O.: *Imitatio pietatis. Motive der christlichen Ikonographie als Modelle zur Verähnlichung* (Berlin, 1983).

Bulst, Neithard: 'Der Schwarze Tod. Demographische, wirtschafts- und kulturgeschichtliche Aspekte der Pestkatastrophe von 1347–1352', in *Saeculum* 30 (1979), pp. 45–67.

Bulst, Neithard, and Robert Jütte, ed.: 'Zwischen Sein und Schein. Kleidung und Identität in der ständischen Gesellschaft', in *Saeculum* 44 (1993), pp. 2–112.

Bumke, Joachim: *Höfische Kultur*, vol. 2 (Munich, 1986), pp. 508–9.

Bunim, Miriam Schild: *Space in Medieval Painting and the Forerunners of Perspective* (New York, 1940) [repr. (New York, 1970)].

Burke, Peter: *The French Historical Revolution. The Annales School. 1929–89* (Cambridge, 1990), pp. 12–31.

Busch, Ralf: 'Die Wasserversorgung des Mittelalters und der frühen Neuzeit', in Cord Meckseper, ed., *Stadt im Wandel*, vol. 4 (Stuttgart, 1985), pp. 301–10.

Buschmann, Arno, and Elmar Wadle, ed.: *Landfrieden. Anspruch und Wirklichkeit*, Rechts- und Staatswissenschaftliche Veröffentlichungen der Görres-Gesellschaft N. F. XCII (Paderborn, 2001).

Bynum, Caroline Walker: 'Did the Twelfth Century Discover the Individual?', in *Journal of Ecclesiastical History* 31 (1980), pp. 1–17.

Callahan, John Leonard: *A Theory of Aesthetics according to the Principles of St. Thomas Aquinas* (Washington, DC, 1927).

Camille, Michael: 'Before the Gaze. The Internal Sense and Late Medieval Practices of Seeing', in Robert S. Nelson, ed., *Visuality Before and Beyond the Renaissance* (Cambridge, 2000), pp. 197–223.

Camporesi, Piero: *La scienza in cucina e l'arte di mangiar bene* (Turin, 1970).

Camporesi, Piero: *Alimentazione, folclore, società* (Parma, 1980).

Camporesi, Piero: *Bread of Dreams. Food and Fantasy in Early Modern Europe* (Cambridge, 1989) [first published (Bologna, 1980)].

Camporesi, Piero: *The Anatomy of the Senses* (Cambridge, 1994) [first published (Milan, 1985)].

Cardini, Franco, and Massimo Miglio, ed.: *Nostalgia del paradiso. Il giardino medievale* (Bari, 2002).

Carlin, Martha, and Joel Thomas Rosenthal, ed.: *Food and Eating in Medieval Europe* (London, 1998).

Carozzi, Claude: 'La tripartition sociale et l'idée de paix au XIe siècle', in *La guerre et la paix. Frontières et violences au Moyen Age. Actes du 101e Congrès National des Sociétés Savantes Lille 1976* (Paris, 1978), pp. 9–22.

Carruthers, Mary: *The Book of Memory* (Cambridge, 1990).

Carruthers, Mary: 'Reading with Attitudes. Remembering the Book', in Dolores Warwick Frese and Katherine O'Brien O'Keeffe, ed., *The Book and the Body* (Notre Dame and London, 1997), pp. 1–33.

Carruthers, Mary: *The Craft of Thought. Meditation, Rhetoric, and the Making of Images. 400 – 1200* (Cambridge, 1998), pp. 171–220 [repr. (Cambridge, 2000)].

Cauchies, Jean-Marie, ed.: *A la cour de Bourgogne. Le duc, son entourage, son train* (Turnhout, 1999) [first published in *Publications du Centre Européen des études bourguignonnes* 34 (1994)].

Chambas-Ploton, Mic: *Jardins médiévaux* (Paris, 2000).

Chapeaurouge, Donat de: *'Das Auge ist ein Herr, das Ohr sein Kecht'. Der Weg von der mittelalterlichen zur abstrakten Malerei* (Wiesbaden, 1983).

Chapman, Emmanuel: 'Some Aspects of St. Augustine's Philosophy of Beauty', in *Journal of Aesthetics and Art Criticism* 1 (1941/42), pp. 46–51.

Chidester, David: *Word and Light. Seeing, Hearing and Religious Discourse* (Urbana, 1992).

Ciggaar, Krijnie Nelly: *Western Travellers to Constantinople. The West and Byzantium. 962–1204* (Leiden, New York and Cologne, 1996).

Clanchy, Michael T.: *From Memory to Written Record* (Oxford, 1992).

Classen, Albrecht, ed.: *The Book and the Magic of Reading in the Middle Ages*, Garland Medieval Casebooks XXIV (New York, 1999).

Claude, Dietrich: *Der Handel im westlichen Mittelmeer während des Frühmittelalters*, Abhandlungen der Akademie der Wissenschaften in Göttingen, Philol.-Hist. Kl. 3. F. CXLIV = Untersuchungen zu Handel und Verkehr der vor- und frühgeschichtlichen Zeit in Mittel- und Nordeuropa, vol. 2 (Göttingen, 1985).

Clausberg, Karl: 'Scheibe, Rad, Zifferblatt. Grenzübergänge zwischen Weltkarten und Weltbildern', in Hartmut Kugler, ed., *Ein Weltbild vor Columbus. Die Ebstorfer Weltkarte* (Berlin, 1991), pp. 260–313.

Cohen, Ted, and Paul Guyer, ed.: *Essays in Kant's Aesthetics* (Chicago, 1982).

Coleman, Janet: 'The Individual and the Medieval State', in Coleman, ed., *The Individual in Political Theory and Practice* (Oxford and New York, 1996), pp. 1–34.

Colombier, Pierre du: 'Les triomphes en images de l'empereur Maximilian Ier', in Jaques Jaquot, ed., *Les fêtes de la Renaissance*, vol. 2 (Paris, 1960), pp. 99–112.

Comito, Terry: *The Idea of the Garden in the Renaissance* (New Brunswick, 1978).

Conley, Tom: 'The Wit of the Letter. Holbein's Lacan', in Teresa Brennan and Martin Jay, ed., *Vision in Context* (New York and London, 1996), pp. 45–61.

Constable, Olivia Remie: *Housing the Stranger in the Mediterranean World* (Cambridge, 2003).

Contamine, Philippe, Marc Bompaire, Stéphane Lebecq and Jean-Luc Sarrazin: *L'économie médiévale* (Paris, 1997).

Contreni, John J., and Santa Casciani, ed.: *Word, Image, Number. Communication in the Middle Ages*, Micrologus Library VIII (Turnhout, 2002).

Corbin, Alain: *The Foul and the Fragrant* (Cambridge, 1986) [first published (Paris, 1982)].

Cormeau, Christoph: 'Essen und Trinken in den deutschen Predigten Bertholds von Regensburg', in Irmgard Bitsch, Trude Ehlert and Xenja von Ertzdorff, ed., *Essen und Trinken in Mittelalter und Neuzeit* (Sigmaringen, 1990), pp. 77–83.

Cosman, Madeleine Pelner: *Fabulous Feasts. Medieval Cookery and Ceremony* (New York, 1976).

Coulet, Noel: 'Les entrées solennelles en Provence au XIVe siècle', in *Ethnologie française* 8 (1977), pp. 63–82.

Cramer, Johannes: 'Badehäuser. Ein städtischer Bautyp', in *Hausbau im Mittelalter*, vol. 2 = *Jahrbuch für Hausforschung* Sonderband (Sobernheim, 1985), pp. 9–58.

Crane, Susan: *The Performance of Self. Ritual, Clothing and Identity during the Hundred Years War* (Philadelphia, 2002).

Crantz, Albert: *Saxonia et metropolis* (Cologne, 1574).

Crick, Julia C.: 'Posthumous Obligation and Family Identity', in William O. Frazer and Andrew Tyrell, ed., *Social Identity in Early Medieval Britain* (London and New York, 2000), pp. 193–208.

Croce, Benedetto: *Aesthetic as Science of Experience and General Linguistics* (London, 1909) [first published (Milan, 1902)].

Croce, Benedetto: 'Rileggendo L'"Aesthetica" del Baumgarten', in *La Critica* 31 (1933), pp. 2–19.

Crocker, Richard Lincoln: *Studies in Medieval Music Theory and the Early Sequence* (Aldershot, 1997).

La croissance agricole du haut Moyen Age (Auch, 1990).

Crossley, Paul: 'Medieval Architecture and Meaning. The Limits of Iconography', in *Burlington Magazine* (1988), pp. 116–21.

Dagenais, John: *The Ethics of Reading in Manuscript Culture. Glossing the* Libro de buen amor (Princeton, 1994)

Damisch, Hubert: *The Origin of Perspective* (Cambridge, MA, and London, 1994) [first published (Paris, 1987)].

Davies, Wendy: *Small Worlds. The Village Community in Early Medieval Brittany* (Berkeley and Los Angeles, 1988), pp. 29–60.

Davis, Scott, Scott MacDonald and Jill Kraye: 'History of Western Ethics', cap. 5–7, in *Encyclopedia of Ethics*, vol. 1 (New York and London, 1992), pp. 480–500.

Daxelmüller, Christoph: 'Narratio, Illustratio, Argumentatio. Exemplum und Bildungstechnik in der frühen Neuzeit', in Walter Haug and Burghard Wachinger, ed., *Exempel und Exempelsammlungen*, Fortuna vitrea II (Tübingen, 1991), pp. 77–95.

Debes, Dietmar: *Das Figurenalphabet* (Munich, 1968).

Deist, Rosemarie: *Gender and Power. Counsellors and Their Masters in Antiquity and Medieval Courtly Romance* (Heidelberg, 2003).

Deluz, Jacques: 'Le paradis terrestre, image de l'Orient lointain dans quelques documents géographiques médiévaux', in *Images et signes de l'Orient dans l'Occident médiéval* (Marseille, 1982), pp. 143–61.

Dempf, Alois: *Ethik des Mittelalters* (Munich, 1927).

Deshman, Robert: 'The Iconography of the Full-page Miniatures of the Benedictional of Aethelwold'. Ph.D. Diss., typescript (Princeton University, 1970).

Deshman, Robert: 'The Imagery of the Living Ecclesia and the English Monastic Reform', in Paul E. Szarmach, ed., *Sources of Anglo-Saxon Culture*, Studies in Medieval Culture XX (Kalamazoo, MI, 1986), pp. 261–82.

Deshman, Robert: *The Benedictional of Aethelwold*, Studies in Manuscript Illumination IX (Princeton, 1995).

Deutsch, Samuel Martin: *Peter Abälard, ein kritischer Theologe des 12. Jahrhunderts* (Leipzig, 1883).

Devroey, Jean-Pierre: 'Les services de transport à l'abbaye de Prüm au IXe siècle', in *Revue du Nord* 61 (1979), pp. 543–69.

Devroey, Jean-Pierre: *Etudes sur le grand domaine carolingien* (Aldershot, 1993).

Dickenmann, Joahnn J.: 'Das Nahrungswesen in England vom 12. bis 15. Jahrhundert', in *Anglia* 27 (1904), pp. 453–515.

Dijksterhuis, Eduard Jan: *The Mechanization of the World Picture* (Oxford, 1961) [repr. (Princeton, 1986); first published (Amsterdam, 1950)].

Dilcher, Gerhard: 'Marktrecht und Kaufmannsrecht in Frühmittelalter', in Klaus Düwel, Herbert Jankuhn, Harald Siems and Dieter Timpe, ed., *Untersuchungen zu Handel und Verkehr der vor- und frühgeschichtlichen Zeit in Mittel- und Nordeuropa*, vol. 3, Abhandlungen der Akademie der Wissenschaften in Göttingen, Philol.-Hist. Kl. 3. F. CL (Göttingen, 1985), pp. 392–7.

Dilthey, Wilhelm: 'Die drei Epochen der modernen Ästhetik und ihre heutige Aufgabe', in *Deutsche Rundschau* 72 (1892), pp. 200–36.

Dilthey, Wilhelm: 'Auffassung und Analyse des Menschen im 15. und 16. Jahrhundert', in Dilthey, *Gesammelte Schriften*, vol. 2 (Stuttgart, 1957; new edn 1969), pp. 1–89.

Dinges, Martin: 'Der "feine Unterschied". Die soziale Funktion der Kleidung in der höfischen Gesellschaft', in *Zeitschrift für historische Forschung* 19 (1992), pp. 49–76.

Dinzelbacher, Peter: *Visionen und Visionsliteratur im Mittelalter*, Monographien zur Geschichte des Mittelalters XXIII (Stuttgart, 1981).

Dirlmeier, Ulf: 'Die kommunalpolitischen Zuständigkeiten und Leistungen süddeutscher Städte im Spätmittelalter', in Jürgen Sydow, ed., *Städtische Versorgung und Entsorgung im Wandel der Geschichte*, Stadt in der Geschichte VIII (Sigmaringen, 1981), pp. 113–50.

Dirlmeier, Ulf: 'Zu den Lebensbedingungen in der mittelalterlichen Stadt. Trinkwasserversorgung und Abfallbeseitigung', in Bernd Herrmann, ed., *Mensch und Umwelt im Mittelalter*, 3rd edn (Stuttgart, 1987), pp. 150–9 [first published (Stuttgart, 1986)].

Dirlmeier, Ulf: 'Zu den materiellen Lebensbedingungen in deutschen Städten des Spätmittelalters', in Reinhard Elze and Gina Fasoli, ed., *Stadtadel und Bürgertum in den italienischen und deutschen Städten des Spätmittelalters*, Schriften des Italienisch-Deutschen Instituts in Trient XIV (Berlin, 1991), pp. 59–80.

Dittrich, Ottmar: *Geschichte der Ethik*, vol. 3 (Leipzig, 1926) [repr. (Aalen, 1964)].

Dixon, Robert: *The Baumgarten Corruption* (London and East Haven, CT, 1995).

Döbert, Rainer: 'Max Webers Handlungstheorien und die Ebenen des Rationalitätskomplexes', in Johannes Weiss, ed., *Max Weber heute. Erträge und Probleme der Forschung* (Frankfurt, 1989), pp. 210–49.

Doehard, René: *Le Haut Moyen Age occidental. Economies et sociétés* (Paris, 1971).

Dolnikowski, Edith Wilks: *Thomas Bradwardine. A View of Time and a Vision of Eter-*

nity in Fourteenth-century Thought, Studies in the History of Christian Thought LXV (Leiden, Boston and Cologne, 1995).

Donato, Maria Monica: 'La "bellissima inventive". Imagini e idee nella Sala della Pace', in Enrico Castelnuovo, ed., *Ambrogio Lorenzetti. Il buon governo* (Milan, 1995), pp. 23–41.

Donckel, Emil: 'Martin Bucer und die "Springenden Heiligen" von Echternach', in *Kurtrierisches Jahrbuch* (1968), pp. 137–40.

Dondaine, Hyacinthe François: *Le corpus dionysien de l'Université de Paris au XIIIe siècle* (Rome, 1953).

Dorn, Franz: *Die Landschenkungen der fränkischen Könige*, Rechts- und Staatswissenschaftliche Veröffentlichche der Görres-Gesellschaft. N. F. LX (Paderborn, 1991).

Douglas, Mary, ed.: *Food in the Social Order* (New York, 1984).

Dray, William: 'R[obin] G[eorge] Collingwood and the Understanding of Actions in History', in Dray, *Perspectives on History* (London, Boston and Henley, 1980), pp. 9–26, 126–7 [first published in *Dialogue* 17 (1978), pp. 659–82].

Duby, Georges: 'Les laics et la paix de Dieu', in *I laici nella 'societas christiana' dei secoli XI e XII* (Milan, 1968), pp. 448–61 [repr. in Duby, *Hommes et structures au Moyen Age* (Paris and The Hague, 1977), pp. 227–40].

Duby, Georges: *Hommes et structures du Moyen Age* (The Hague and Paris, 1973).

Dülmen, Richard van: 'Norbert Elias und der Prozess der Zivilisation', in Dülmen, ed., *Gesellschaft der Frühen Neuzeit* (Frankfurt, 1993), pp. 361–71.

Duerr, Hans Peter: *Nacktheit und Scham* = Duerr, *Der Mythos vom Zivilisationsprozess*, vol. 1 (Frankfurt, 1988).

Duerr, Hans Peter: *Intimität* = Duerr, *Der Mythos vom Zivilisationsprozess*, vol. 2 (Frankfurt, 1990).

Duerr, Hans Peter: *Obzönität und Gewalt* = Duerr, *Der Mythos vom Zivilisationsproeezss*, vol. 3 (Frankfurt, 1993).

Düwel, Klaus: 'Buchstabenmagie und Alphabetzauber', in *Frühmittelalterliche Studien* 22 (1988), pp. 70–110.

Düwel, Klaus: 'Über Nahrungsgewohnheiten und Tischzuchtsitten des Mittelalters', in Bernd Herrmann, ed., *Umwelt in der Geschichte* (Göttingen, 1989), pp. 129–49.

Düwel, Klaus: 'Epigraphische Zeugnisse für die Macht der Schrift im östlichen Frankenreich', in Karin von Welck, Alfred Wieczorek and Hermann Ament, ed., *Die Franken. Wegbereiter Europas*, (Mainz, 1996), pp. 540–52.

Duindam, Jerome: *Myths of Power. Norbert Elias and the Early Modern European Court* (Amsterdam, 1995).

Durliat, Jean: 'Le mense dans le polyptyque d'Irminon', in Hartmut Atsma, ed., *La Neustrie*, vol. 1, Beihefte zur Francia XVI (Sigmaringen, 1989), pp. 467–503.

Durliat, Jean: 'Qu'est-ce qu'un polyptyque?', in *Media in Francia. Recueil de melanges offert à Karl Ferdinand Werner* (Paris, 1989), pp. 129–38.

Ebel, Else: 'Altnordische Quellen zu den skandinavischen Händlerorganisationen', in Ebel and Herbert Jankuhn, ed., *Untersuchungen zu Handel und Verkehr des vor- und frühgeschichtlichen Zeit in Mittel- und Nordeuropa*, vol. 6, Abhandlungen der Akademie der Wissenschaften in Göttingen, Philol.-Hist. Kl. 3. F. CLXXXIII (Göttingen, 1989), pp. 146–72.

Eberle, Matthias: *Individuum und Landschaft*, Kunstwissenschaftliche Unter-suchungen des Ulmer Vereins VIII (Giessen, 1980).

Ebersolt, Jean: *Constantinople Byzantine et les voyageurs du Levant* (Paris, 1918).

Ebner, Herwig: 'Friedenssehnsucht, Friedensprogramme und friedenssichernde

Maßnahmen im hohen und späten Mittelalter', in *Schriftenreihe des Instituts für Geschichte*, vol. 2 (Graz, 1988), pp. 55–74.

Ebner, Herwig: 'Wasser und Siedlung', and 'Wasserversorgung und Entsorgung' in Gerhard Michael Dienes and Franz Leitgeb, ed., *Wasser* (Graz, 1990), pp. 46–58, 76–86.

Eco, Umberto: 'Sviluppo dell' estetica medievale', in *Momenti e problemi di storia dell' estetica*, vol. 1 (Milan, 1959), pp. 115–229.

Eco, Umberto: *The Aesthetics of Thomas Aquinas* (Cambridge, MA, 1988) [first published (Milan, 1970)].

Edgerton Samuel Youngs, Jr: *The Renaissance Rediscovery of Linear Perspective* (New York, 1975).

Edgerton, Samuel Youngs, Jr: *Pictures and Punishment. Art and Criminal Prosecution during the Florentine Renaissance* (Ithaca and London 1985).

Edgerton, Samuel Youngs, Jr: 'From Mental Matrix to Mappamundi to Christian Empire. The Heritage of Ptolemaic Cartography in the Renaissance', in David Woodward, ed., *Art and Cartography* (Chicago and London, 1987), pp. 10–50.

Edson, Evelyn: *Mapping Time and Space. How Medieval Mapmakers Viewed Their World* (London, 1997).

Effros, Bonnie: *Caring for Body and Soul. Burial and Afterlife in the Merovingian World* (University Park, PA, 2002).

Effros, Bonnie: *Creating Community with Food and Drink in Merovingian Gaul* (Basingstoke, 2002).

Eggebrecht, Hans Heinrich: 'Die Mehrstimmigkeitslehre von ihren Anfängen bis zum 12. Jahrhundert', in Frieder Zaminer, ed., *Geschichte der Musiktheorie*, vol. 5 (Darmstadt, 1984), pp. 9–87.

Ehler, Christine, and Ursula Schaefer, ed.: *Verschriftung und Verschriftlichung*, ScripOralia XCIV (Tübingen, 1998).

Ehlers, Eckhard: *Ernährung und Gesellschaft* (Stuttgart, 1983).

Eichberg, Henning: 'Dansens energi. Kulturens sving i kroppens felt', in *Centring* 8,2 (1987), pp. 200–1.

Eisenbart, Liselotte Constanze: *Kleiderordnungnen der deutsche Städte zwischen 1350 und 1700*, Göttinger Bausteine zur Geschichtswissenschaft XXXII (Göttingen, 1962).

Eisenstein, Elizabeth Lewisohn: *The Printing Revolution in Early Modern Europe* (Cambridge, 1983).

Ekenberg, Anders: *Cur Cantatur? Die Funktionen des liturgischen Gesanges nach den Autoren der Karolingerzeit*, Bibliotheca theologiae practicae LXI (Stockholm, 1987).

Ellermeyer, Jürgen: 'Sozialgruppen, Selbstverständnis, Vermögen und städtische Verordnungen', in *Blätter für deutsche Landesgeschichte* 113 (1977), pp. 243–75.

Elliott, John Huxtable: 'Final Reflections. The Old World and the New Revisited', in Karen Ordahl Kupperman, ed., *America in European Consciousness. 1493–1750* (Chapel Hill and London, 1995), pp. 391–408.

Elmshäuser, Konrad, and Andreas Hedwig: *Studien zum Polytychon von Saint-Germain-des-Près* (Cologne and Vienna, 1993).

Elze, Reinhard: 'Über die Leistungsfähigkeit von Gesandtschaften und Boten im 11. Jahrhundert', in Werner Paravicini and Karl Ferdinand Werner, ed., *Histoire comparée de l'administration (IVe–XVIIIe siècle)*, Beihefte der Francia IX (Sigmaringen, 1980), pp. 3–10.

Enright, Michael Joseph: *Iona, Tara and Soissons*, Arbeiten zur Frühmittel-alterforschung XVII (Berlin, New York, 1985).

Enright, Michael Joseph: *Lady with a Meadcup* (Dublin, 1996).

Epperlein, Siegfried: *Waldnutzung, Waldstreitigkeiten und Waldschutz in Deutschland im hohen Mittelalter,* Vierteljahrschrift für Sozial- und Wirtschaftsgeschichte. Beiheft CIX (Stuttgart, 1993).

Erbe, Michael: *Zur neueren französischen Sozialgeschichtsforschung* (Darmstadt, 1979), pp. 27–46.

Etudes sur la sensibilité au Moyen Age (Limoges, 1989).

Faes de Mottoni, Barbara de: *Il 'Corpus Dionysianum' nel medioevo. Rassegna di studi. 1900–1972,* Pubblicazioni del Centro di studio per la storia della storiografia filosofica III (Bologna, 1977).

Falk, Alfred, Manfred Gläser, and Cornelia Moeck-Schlösser: 'Wasserversorgung und Abfallbeseitigung in den Hansestädten', in *Hanse* 1 (1989), pp. 409–13.

Falk, Pasi: 'Essen und Trinken. Über die Geschichte der Mahlzeit', in Alexander Schuller and Jutta Anna Kleber, ed., *Verschlemmte Welt* (Göttingen, 1994), pp. 103–31.

Farago, Claire: '"Vision Itself Has Its History". "Race", Nation and Renaissance Art History', in Farago, ed., *Reframing the Renaissance. Visual Culture in Europe and Latin America. 1450–1650* (New Haven and London, 1995), pp. 67–88.

Fehring, Günter Peter: 'Missions- und Kirchenwesen in archäologischer Sicht', in Herbert Jankuhn and Reinhard Wenskus, ed., *Geschichtswissenschaft und Archäologie,* Vorträge und Forschungen, herausgegeben vom Konstanzer Arbeitskreis für mittelalterliche Geschichte XXII (Sigmaringen, 1979), pp. 556–67.

Fell, Christine Elizabeth, Cecily Clark and Elizabeth Williams: *Women in Anglo-Saxon England and the Impact of 1066* (London, 1984).

Fellmann, Ferdinand: 'Der Geltungsanspruch des ästhetischen Urteils', in *Zeitschrift für Ästhetik und Allgemeine Kunstwissenschaft* 34 (1989), pp. 155–73.

Fichtenau, Heinrich: *Askese und Laster in der Anschauung des Mittelalters* (Vienna, 1948).

Fichtenau, Heinrich: *Arenga,* Mitteilungen des Instituts für Österreichische Geschichtsforschung. Ergänzungsband XVIII (Graz and Cologne, 1957).

Ficker, Julius: *Beiträge zur Urkundenlehre,* 2 vols (Innsbruck, 1877–78), esp. vol. 1, pp. 294–97, vol. 2, pp. 214–21.

Finucane, Ronald C.: *Miracles and Pilgrims. Popular Beliefs in Medieval England* (London, Melbourne and Toronto, 1977).

Flint, Valerie Irene Jane: *The Rise of Magic in Early Medieval Europe* (Princeton, 1991).

Förstemann, Ernst Günther: 'Versuch einer Geschichte der christlichen Geißlergesellschaften. Geschichte mit den Geißlern verwechselter Gesellschaften, I.: Rasende Tänzer', in *Archiv für alte und neuere Kirchengeschichte* (1817), pp. 640–65.

Foot, Sarah: 'Wilton, Wiltshire', in Foot, *Veiled Women,* vol. 2 (Aldershot, 2000), pp. 221–37.

Fossier, Robert: *Polyptyques et censiers,* Typologie des sources du Moyen Age occidental XXVIII (Turnhout, 1978).

Fouquet, Gerhard: *Bauen für die Stadt. Finanzen, Organisation und Arbeit in kommunalen Baubetrieben des Spätmittelalters,* Städteforschung. Reihe A, vol. XLVIII (Cologne, Weimar, and Vienna, 1999).

France, John: 'War and Christendom in the Thought of Rodulfus Glaber', in *Studia monastica* 30 (1988), pp. 105–19.

Frank, Barbara, Thomas Haye and Doris Tophinke, ed.: *Gattungen mittelalterlicher Schriftlichkeit,* ScripOralia XCIX (Tübingen, 1998).

Franke, Ursula: *Kunst als Erkenntnis. Die Rolle der Sinnlichkeit in der Ästhetik des*

Alexander Gottlieb Baumgarten, Studia Leibnitiana. Supplementa IX (Wiesbaden, 1972).

Freedberg, David: *The Power of Images* (Chicago and London, 1989).

Freeman, Ann: 'Theodulf of Orleans and the *Libri Carolini*', in *Speculum* 32 (1957), pp. 663–705.

Fricker, Bartolomaus: *Geschichte der Stadt und Bäder zu Baden* (Aarau, 1880).

Fried, Johannes: 'Die Kunst der Aktualisierung in der oralen Gesellschaft. Die Königserhebung Heinrichs I als Exempel', in *Geschichte in Wissenschaft und Unterricht* 44 (1993), pp. 493–503. [an enlarged version appeared s. t. 'Die Königserhebung Heinrichs I. Erinnerung, Mündlichkeit und Traditionsbildung im 10. Jahrhundert', in Michael Borgolte, ed., *Mittelalterforschung nach der Wende*, Beihefte zur Historischen Zeitschrift XX (Munich, 1995), pp. 267–318].

Fried, Johannes, ed.: *Träger und Instrumentarien des Friedens im hohen und späten Mittelalter*, Vorträge und Forschungen, hrsg. vom Konstanzer Arbeitskreis für mittelalterliche Geschichte XLIII (Sigmaringen, 1996).

Friedman, Jeffrey, ed.: *The Rational Choice Controversy* (New Haven and London, 1996).

Friedman, John Block: 'Cultural Conflicts in Medieval World Maps', in Stuart B. Schwartz, ed., *Implicit Understanding. Observing, Reporting and Reflecting on the Encounters between Europeans and Other Peoples in the Early Modern Era* (Cambridge, 1994), pp. 64–95.

Fritze, Wolfgang H.: 'Untersuchungen zur frühslawischen und frühfrankischen Geschichte bis ins 7. Jahrhundert', Ph.D. Diss. typescript (University of Marburg, 1952) [new edn by Dietrich Kurze, Winfried Schich and Reinhard Schneider (Frankfurt, 1994)].

Frugoni, Chiara: *Das Mittelalter auf der Nase* (Munich, 2003), pp. 21–31.

Fudge, Erica: *Perceiving Animals. Humans and Beasts in Early Modern English Culture* (Urbana and Chicago, 2002).

Fudge, Erica: 'How a Man Differs from a Dog', in *History Today* 53, no. 6 (2003), pp. 38–44.

Fuller, Sarah: 'Theoretical Foundations of Early Organum Theory', in *Acta Musicologica* 53 (1981), pp. 52–84.

Gadol, Joan: *Leon Battista Alberti. Universal Man of the Early Renaissance* (Chicago and London, 1969).

Galetti, Paola: 'Un caso particolare. Le prestazioni d'opera nei contratti agrari piacentni dei secoli VIII–X', in Vito Fumagalli, ed., *Le prestazioni d'opera nelle campagne italiane del Medioevo*, Biblioteca di storia agraria medievale III (Bologna, 1987), pp. 69–103.

Ganshof, François-Louis: 'Merowingisches Gesandtschaftswesen', in *Aus Geschichte und Landeskunde. Forschungen und Darstellungen. Franz Steinbach zum 65. Geburtstag gewidmet* (Bonn, 1960), pp. 166–83.

Ganshof, François-Louis: *De internationale betrekkeningen van het Frankisch Rijk onder de Merowingen*, Mededelingen van de Koninklijke Vlaamse Academie vor Wetenschappen, Letteren Schone Kunsten van België, Klasse der Letteren XXV, 2 (Brussels, 1963).

Ganz, David: 'Temptabat et scribere. Vom Schreiben in der Karolingerzeit', in Rudolf Schieffer, ed., *Schriftkultur und Reichsverwaltung unter den Karolingern*, Abhandlungen der Nordrhein-Westfälischen Akademie der Wissenschaften XCIII (Opladen, 1996), pp. 13–33.

Ganz, Peter. ed.: *Das Buch als magisches und Repräsentationsobjekt* (Wiesbaden, 1992).

Gass, Wilhelm: 'Zur Geschichte der Ethik', in *Zeitschrift für Kirchengeschichte* 1 (1877), pp. 332–96, 510–30.

Gass, Wilhelm: *Geschichte der christlichen Ethik*, vol. 1 (Berlin, 1881).

Gautier Dalché, Patrick: 'Tradition et renouvellement dans la représentation de l'espace géographique au IXe siècle', in *Studi medievali*, 3rd ser., 24 (1983), pp. 121–65.

Gautier Dalché, Patrick: 'Un problème d'histoire culturelle. Perception et représentation de l'espace au Moyen Age', in *Médiévales. Language, Textes, Histoire* 18 (1990), pp. 5–15.

Gay, Peter: *The Bourgeois Experience*, vol. 1: *Education of the Senses* (Oxford, 1984).

Geary, Patrick J.: *Phantom of Remembrance. Memory and Oblivion at the End of the First Millennium* (Princeton, 1994).

Gebser, Jean: *Ursprung und Gegenwart*, vol. 1 (Stuttgart, 1959).

Gechter, Marianne: 'Wasserversorgung und Entsorgung in Köln vom Mittelalter bis zur frühen Neuzeit', in *Kölner Jahrbuch für Vor- und Frühgeschichte* 20 (1987), pp. 219–70.

Geertz, Clifford: 'The Way We Think Now. Toward an Ethnography of Modern Thought', in Geertz, *Local Knowledge* (London, 1993), pp. 147–63 [first published (New York, 1983)].

Gelling, Margaret: 'The Place-Names Burton and Variants', in Sonia Chadwick Hawkes, ed., *Weapons and Warfare in Anglo-Saxon England* (Oxford, 1989), pp. 145–8.

Gellrich, Jesse M.: *The Idea of the Book in the Middle Ages* (Ithaca and London, 1986).

Genova, Anthony C.: 'Kant's Transcendental Deduction of Aesthetic Judgments', in *Journal of Aesthetics and Art Criticism* 30 (1971/72), pp. 459–75.

Gernhuber, Joachim: *Die Landfriedensbewegung in Deutschland bis zum Mainzer Landfrieden von 1235*, Bonner rechtswissenschaftliche Abhandlungen XLIV (Bonn, 1952).

Gethmann-Siefert, Annemarie: 'Zur Begründung einer Ästhetik durch Hegel', in *Hegel-Studien* 13 (1978), pp. 237–89.

Gethmann-Siefert, Annemarie: 'Kunst und Philosophie. Zur Kritik der Hegelschen Ästhetik', in *Zeitschrift für Ästhetik und Allgemeine Kunstwissenschaft* 28 (1983), pp. 62–85.

Gilbert, Katherine Everett, and Helmut Kuhn: *A History of Esthetics* (New York, 1939) [rev. edn (Bloomington, 1953)].

Gioseffi, Decio: *Perpectiva artificialis. Per la storia della prospettiva spigolature e appunti* (Triest, 1957)

Girndt, Helmut: *Das soziale Handeln als Grundkategorie erfahrungswissenschaftlicher Soziologie*, Veröffentlichungen des Max-Weber-Instituts der Universitat München I (Tübingen, 1967), pp. 22–4.

Girndt, Helmut: 'Handeln, soziales', in Joachim Ritter, ed., *Historisches Wörterbuch der Philosophie*, vol. 3 (Basle and Stuttgart, 1974), cols 994–6.

Glunz, Hans Hermann: *Die Literarästhetik des europäischen Mittelalters. Wolfram, Rosenroman, Chaucer, Dante* (Bochum, 1937) [2nd edn (Frankfurt, 1963)].

Göggelmann, Hans Erich: 'Das Strafrecht der Reichsstadt Ulm bis zur Carolina'. LL.D. Diss., typescript (University of Tübingen, 1984).

Göttert, Karl-Heinz: 'Rhetorik und Konversationsatheorie', in Joachim Dyck, Walter Jens and Gert Ueding, ed., *Rhetorik der frühen Neuzeit*, Rhetorik X (Tübingen, 1991), pp. 45–56.

Goetz, Hans-Werner: *Strukturen der spätkarolingischen Epoche im Spiegel der Vorstellungen eines zeitgenössischen Mönchs* (Bonn, 1981).

Goetz, Hans-Werner: 'Kirchenschutz, Rechtswahrung und Reform. Zu Zielen und zum Wesen der frühen Gottesfriedensbewegung in Frankreich', in *Francia* 11 (1983), pp. 193–239.

Goetz, Hans-Werner: 'Der Kölner Gottesfriede von 1083', in *Jahrbuch des Kölnischen Geschichtsvereins* 55 (1984), pp. 39–76.

Goetz, Hans-Werner: 'Herrschaft und Raum in der frühmittelalterlichen Grundherrschaft', in *Annalen des Historischen Vereins für den Niederrhein* 190 (1987), pp. 7–33.

Goetz, Hans-Werner: 'Gottesfriede und Gemeindebildung', in *Zeitschrift der Savigny-Stiftung für Rechtsgeschichte*, Germanistische Abteilung 105 (1988), pp. 122–44.

Goetz, Hans-Werner: 'La paix de Dieu en France autour de l'an Mil', in *Le roi de France et son royaume autour de l'an Mil. Actes du colloque international Hugues Capet. 987–1987* (Paris, 1988), pp. 131–45.

Goldstein, Carl: *Visual Fact over Verbal Fiction. A Study of the Carraci and the Criticism. Theory and Practice of Art in Renaissance and Baroque Italy* (Cambridge, 1988).

Gollwitzer, Peter Max: *Abwägen und Planen. Bewusstsein in verschiedenen Handlungsphasen*, Motivationsforschung XIII (Göttingen, 1991).

Gombrich, Ernst Hans: *Art and Illusion*, 5th edn (Oxford, 1972) [first published (Washington, 1959)].

Gombrich, Ernst Hans: *Norm and Form*, = Gombrich, *Studies on the Art of the Renaissance*, vol. 1, 4th edn (Oxford, 1985) [first published (Oxford, 1966)].

Goody, Jack, and Ian Watt: 'The Consequences of Literacy', in *Comparative Studies in Society and History* 5 (1963), pp. 304–45.

Gosselin, Marie Dominique Roland: *La Morale de St. Augustin*, Etudes philosophiques IV (Paris, 1925).

Gottfried, Robert Steven: *The Black Death. Natural and Human Disaster in Medieval Europe* (London, 1983).

Gougaud, Louis: 'La danse dans les églises', in *Revue d'histoire ecclésiastique* 15 (1914), pp. 229–30.

Goul, Penelope: 'Music, Melancholy, and Medical Spirits in Early Modern Thought', in Peregrine Horden, ed., *Music as Medicine. The History of Music Therapy since Antiquity* (Aldershot, 2000), p. 181 [Commentary by Peregrine Horden, pp. 249–54].

Gramme, Willi: *Die Körperpflege bei den Angelsachsen*, Anglistische Forschungen LXXXVI (Heidelberg, 1938).

Greenhalgh, Michael, and Vincent Megaw, ed.: *Art in Society* (London, 1978).

Guenée, Bernard: 'Les généalogies entre l'histoire et la politique', in *Annales* 33 (1978), pp. 450–77.

Gullick, Mark: 'A Bibliography of Medieval Painting Treatises', in Linda L. Brownrigg, ed., *Making the Medieval Book. Techniques of Production*, Mikrokosmos IV (Los Altos Hills, CA, 1995), pp. 241–4.

Guyer, Paul: *Kant on the Claims of Taste* (Cambridge, MA, 1979).

Haas, Michael: 'Organum', in: *Die Musik in Geschichte und Gegenwart. Sachteil*, 2nd edn, ed. Ludwig Finscher, vol. 7 (Kassel, 1997), cols 853–81.

Hägermann, Dieter: 'Eine Grundherrschaft des 13. Jahrhunderts im Spiegel des

Frühmittelalters. Caesarius von Prüm und seine kommentierte Abschrift des Urbars von 893', in *Rheinische Vierteljahrsblätter* 45 (1981), pp. 1–34.

Hägermann, Dieter: 'Anmerkungen zum Stand und den Aufgaben frühmittelalterlicher Urbarforschung', in *Rheinische Vierteljahrsblätter* 50 (1986), pp. 32–58.

Hägermann, Dieter: 'Der Abt als Grundherr. Kloster und Wirtschaft im frühen Mittelalter', in Friedrich Prinz, ed., *Herrschaft und Kirche* (Stuttgart, 1988), pp. 345–85.

Hägermann, Dieter, and Karl Heinz Ludwig: 'Verdichtung von Technik als Periodisierungsindikatoren des Mittelalters', in *Technikgeschichte* 57 (1990), pp. 315–28.

Hägermann, Dieter: 'Technik im frühen Mittelalter zwischen 500 und 1000', in Hägermann and Helmuth Schneider, *Landbau und Handwerk. 750 v. Chr. bis 1000 n. Chr.*, Propyläen Technikgeschichte I (Berlin, 1997), pp. 317–45.

Haftlmeier-Seiffert, Renate: *Bauerndarstellungen auf deutschen Flugblättern des 17. Jahrhunderts*, Mikrokosmos XXV (Frankfurt, Bern, New York and Paris, 1991).

Hagel, Jürgen: 'Stuttgarter Wasser- und Umweltprobleme in der frühen Neuzeit', in *Zeitschrift für Württembergische Landesgeschichte* 42 (1983), pp. 217–54.

Hagenlocher, Albrecht: 'Quellenberufungen als Mittel der Legitimation in deutschen Chroniken des 13. Jahrhunderts', in *Jahrbuch des Vereins für niederdeutsche Sprachforschung* 102 (1979), pp. 15–71.

Hagenlocher, Albrecht: *Der guote vride. Idealer Friede in der deutschen Literatur bis ins frühe 14. Jahrhundert*, Historische Wortforschung II (Berlin and New York, 1992).

Hahn, Cynthia: 'Purification, Sacred Action, and the Vision of God', in *Word and Image* 5 (1989), pp. 71–84.

Hahn, Cynthia: 'Visio Dei. Changes in Medieval Visuality', in Robert S. Nelson, ed., *Visuality Before and Beyond the Renaissance* (Cambridge, 2000), pp. 169–96.

Hallpike, Christopher Robert: *The Foundations of Primitive Thought* (Oxford, 1979).

Hansen, Inge Lyse, and Chris Wickham, ed.: *The Long Eighth Century*, The Transformation of the Roman World XI (Leiden, New York and Cologne, 2000).

Hartlaub, Gustav Friedrich: 'Körper, Raum und Ton im frühen Mittelalter', in *Zeitschrift für Ästhetik und allgemeine Kunstwissenschaft* [A.F.] 35 (1941), pp. 1–16.

Hartmann, Eduard von: *Die deutsche Aesthetik seit Kant* = Hartmann, *Ausgewählte Werke*, 2nd edn, vol. 3 (Leipzig, 1888), pp. 1–27 [first published (Leipzig, 1886)].

Hartmann, Wilfried: *Der Frieden im früheren Mittelalter*, Beiträge zur Friedensethik (Barsbüttel, 1992), pp. 19–46.

Haseloff, Günther: *Der Tassilokelch*, Münchner Beiträge zur Vor- und Frühgeschichte I (Munich, 1951).

Haseloff, Günther: 'Zum Ursprung der germanischen Tierornamentik. Die spätrömische Wurzel', in *Frühmittelalterliche Studien* 7 (1973), pp. 406–42.

Haseloff, Günther: *Die germanische Tierornamentik der Völkerwanderungszeit. Studien zu Salin's Stil I.*, 3 vols, Vorgeschichtliche Forschungen XVII (Berlin, 1979–81).

Hasenfratz, Hans Peter: *Die toten Lebenden*, Zeitschrift für Religions- und Geistesgeschichte. Beiheft XXIV (Leiden, 1982).

Haskell, Francis: *History and Its Images* (New Haven and London, 1993).

Hauck, Karl: 'Die Wiedergabe von Göttersymbolen und Sinnzeichen der A-, B- und C-Brakteaten auf D- und F-Brakteaten, exemplarisch erhellt mit Speer und Kreuz', in *Frühmittelalterliche Studien* 20 (1986), pp. 474–512.

Haug, Walter, and Rainer Warning, ed.: *Das Fest*, Poetik und Hermeneutik XIV (Munich, 1989).

Head, Thomas, and Richard Landes, ed.: 'Essays on the Peace of God', in *Historical Reflections* 14, no. 3 (1987), pp. 379–549.

Head, Thomas, and Richard Landes, ed.: *The Peace of God. Social Violence and Religious Response in France around the Year 1000* (Ithaca and London, 1992).

Hecker, Justus Friedrich Carl: *Der Schwarze Tod im vierzehnten Jahrhundert* (Berlin, 1832).

Hecker, Justus Friedrich Carl: 'Die Tanzwuth', in August Hirsch, ed., *Die grossen Volkskrankheiten des Mittelalters* (Berlin, 1865), pp. 143–92.

Heers, Jacques: *Family Clans in the Middle Ages* (Amsterdam and New York, 1977) [first published (Paris, 1974)].

Heers, Jacques: *Fêtes des fous et carnavals* (Paris, 1983).

Heffner, Karl: 'Über die Baderzunft im Mittel-Alter und später, besonders in Franken', in *Archiv des Historischen Vereins von Unterfranken und Aschaffenburg* 6 (1864), pp. 155–246.

Hehl, Ernst-Dieter: 'Kirche, Krieg und Staatlichkeit im hohen Mittelalter', in Werner Rösener, ed., *Staat und Krieg* (Göttingen, 2000), pp. 17–36.

Heidecker, Karl, ed.: *Charters and the Use of the Written Word in Medieval Society*, Utrecht Studies in Medieval Literacy XIV (Turnhout, 2000).

Heine, Günter: 'Umweltschutzrecht aus historischer Sicht', in Ernst Schubert and Bernd Herrmann, ed., *Von der Angst zur Ausbeutung. Umwelterfahrung zwischen Mittelalter und Neuzeit* (Frankfurt, 1994), pp. 157–83.

Hemardinquer, Jean-Jacques, ed.: *Pour une histoire de l'alimentation*, Cahiers des Annales XXVIII (Paris, 1971).

Henderson, George: *Vision and Image in Early Christian England* (Cambridge, 1998).

Hennebo, Dieter: *Gärten des Mittelalters* (Munich, 1967).

Hentschel, Beate: 'Zur Genese einer optimistischen Anthropologie in der Renaissance', in Klaus Schreiner and Norbert Schnitzler, ed., *Gepeinigt, begehrt, vergessen. Symbolik und Sozialbezug des Körpers im späten Mittelalter und in der frühen Neuzeit* (Munich, 1992), pp. 85–105.

Hermann, Jean Frédéric: *Notices historiques, statistiques et litéraires sur la ville de Strasbourg*, vol. 2 (Strasbourg, 1819), pp. 451–3.

Hermeren, Göran: *Representation and Meaning in the Visual Arts* (Lund, 1969).

Heslop, T. A.: 'Attitudes to the Visual Arts. The Evidence from Written Sources', in Jonathan J. Alexander and Paul Binski, ed., *Age of Chivalry. Art in Plantagenet England. 1200–1400* (London, 1987), pp. 26–32.

Heyne, Moritz: *Körperpflege und Kleidung bei den Deutschen* (Leipzig and Munich, 1903), pp. 35–61.

Higounet, Charles: 'A propos de la perception de l'espace au Moyen Age', in *Media in Francia Recueil de melanges offert à Karl Ferdinand Werner* (Paris, 1989), pp. 257–68.

Hill, David, and Alexander R. Rumble, ed.: *The Defense of Wessex* (Manchester, New York, 1996).

Hiller, Bruno: 'Abälard als Ethiker', Ph.D. Diss. (University of Erlangen, 1900).

Hillman, David, and Carla Mazzio, ed.: *The Body in Parts. Fantasies of Corporeality in Early Modern Europe* (London and New York, 1997).

Hines, John: 'North Sea Trade and the Proto-Urban Sequence', in *Archaeologia Polona* 32 (1994), pp. 7–26.

Hinz, Hermann: 'Baderäume', in *Reallexikon der Germanischen Altertumskunde*, 2nd edn, vol. 1 (Berlin and New York, 1973), pp. 579–83.

Hirschfelder, Günter: *Europäische Eßkultur* (Frankfurt, 2003), pp. 95–112.

Hirschmann, Gerhard: 'Nürnberger Gartenkultur im Barockzeitalter', in Bernhard Kirchgässner and Joachim Berrnhard Schultis, ed., *Wald, Garten und Park* (Sigmaringen, 1993), pp. 35–50.

His, Rudolf: *Das Strafrecht der Friesen im Mittelalter* (Leipzig, 1901).

His, Rudolf: *Das Strafrecht des deutschen Mittelalters*, vol. 2 (Weimar, 1935).

Hodges, Richard: *Primitive Peasant Markets* (Oxford, 1988).

Hodges, Richard: 'In the Shadow of Pirenne. San Vincenzo al Volturno and the Revival of Mediterranean Commerce', in Riccardo Francovich and G. Noyé, ed., *La storia dell' Alto Medioevo Italiano alla luce dell' archeologia* (Florence, 1994), pp. 109–27.

Hodges, Richard: 'Henri Pirenne and the Questions of Demand in the Sixth Century', in Hodges and William Bowden, ed., *The Sixth Century*, The Transformation of the Roman World III (Leiden, Boston and Cologne, 1998), pp. 3–14.

Hoeniger, Robert: *Der Schwarze Tod in Deutschland* (Berlin, 1882) [repr. (Vaduz, 1986)].

Hoffmann, Hartmut: *Gottesfriede und Treuga Dei*, Schriften der Monumenta Germanica Historica XX (Stuttgart, 1964) [repr. (Stuttgart, 1986)].

Hoffmann, Hartmut: *Buchkunst und Königtum im ottonischen und frühsalischen Reich*, Schriften der Monumenta Germaniae Historica XXX, 2 vols (Stuttgart, 1986).

Hoffmann, Robert: 'Die Augsburger Bäder und das Handwerk der Bader', in *Zeitschrift des Historischen Vereins für Schwaben und Neuburg* 12 (1885), pp. 1–35.

Hoffmann-Krayer, Ernst: 'Tänze auf Kirchhöfen', in *Archiv für das Studium der neueren Sprachen und Literaturen* 127 (1911), pp. 197–9.

Hollstein, Ernst: *Mitteleuropäische Eichenchronologie* (Mainz, 1980).

Holschneider, Arno: *Die Organa von Winchester. Studien zum ältesten Repertoire polyphoner Musik* (Hildesheim, 1968).

Holtdorf, Arne: 'Das Tanzlied von Kölbigk', in Günther Jungbluth, ed., *Interpretationen mittelhochdeutscher Lyrik* (Bad Homburg vor der Höhe, Berlin, Zurich, 1969), pp. 13–45.

Holzhauer, Heinz: 'Zum Strafgedanken im frühen Mittelalter', in Stephan Buchholz, Paul Mikat and Dieter Werkmüller, ed., *Überlieferung, Bewahrung und Gestaltung in der rechtsgeschichtlichen Forschung*, Rechts- und staatswissenschaftliche Veröffentlichungen der Görres-Gesellschaft. N. F. LXIX (Paderborn, 1993), pp. 179–92.

Horrox, Rosemary, ed.: *The Black Death* (Manchester and New York, 1994).

Hottinger, Salomon: *Thermae Argovia-Badenses. Das ist Eigentliche Beschreibung der warmen Bäder insgemein, des herrlichen in dem Aargöw gelegenen warmen Bads zu Baden insbesondere* (Baden, 1702).

Hruza, Karel, and Paul Herold, ed.: *Wege zur Urkunde – Wege der Urkunde – Wege der Forschung*, Forschungen zur Kaiser- und Papstgeschichte. Beihefte zu J. F. Böhmer, Regesta Imperii, vol. XXIV (Vienna and Cologne, 2004).

Huberti, Ludwig: *Studien zur Rechtsgeschichte der Gottesfrieden und Landfrieden*, vol. 1: *Zur Rechtsgeschichte der Friedenssatzungen im Mittelalter* (Ansbach, 1892).

Illi, Martin: *Von der Schissgruob zur modernen Stadtentwässerung* (Zurich, 1987).

Illi, Martin, and Edgar Höfler: 'Versorgung und Entsorgung im Spiegel der Schriftquellen', in Marianne and Nikolaus Flüeler, ed., *Stadtluft, Hirsebrei und Bettelmönch. Die Stadt um 1300* (Stuttgart, 1992), pp. 351–63.

Illich, Ivan: *In the Vinyard of the Text* (Chicago, 1993) [first published (Paris, 1990)].

Innes, Matthew: *State and Society in the Early Middle Ages. The Middle Rhine Valley. 400–1000* (Cambridge, 2000).

Irmscher, Johannes: 'Die Anfänge des Begriffs Ästhetik', in *Ästhetik und Urgeschichte*.

Kolloquium der Leibniz-Sozietät zum 90. Geburtstag von Georg Knepler, Sitzungsberichte der Leibniz-Sozietät XXV, no. 6 (Berlin, 1998), pp. 35–7.

Irsigler, Franz: 'Divites und pauperes in der Vita Meinwerci', in *Vierteljahrsschrift für Sozial- und Wirtschaftsgeschichte* 57 (1970), pp. 449–99.

Irsigler, Franz: 'Grundherrschaft, Handel und Märkte zwischen Maas und Rhein im frühen und hohen Mittelalter', in Klaus Fink and Wilhelm Janssen, ed., *Grundherrschaft und Stadtentstehung am Niederrhein*, Klever Archiv IX (Kleve, 1989), pp. 52–78.

Irsigler, Franz, and Arnold Lassotta: *Bettler und Gauner, Dirnen und Henker. Aussenseiter in einer mittelalterlichen Stadt. Köln 1300–1600* (Munich, 1989).

Ivins, William Mills, Jr: *Prints and Visual Communication* (New York, 1969).

Jäger, Michael: *Die Ästhetik als Antwort auf das kopernikanische Weltbild.Die Beziehungen zwischen den Naturwissenschaften und der Ästhetik Alexander Gottlieb Baumgartens und Georg Friedrich Meiers*, Philosophische Texte und Studien X (Hildesheim, 1984).

Jäschke, Kurt-Ulrich: *Burgenbau und Landesverteidigung um 900*, Vorträge und Forschungen, hrsg. vom Konstanzer Arbeitskreis für mittelalterliche Geschichte. Sonderband XVI (Sigmaringen, 1975).

Jahn, Bernhard: 'Genealogie und Kritik. Theologie und Philologie als Korrektive genealogischen Denkens in Cyriakus Spangenbergs historiographischen Werken', in Kilian Heck and Bernhard Jahn, ed., *Genealogie als Denkform in Mittelalter und Früher Neuzeit*, Studien und Texte zur Sozialgeschichte der Literatur LXXX (Tübingen, 2000), pp. 69–85.

Janssen, Wilhelm: 'Ein niederrheinischer Fürstenhof um die Mitte des 14. Jahrhunderts', in *Rheinische Vierteljahresblätter* 34 (1970), pp. 219–51.

Janssen, Wilhelm: 'Friede', in Otto Brunner, Werner Conze and Reinhart Koselleck, ed., *Geschichtliche Grundbegriffe*, vol. 2 (Stuttgart, 1975), pp. 543–91 [abridged version in Dieter Senghaas, ed., *Den Frieden denken* (Frankfurt, 1995), pp. 227–75].

Janssen, Wilhelm: ' ". . . na gesetze unser lande . . .". Zur territorialen Gesetzgebung im späten Mittelalter', in Dietmar Willoweit, ed., *Gesetzgebung als Faktor der Staatsentwicklung*, Der Staat. Beiheft VII (Berlin, 1984), pp. 7–40.

Janssen, Walter, and Dietrich Lohrmann, ed.: *Villa – curtis – grangia. Landwirtschaft zwischen Loire und Rhein von der Römerzeit zum Hochmittelalter*, Beihefte der Francia XI (Sigmaringen, 1983).

Jardins et vergers en Europe occidentale (VIIIe–XVIIIe siècles) (Auch, 1989).

Jaritz, Gerhard, ed.: *Pictura quasi fictura. Die Rolle des Bildes in der Erforschung von Alltag und Sachkultur des Mittelalters und der frühen Neuzeit*, Forschungen des Instituts für Realienkunde des Mittelalters und der Frühneuzeit I (Vienna, 1996).

Jauss, Hans Robert: 'Ästhetische Normen und geschichtliche Reflexion in der "querelle des Anciens et des Modernes" ', in Charles Perrault, *Parallèle des Anciens et des Modernes*, ed. Hans Robert Jauss (Munich, 1964), pp. 8–66.

Jeck, Udo Reinhold: *Aristoteles contra Augustinum. Zur Frage nach dem Verhältnis von Zeit und Seele bei den antiken Aristoteleskommentatoren, im arabischen Aristotelismus und im 13. Jahrhundert*, Bochumer Studien zur Philosophie XXI (Amsterdam and Philadelphia, 1994).

Jedin, Hubert: 'Entstehung und Tragweite des Trienter Edikts über die Bilderverehrung', in *Theologische Quartalschrift* 116 (1935), pp. 143–88, 404–29.

Jeggle, Utz: *Der Kopf des Körpers. Eine volkskundliche Anatomie* (Weinheim and Berlin, 1986).

Jeitteles, Ignaz: 'Aesthetik', in Jeitteles, ed., *Aesthetisches Wörterbuch* (Vienna, 1839), pp. 18–19 [repr. (Hildesheim, New York, 1978)].

Jobert, Philippe: *La notion de donation. Convergences 630 – 750* (Paris, 1977).

Jodl, Friedrich: *Geschichte der Ethik*, vol. 1 (Stuttgart, 1882) [repr. of the 4th edn of 1929 (Essen, 1995)].

Johanek, Peter: 'Der "Aussenhandel" des Frankenreichs der Merowingerzeit nach Norden und Osten im Spiegel der Schriftquellen', in Klaus Düwel, Herbert Jankuhn, Harald Siems and Dieter Timpe, ed., *Untersuchungen zu Handel und Verkehr der vor- und frühgeschichtlichen Zeit in Mittel- und Nordeuropa*, vol. 3, Abhandlungen der Akademie der Wissenschaften in Göttingen, Philol.-Hist. Kl. 3. F. CL (Göttingen, 1985), pp. 245–47.

Johanek, Peter: 'Der fränkische Handel der Karolingerzeit im Spiegel der Schriftquellen', in Klaus Düwel, Herbert Jankuhn, Harald Siems and Dieter Timpe, ed., *Untersuchungen zu Handel und Verkehr der vor- und frühgeschichtlichen Zeit in Mittel- und Nordeuropa*, vol. 3, Abhandlungen der Akademie der Wissenschaften in Göttingen, Philol.-Hist. Kl. 3. F. CLVI (Göttingen, 1987), pp. 7–68.

John, Eric: *Land Tenure in Early England*, Studies in Early English History I (Leicester, 1960) [2nd edn (Leicester, 1964)].

John, Eric: 'Some Latin Charters of the Tenth-Century Reformation in England', in *Revue Bénédictine* 70 (1960), pp. 333–59 [repr. in John, *Orbis Britanniae and Other Studies*, Studies in Early English History IV (Leicester, 1966), pp. 181–209].

John, Eric: 'War and Society in the Tenth Century', in *Transactions of the Royal Historical Society*, 5th series 27 (1977), pp. 173–195.

Jolly, Karen, Catharina Raudvere and Edward Peters: *Witchcraft and Magic in Europe*, vol. 3: *The Middle Ages* (London, 2002).

Jung, Vera: *Körperlust und Disziplin. Studien zur Fest- und Tanzkultur im 16. und 17. Jahrhundert* (Cologne, Weimar and Vienna, 2001).

Jung, Vera: ' "Wilde" Tänze – "Gelehrte" Tanzkunst. Wie man im 16. Jahrhundert versuchte, die Körper zu zähmen', in Richard van Dülmen, ed., *Körper-Geschichten* (Frankfurt, 1996), pp. 43–70, 228–33.

Justus, Wolfgang: *Die frühe Entwicklung des säkularen Friedensbegriffs in der mittelalterlichen Chronistik*, Kollektive Einstellungen und sozialer Wandel im Mittelalter [A. F.] IV (Cologne and Vienna, 1975).

Kaden, Christian: 'Tonsystem und Mehrstimmigkeitslehre der Musica enchiriadis', in Martin Kintzinger, Sönke Lorenz and Michael Walter, ed., *Schule und Schüler im Mittelalter*, Archiv für Kulturgeschichte. Beiheft XLII (Cologne, Weimar and Vienna, 1996), pp. 75–87.

Kaeuper, Richard W., ed.: *Violence in Medieval Society* (Woodbridge, 2000).

Kaiser, Reinhold: 'Selbsthilfe und Gewaltmonopol. Königliche Friedenswahrung in Deutschland und Frankreich im Mittelalter', in *Frühmittelalterliche Studien* 17 (1983), pp. 55–72.

Kaiser, Reinhold: 'Gottesfrieden', in *Lexikon des Mittelalters*, vol. 4 (Munich and Zurich, 1989), cols 1587–92.

Kaiser, Reinhold: *Trunkenheit und Gewalt im Mittelalter* (Cologne, Weimar and Vienna, 2002).

Kamper, Dietmar: *Zur Geschichte der Einbildungskraft* (Reinbek, 1990).

Kamper, Dietmar, and Christoph Wulf, ed.: *Das Schwinden der Sinne* (Frankfurt, 1988).

Kapriev, Georgi, and Albert Speer, ed.: *The Reception of Pseudo-Dionysius in the Middle Ages* (Sofia, 1999).

Kasper, Clemens M., and Klaus Schreiner, ed.: *Viva vox et ratio scripta. Mündliche und schriftliche Kommunikationsformen im Mönchtum des Mittelalters*, Vita regularis V (Munster, 1997).

Kasten, Brigitte: 'Erbrechtliche Verfügungen des 8. und 9. Jahrhunderts. Zugleich ein Beitrag zur Organisation und zur Schriftlichkeit bei der Verwaltung adeliger Grundherrschaften am Beispiel des Grafen Heccard aus Burgund', in *Zeitschrift der Savigny-Stiftung für Rechtsgeschichte*, Germanistische Abteilung 107 (1990), pp. 236–338.

Kauffmann, Georg: *Zum Verständnis von Bild und Text in der Renaissance* (Opladen, 1980).

Kaulbach, Friedrich: *Einführung in die Philosophie des Handelns* (Darmstadt, 1982).

Keil, Gundolf: 'Seuchenzüge des Mittelalters', in Bernd Herrmann, ed. *Mensch und Umwelt im Mittelalter*, 3rd edn (Stuttgart, 1987), pp. 109–28 [first published (Stuttgart, 1986)].

Keller, Hagen: 'Vom heiligen Buch zur "Buchführung"', in *Frühmitteltalerliche Studien* 26 (1992), pp. 1–31.

Keller, Hagen, and Klaus Grubmüller, ed.: *Pragmatische Schriftlichkeit im Mittelalter*, Münsterische Mittelalter-Schriften LXV (Munich, 1992).

Keller, Hagen, and Nikolaus Staubach, ed.: *Iconologia sacra. Bildkunst und Dichtung in der Religions- und Sozialgeschichte Alteuropas [Festschrift für Karl Hauck zum 75. Geburtstag]* (Berlin and New York, 1994).

Kellner, Beate: *Ursprung und Kontinuität. Studien zum genealogischen Wissen im Mittelalter* (Munich, 2004).

Kemp, Martin: 'From "Mimesis" to "Fantasia". The Quattrocento Vocabulary of Creation', in: *Viator* 8 (1977), pp. 347–98.

Kemp, Martin: 'Medieval Pictorial Systems', in Brendan Cassidy, ed., *Iconography at Crossroads. Papers from the Colloquium Sponsored by the Index of Christian Art, Princeton University, 23–24 March 1990* (Princeton, 1993), pp. 121–27.

Kempers, Bram: 'Ambrogio Lorenzettis Fresken im Palazzo Pubblico in Siena', in Hans Belting and Dieter Blume, ed., *Malerei und Stadtkultur in der Dantezeit. Die Argumentation der Bilder* (Munich, 1989), pp. 71–84.

Kennelly, Dolorosa: 'Medieval Towns and the Peace of God', in *Medievalia et Humanistica* NS 15 (1963), pp. 35–53.

Kennelly, Karen: 'Sobre la paz de Dios y la sagrera en el condado de Barcelona (1030–1130)', in *Anuario de estudios medievales* 5 (1968), pp. 107–36.

Kent, Bonnie: *The Virtues of Will. The Transformation of Ethics in the Late Thirteenth Century* (Washington, 1995).

Kieckhefer, Richard: *Magic in the Middle Ages* (Cambridge, 1989).

Kieckhefer, Richard: 'The Specific Rationality of Medieval Magic', in *American Historical Review* 99 (1994), pp. 813–36.

Kießling, Rolf: *Die Stadt und ihr Umland*, Städteforschung. Reihe A., vol. XXIX (Cologne and Vienna, 1989).

Kirstein, Anton: *Entwurf einer Ästhetik der Natur und Kunst* (Paderborn, 1896).

Kitzinger, Ernst: 'World Map and Fortune's Wheel', in *Proceedings of the American Philosophical Society* 117 (1973), pp. 343–73 [repr. in Kitzinger, *The Art of Byzantium and the Medieval West*, ed. W. Eugene Kleinbauer (Bloomington and London 1976), pp. 327–56].

Kivy, Peter: *The Seventh Sense. A Study of Francis Hutcheson's Aesthetics and Its Influence in Eighteenth-Century Britain* (New York, 1976).

Kleinschmidt, Harald: 'Wordhord onleac. Bemerkungen zur Geschichte der sprechsprachlichen Kommunikation im Mittelalter', in *Historisches Jahrbuch* 108 (1988), pp. 37–62.

Kleinschmidt, Harald: *Tyrocinium militare* (Stuttgart, 1989).

Kleinschmidt, Harald: 'Die Bedeutung der Historischen Verhaltensforschung für die Geschichte der Unterschichten im Mittelalter. Wege zur Geschichte der sprechsprachlichen Kommunikation', in *Mediaevalia historica Bohemica* 1 (1991), pp. 317–54.

Kleinschmidt, Harald:: 'Magie des Sprechens. Plädoyer für einen historischen Magiebegriff', in *Rekishi jinrui (History and Anthropology)* 24 (1996), pp. 3–26.

Kleinschmidt, Harald: 'Thinking as Action. Some Principal Changes in Medieval and Early Modern Europe', in *Ethnologia Europaea* 27 (1997), pp. 1–20.

Kleinschmidt, Harald: 'William Henry Stevenson and the Continental Diplomatics of His Time', in *Rekishi jinrui (History and Anthropology)* 26 (1998), pp. 3–39.

Kleinschmidt, Harald: 'The Fragmentation of the Integrated Process of Communicative Action. Notes on the Conceptual History of Communication in Medieval Europe', in *NOWELE [Northwest European Language Evolution]* 35 (1999), pp. 77–114.

Kleinschmidt, Harald: *Understanding the Middle Ages* (Woodbridge, 2000), pp. 214–39.

Klinck, Anne L.: 'Anglo-Saxon Women and the Law', in *Journal of Medieval History* 8 (1982), p. 109.

Knefelkamp, Ulrich: *Das Gesundheits- und Fürsorgewesen der Stadt Freiburg im Breisgau im Mittelalter*, Veröffentlichungen aus dem Archiv der Stadt Freiburg XVII (Freiburg, 1981).

Knichel, Martina: *Geschichte des Fernbesitzes der Abtei Prüm in den heutigen Niederlanden, in der Picardie, in Revin, Fumay und Pépin sowie in Awans und Loncin*, Quellen und Abhandlungen zur mittelrheinischen Kirchengeschichte LVI (Mainz, 1987).

Knight, William: *The Philosophy of the Beautiful. Being an Outline of the History of Aesthetics* (London, 1895), pp. 43–9 [on 'Mediaevalism'].

Kobialka, Michal: *This is My Body. Representational Practices in the Early Middle Ages* (Ann Arbor, 1999), pp. 35–99.

Kochendorffer, Karl: 'Zum mittelalterlichen Badewesen', in *Zeitschrift für deutsche Philologie* 24 (1892), pp. 492–502.

Körner, Theodor: *Iuramentum und frühe Friedensbewegung (10.–12. Jahrhundert)*, Münchener Universitätsschriften, Juristische Fakultät. Abhandlungen zur rechtswissenschaftlichen Grundlagenforschung XXVI (Berlin, 1977).

Körte, Konrad: 'Die Orgel von Winchester', in *Kirchenmusikalisches Jahrbuch* 57 (1973), pp. 1–24.

Kolmer, Lothar, and Christian Rohr, ed.: *Mahl und Repräsentation. Der Kult ums Essen*, 2nd edn (Paderborn, 2002) [first published (Paderborn, 2000)].

Kosto, Adam J.: *Making Agreements in Medieval Catalonia. Power, Order and the Written Word* (Cambridge, 2001).

Kralik, Dietrich von: 'Die deutschen Bestandteile der lex Baiuvariorum', in *Neues Archiv der Gesellschaft für ältere deutsche Geschichtskunde* 38 (1913), pp. 439–40.

Krieger, Josef: *Beiträge zur Geschichte der Volksseuchen und zur medicinischen Topographie von Strassburg*, Statistische Mitteilungen über Elsaß-Lothringen X (Strasbourg, 1879).

Kristeller, Paul Oskar: 'The Modern System of the Arts', in *Journal of the History of Ideas* 12 (1951), pp. 496–527, 13 (1952), pp. 17–46.

Kristeller, Paul Oskar: 'The Dignity of Man', in Kristeller, *Renaissance Concepts of Man, and Other Essays* (New York, 1972), pp. 66–79.

Kristeller, Paul Oskar: *Humanismus und Renaissance*, 2 vols, ed. Eckard Kesler (Munich, 1974–76).

Kruger, Steven F.: *Dreaming in the Middle Ages* (Cambridge, 1992).

Kuchenbuch, Ludolf: *Bäuerliche Gesellschaft und Klosterherrschaft im 9. Jahrhundert. Studien zur Sozialstruktur der Familia der Abtei Prüm*, Vierteljahrschrift für Sozial- und Wirtschaftsgeschichte, Beihefte LXVI (Wiesbaden, 1978).

Kuchenbuch, Ludolf: 'Die Klostergrundherrschaft im Mittelalter', in Friedrich Prinz, ed., *Herrschaft und Kirche* (Stuttgart, 1988), pp. 297–343.

Kuchenbuch, Ludolf: *Grundherrschaft im früheren Mittelalter* (Idstein, 1991).

Kuchenbuch, Ludolf: '*bene laborare*. Zur Sinnordnung der Arbeit, ausgehend vom *Capitulare de villis*', in Bea Lundt and Helma Reimöller, ed., *Von Aufbruch und Utopie. Perspektiven einer neuen Gesellschaftsgeschichte des Mittelalters. Für und mit Ferdinand Seibt* (Cologne, 1992), pp. 337–52.

Kuchenbuch, Ludolf: 'Teilen, Aufzählen, Summieren. Zum Verfahren in ausgewählten Güter- und Einkünfteverzeichnissen des 9. Jahrhunderts', in Ursula Schaefer, ed., *Schriftlichkeit im frühen Mittelalter*, ScripOralia LII (Tübingen, 1993), pp. 178–206.

Kuchenbuch, Ludolf: 'Die Achtung vor dem alten Buch und die Furcht vor dem neuen. Cesarius von Milendonk erstellt 1222 eine Abschrift des Prümer Urbars von 893', in *Historische Anthropologie* 3 (1995), pp. 175–202.

Kuchenbuch, Ludolf: 'Potestas und Utilitas. Ein Versuch über Stand und Perspektiven der Forschung zur Grundherrschaft im 9.–13. Jahrhundert', in *Historische Zeitschrift* 265 (1997), pp. 117–46.

Kuchenbuch, Ludolf: 'Sind mediävistische Quellen mittelalterliche Texte?', in Hans-Werner Goetz, ed., *Die Aktualität des Mittelalters* (Bochum, 2000), pp. 348–52.

Kühnel, Harry: 'Das Alltagsleben im Hause der spätmittelalterlichen Stadt', in Alfred Haverkamp, ed., *Haus und Familie in der spätmittelalterlichen Stadt*, Städteforschung, Reihe A, vol. XVIII (Cologne and Vienna, 1984), pp. 37–65.

Kühnemann, Eugen: *Kants und Schillers Begründung der Ästhetik* (Munich, 1895).

Kümmel, Werner Friedrich: *Musik und Medizin. Ihre Wechselbeziehungen in Theorie und Praxis von 800 bis 1800*, Freiburger Beiträge zur Wissenschafts- und Universitätsgeschichte II (Freiburg and Munich, 1977).

Kuhn, Rudolf: 'Lionardos Lehre über die Grenzen der Malerei gegen andere Künste und Wissenschaften', in *Zeitschrift für Ästhetik und Allgemeine Kunstwissenschaft* 33 (1988), pp. 215–46.

Kuhn, Rudolf: 'Cennino Cennini. Sein Verständnis dessen, was die Kunst in der Malerei sei, und seine Lehre vom Entwurfs- und Werkprozess', in *Zeitschrift für Ästhetik und Allgemeine Kunstwissenschaft* 36 (1991), pp. 104–53.

Kuhnert, Reinhold P.: *Urbanität auf dem Lande. Badereisen nach Pyrmont im 18. Jahrhundert*, Veröffentlichungen des Max-Planck-Instituts für Geschichte LXXVII (Göttingen, 1984).

Kulenkampff, Jens: *Kants Logik des ästhetischen Urteils*, Philosophische Abhandlungen LXI (Frankfurt, 1978).

Kunow, Jürgen: *Negotiator et vectura. Händler und Transport im Freien Germanien*, Kleine Schriften des Vorgeschichtlichen Seminars Marburg VI (Marburg, 1980).

Kunow, Jürgen: 'Zum Handel mit römischen Importen in der Germania libera', in Klaus Düwel, Herbert Jankuhn, Harald Siems and Dieter Timpe, ed., *Untersuchungen zu Handel und Verkehr in vor- und frühgeschichtlicher Zeit in*

Mittel- und Nordeuropa, vol. 1, Abhandlungen der Akademie der Wissenschaften in Göttingen, Philol.-Hist. Kl. 3. F. CLXIII (Göttingen 1985), pp. 430–59.

Kupfer, Marcia: 'Medieval World Maps. Embedded Images, Interpretative Frames', in *Word and Image* 10 (1994), pp. 262–88.

Kurze, Dietrich: 'Krieg und Frieden im mittelalterlichen Denken', in Heinz Duchhardt, ed., *Zwischenstaatliche Friedenswahrung in Mittelalter und Früher Neuzeit*, Münsterische Hiostorische Forschungen I (Cologne and Vienna, 1991), pp. 1–44.

Kusche, Johann: 'Verfall und Wiederaufbau des deutschen Badewesens', Med.D. Diss. (Berlin, 1929).

Kyll, Nikolaus: *Tod, Grab, Begräbnisplatz, Totenfeier. Zur Geschichte ihres Brauchtums im Trierer Landes und in Luxemburg unter besonderer Berücksichtigung des Visitationshandbuchs des Regino von Prüm*, Rheinisches Archiv LXXXI (Bonn, 1972).

Lachaud, Frédérique: 'Dress and Social Status in England before the Sumptuary Laws', in Peter Coss and Maurice Keen, ed., *Heraldry, Pageantry and Social Display in Medieval England* (Woodbridge, 2002), pp. 105–23.

Ladner, Gerhart Burian: 'Der Bilderstreit und die Kunst-Lehren der byzantinischen und der abendländischen Theologie', in *Zeitschrift für Kirchengeschichte* 50 (1931), pp. 1–23.

Laird, Marc, and Hugh Palmer: *Formal Garden* (London, 1992).

Lang, Berel: 'Kant and the Subjective Objects of Taste', in *Journal of Aesthetics and Art Criticism* 25 (1966/67), pp. 247–53

Langini, Alex: *La procession dansante d'Echternach* (Echternach, 1977).

Lebecq, Stéphane: *Marchands et navigateurs frisons au haut Moyen Age*, vol. 1 (Lille, 1983).

Leclercq, Jean: *The Love of Learning and Desire for God. A Study of Monastic Culture*, trans. and 2nd edn (New York, 1974) [first published (Paris, 1957)].

Lecoq, Danielle: 'La "mappemonde" du *De arca noe mystica* de Hugues de Saint-Victor', in Monique Pelletier, ed., *Géographie du monde au Moyen Age et à la Renaissance* (Paris, 1989), pp. 9–31.

Lecouteux, Claude: *Les monstres dans la littérature allemande du moyen âge (1150–1350)*, 3 vols, Göppinger Arbeiten zur Germanistik CCCXXX (Göppingen, 1982).

Lecouteux, Claude: *Geschichte der Gespenster und Wiedergänger im Mittelalter* (Cologne and Vienna, 1987).

Lecouteux, Claude: *Witches, Werewolves and Fairies. Shapeshifters and Astral Doubles in the Middle Ages* (Rochester, VT, 2003) [first published (Paris, 1992)].

Le Goff, Jacques: 'Labor, Techniques, and Craftsmen in the Value Systems of the Early Middle Ages', in Le Goff, *Time, Work and Craftsmen in the Middle Ages* (Chicago, 1980), pp. 71–86 [first published (Paris, 1977)].

Le Goff, Jacques: 'Das Christentum und die Träume', in Le Goff, *Phantasie und Realität des Mittelalters* (Stuttgart, 1990), pp. 271–322 [first published in *I sogni nel medioevo* (Rome, 1983); repr. (Paris, 1985)].

Lehnert, Walter: 'Entsorgungsprobeme der Reichsstadt Nürnberg', in Jürgen Sydow, ed., *Städtische Versorgung und Entsorgung im Wandel*, Stadt in der Geschichte VIII (Sigmaringen, 1981), pp. 151–63.

Leinkauf, Thomas: 'Athanasius Kircher', in Helmut Holsten and Wilhelm Schmidt-Biggemann, ed., *Die Philosophie des 17. Jahrhunderts*, vol. 4 (Basle and Stuttgart, 2001), pp. 269–90.

Leisering, Walter, and Berent Schwineköper: 'Kölbigk', in *Handbuch der historischen Stätten Deutschlands*, vol. 11: *Provinz Sachsen Anhalt* (Stuttgart 1975), pp. 246–7.

Lenk, Hans, ed.: *Handlungstheorie interdiziplinär*, 4 vols in 6 parts (Munich, 1977–81).

Lentz, Matthias: 'Schmähbriefe und Schandbilder als Medien außergerichtlicher Konfliktbewältigung', in Hans Schlosser and Dietmar Willoweit, ed., *Neue Wege strafrechtsgeschichtlicher Forschung*, Konflikt, Verbrechen und Sanktion in der Gesellschaft Alteuropas. Symposien und Synthesen II (Cologne, 1999), pp. 55–81.

Lentz, Matthias: 'Defamatory Pictures and Letters in Late Medieval Germany. The Visualisation of Disorder and Infamy', in *Medieval History Journal* 3, no. 1 (2000), pp. 139–60.

Lentz, Matthias: 'Schmähbriefe und Schandbilder. Realität, Fiktionalität und Visualität spätmittelalterlicher Normenkonflikte', in Klaus Schreiner and Gabriela Signori, ed., *Bilder, Texte, Rituale*, Zeitschrift für Historische Forschung. Beiheft XXIV (Berlin, 2000), pp. 35–67.

Lersch, Bernhard Maximilian: *Geschichte der Balneologie, Hydroposie und Pegologie* (Würzburg, 1863).

Levi, Margaret: 'A Model, a Method and a Map. Rational Choice in Comparative and Historical Perspective', in Mark Irving Lichbach and Alan S. Zuckerman, ed., *Comparative Politics. Rationality, Culture and Structure* (Cambridge, 1997), pp. 19–41.

Lewin, Leif, and Evert Vedung, ed.: *Politics as Rational Action*, Theory and Decision Library XXIII (Dordrecht and Boston, 1980).

Lewis, Susan: 'Vision and Revision. On "Seeing" and "Not Seeing" God in the Dublin Apocalypse', in *Word and Image* 10 (1994), pp. 289–311.

Leyser, Karl: 'Early Medieval Warfare', in Janet Cooper, ed., *The Battle of Maldon* (London, 1993), pp. 87–108 [repr. in Leyser, *Communication and Power in Medieval Europe*, ed. Timothy Reuter (London and Rio Grande, 1994), pp. 29–50].

Liebsch, Dietmar: *Die Geburt der ästhetischen Bildung aus dem Körper der antiken Plastik*, Archiv für Begriffsgeschichte. Sonderheft 2001 (Hamburg, 2001).

Lindberg, David Charles: 'Lines of Influence in Thirteenth-Century Optics', in *Speculum* 46 (1971), pp. 66–83.

Lindberg, David Charles: *Theories of Vision from Al-Kindi to Kepler* (Chicago and London, 1976).

Lindberg, David Charles: *Studies in the History of Medieval Optics* (London, 1983).

Lindberg, David Charles, and Nicholas H. Steneck: 'The Sense of Vision and the Origins of Modern Science', in Allen George Debus, ed., *Science, Medicine and Society in the Renaissance. Essays to Honor Walter Pagel* (New York, 1972), pp. 29–45.

Lindquist, Sven-Olof, and Birgitta Radhe, ed.: *Society and Trade in the Baltic during the Viking Age*, Acta Visbyensia VII (Visby, 1985).

Löwenstein, Uta: 'Voraussetzungen und Grundlagen von Tafelzeremonien und Zeremonientafeln', in Jörg Jochen Berns and Thomas Rahn, ed., *Zeremoniell als höfische Ästhetik in Spätmittelalter und Früher Neuzeit* (Tübingen, 1995), pp. 266–79.

Lottin, Odon: 'Saint Albert le Grand et l'Ethique à Nicomaque', in Albert Lang, Josef Lechner and Michael Schmaus, ed., *Aus der Geisteswelt des Mittelalters. Studien und Texte. Martin Grabmann zur Vollendung des 60. Lebensjahres*, Beiträge zur Geschichte der Philosophie und Theologie des Mittelalters. Supplement bd III, no. 1 (Munster, 1935), pp. 611–26.

Lottin, Odon: *Psychologie et morale aux XIIe et XIIIe siècles*, 6 vols (Louvain and Gembloux, 1942–60).

Lotze, Hermann: *Geschichte der Aesthetik in Deutschland* (Munich, 1868).

Lucas, A. T.: 'Washing and Bathing in Ancient Ireland', in *Journal of the Royal Society of Antiquaries of Ireland* (1969), pp. 65–114.

[Lunges] Lounghis, Telemachos K.: *Les ambassades byzantines en Occident depuis la foundation des états barbares jusqu'aux Croisades* (Athens, 1980).

Lutterbach, Hubertus: 'Intentions- oder Tathaftung? Zum Bussverständnis in den frühmittelalterlichen Bussbüchern', in *Frühmittelalterliche Studien* 29 (1995), pp. 120–43.

McCarthy, Edward Randall: 'Medieval Light Theories and Optics and Duns Scotus' Treatment of Light in D. 13 of Book II of His Commentary on the Sentences', Ph.D. Diss., typescript (City University of New York, 1976).

McCartney, William: *Olfaction and Odours* (Berlin, Heidelberg and New York, 1968).

McCormick, Michael: *Eternal Victory. Triumphal Rulership* (Cambridge, 1985).

McCormick, Michael: 'Clovis at Tours, Byzantine Public Ritual and the Origins of Medieval Ruler Symbolism', in Evangelos Chrysos and Alexander Schwarcz, ed., *Das Reich und die Barbaren* (Vienna, 1989), pp. 155–80.

McCormick, Michael: 'Diplomacy and the Carolingian Encounter with Byzantium down to the Accession of Charles the Bald', in Bernhard McGinn and Willemien Otten, ed., *Eriugena, East and West*, Notre Dame Conferences in Medieval Studies V (Notre Dame 1994), pp. 15–48.

McGrade, Stephen A.: 'Seeing Things. Ockham and Representationalism', in Christian Wenin, ed., *L'homme et son universe au Moyen Age* (Louvain-la-Neuve, 1986), pp. 591–7.

McIntyre, Alasdair: *A Short History of Ethics* (London, 1990).

MacKinney, Loren: 'The People and Public Opinion in the Eleventh Century Peace Movement', in *Speculum* 5 (1930), pp. 181–206.

McKinnon, James William: 'The Tenth-Century Organ at Winchester', in *Organ Yearbook* 5 (1974), pp. 4–19.

McKitterick, Rosamond: *The Carolingians and the Written Word* (Cambridge, 1989).

McKitterick, Rosamond, ed.: *The Uses of Literacy in Early Medieval Europe* (Cambridge, 1989).

McKitterick, Rosamond: 'Text and Image in the Carolingian World', in McKitterick, ed., *The Uses of Literacy in Early Medieval Europe* (Cambridge, 1989), pp. 297–318.

McLaughlin, Mary: 'Abelard as Autobiographer. The Motives and Meaning of His "Story of Calamities"', in *Speculum* 42 (1967), pp. 463–88.

MacManmon, John: 'Francis Hutcheson's *Inquiry* and the Controversy over the Basis of Morality. 1700–1750', in *Eighteenth-Century Life* 5 (1979), pp. 1–13.

McVaugh, Michael R.: *Renaissance Medical Learning*, ed. Nancy G. Siraisi, Osiris VI (Philadelphia, 1990).

McVaugh, Michael R: 'Smells and the Medieval Surgeon', in *Micrologus* 10 (2002), pp. 113–32.

Magnou-Nortier, Elisabeth: 'Les évêques et la paix dans l'espace Franc (VIe–XIe siècles)', in *L'évêque dans l'histoire de l'église* (Angers, 1984), pp. 33–50.

Mann, Hans-Dieter: *Lucien Fèbvre. La pensée vivante d'un historien* (Paris, 1971).

Marcuse, Julian: *Bäder und Badewesen in Vergangenheit und Gegenwart* (Stuttgart, 1903).

Marenbon, John: *Early Medieval Philosophy*, 2nd edn (London, 1988) [first published (London, 1983)].

Marenbon, John: *The Philosophy of Peter Abelard* (Cambridge, 1997).

Martin, Alfred: *Deutsches Badewesen in vergangenen Tagen* (Jena, 1906).

Martin, Alfred: 'Geschichte der Tanzkrankheit in Deutschland', in *Zeitschrift des Vereins für Volkskunde* 24 (1914), pp. 238–9.

Martin, Alfred: 'Bad', in *Handwörterbuch des deutschen Aberglaubens*, vol. 1 (Berlin, 1927–28), pp. 796–850.

Martin, Alfred: 'Ins Bad schlagen, rufen, blasen', in *Zeitschrift für Volkskunde* 3 (1931), pp. 59–60.

Martino, Ernesto de: *La terra del rimorso. Contributo a una storia religiosa del Sud*, La cultura XLII (Milan, 1961).

Marx, Susanne: 'Studien zur Tierornamentik insularer Handschriften'. Ph.D. Diss., typescript (University of Munich 1995).

Marx, Susanne: 'Studies in Insular Animal Ornament in late 7th and 7th Century Manuscripts', in Cormac Bourke, ed., *From the Isles to the North. Early Medieval Art in Ireland and Britain* (Belfast, 1995), pp. 105–10.

Marx, Susanne: 'The Miserable Beasts. Animal Art in the Gospels of Lindisfarne, Lichfield and St. Gallen', in *Journal of the Medieval Academy of Ireland* 9 (1995), pp. 234–44.

Mattenklott, Gert: 'Mund', in Christoph Wulf, ed., *Vom Menschen. Handbuch Historische Anthropologie* (Weinheim and Basle, 1997), pp. 471–8.

Mattenklott, Gert: 'Nase', in Christoph Wulf, ed., *Vom Menschen. Handbuch Historische Anthropologie* (Weinheim and Basle, 1997), pp. 464–70.

Mattl, Siegfried: 'Sichtbares und Unsichtbares. Konzepte zum Sehsinn', in Elisabeth Vavra, ed., *Bild und Abbild vom Menschen im Mittelalter*, Schriften der Akademie Friesach VI (Klagenfurt, 1999), pp. 31–45.

Maurer, Michael: 'Der Prozeß der Zivilisation. Bemerkungen eines Historikers zur Kritik des Ethnologen Hans Peter Duerr an der Theorie des Soziologen Norbert Elias', in *Geschichte in Wissenschaft und Unterricht* 40 (1989), pp. 225–38.

Maurer, Michael, ed.: *Das Fest* (Cologne, Weimar and Vienna, 2004).

Mausbach, Joseph: *Die Ethik des heiligen Augustinus* (Freiburg, 1909).

Mazzini, Guido: 'Una leggenda germanica ed un episodio dantesco', in *Studi medievali* NS 1 (1928), pp. 181–5.

Mead, William Edward: *The English Medieval Feast* (London, 1931) [repr. (London, 1967)].

Medicus, Fritz: 'Über den Begriff der Ästhetik', in Medicus, *Grundfragen der Ästhetik* (Jena, 1917), pp. 87–121.

Medieval Gardens, Dumbarton Oaks Research Library and Collection (Washington, DC, 1986).

Meier, Christel, and Uwe Ruberg, ed.: *Text und Bild* (Wiesbaden, 1980).

Meier, Hans Georg: 'Leibniz und Baumgarten als Begründer der deutschen Ästhetik', Ph.D. Diss. (University of Halle, 1875).

Meier, John: 'Das Tanzlied der Tänzer von Kölbigk', in *Schweizerisches Archiv für Volkskunde*: 33 (1934), pp. 152–65.

Meier, Ulrich: 'The Iconography of Justice and Power in the Sculptures and Paintings of Town Halls in Medieval Germany', in *Medieval History Journal* 3, no 1 (2000), pp. 161–74.

Meisen, Karl: 'Springprozessionen und Schutzheilige gegen den Veitstanz und ähnliche Krankheiten im Rheinlande und in seinen Nachbargebieten', in *Rheinisches Jahrbuch für Volkskunde*: 2 (1951), pp. 164–78.

Melville, Gert, and Karl-Siegbert Rehberg, ed.: *Gründungsmythen – Genealogien – Memorialzeichen. Beiträge zur institutionellen Konstruktion von Kontinuität* (Cologne, Weimar and Vienna, 2004).

Menuge, Noël James, ed.: *Medieval Law and Women* (Manchester, New York, 2003).

Menzel, Viktor: *Deutsches Gesandtschaftswesen im Mittelalter* (Hanover, 1892).

Mercati e mercanti nell' alto medioevo, Settimane di studio del Centro Italiano di Studi sull' Alto Medioevo XL (Spoleto, 1993).

Metzner, Ernst-Erich: *Zur frühesten Geschichte der europäischen Balladendichtung. Der Tanz von Kölbigk*, Frankfurter Beiträge zur Germanistik XIV (Frankfurt, 1972).

Meyvaert, Paul: 'The Authorship of the "Libri Carolini"', in *Revue bénédictine* 89 (1979), pp. 29–57.

Michael, Emily: 'Francis Hutcheson on Aesthetic Perception and Aesthetic Pleasure', in *British Journal of Aesthetics* 24 (1984), pp. 241–55.

Miles, Margaret: 'Vision. The Eye of the Body and the Eye of the Mind in Saint Augustine's *De trinitate* and *Confessions*', in *Journal of Religion* 63 (1983), pp. 125–42.

Miller, William Ian: 'Dreams, Prophecy and Sorcery. Blaming the Secret Offender in Medieval Iceland', in *Scandinavian Studies* 58 (1986), pp. 101–23.

Mitterauer, Michael: *Ahnen und Heilige* (Munich, 1993).

Möbius, Friedrich, and Helga Scurie: *Symbolwerte mittelalterlicher Kunst* (Leipzig, 1984).

Monjot, Denis, ed.: *Manger et boire au Moyen Age*, Publications de la Faculté des Lettres et Sciences Humaines de Nice XXVIII (Nice, 1984).

Morimoto, Yoshiki: 'Autour du polyptyque de Saint-Bertin (844–859)', in Adriaan Verhulst, ed., *Le grand domaine aux époques merovingienne et carolingienne*, Publications du Centre belge d'histoire rurale LXXXI (Gent, 1985), pp. 125–51.

Morimoto, Yoshiki: 'Le polyptyque de Prüm, n'a-t-il pas été interpolé?', in *Le Moyen Age* 92 (1986), pp. 265–76.

Morimoto, Yoshiki: 'Etat et perspectives des recherches sur les polyptyques carolingiens', in *Annales de l'Est* 40 (1988), pp. 99–149.

Morimoto, Yoshiki: 'Considérations nouvelles sur les "villes et campagnes" dans le domaine de Prüm au haut Moyen Age', in Jean-Marie Duvosquel and Alain Dierkens, ed., *Villes et campagnes au Moyen Age. Melanges Georges Despy* (Liège, 1991), pp. 515–31.

Morimoto, Yoshiki: 'Die Bedeutung des Prümer Urbars für die heutige Forschung', in Reiner Nolden, ed., *'anno verbi incarnati DCCCXCIII conscriptum'. Im Jahre des Herrn 893 geschrieben. 1100 Jahre Prümer Urbar* (Trier, 1993), pp. 127–36.

Morimoto, Yoshiki: 'Autour du grand domaine carolingien. Aperçu critique des recherches récentes sur l'histoire rurale du haut Moyen Age', in Morimoto and Adriaan Verhulst, ed., *Economie rurale et économie urbaine au Moyen Age* (Gent and Fukuoka, 1994), pp. 25–79.

Morimoto, Yoshiki: 'L'assolement triennal au haut Moyen Age. Une analyse des données des polyptyques carolingiens', in Morimoto and Adriaan Verhulst, ed., *Economie rurale et économie urbaine au Moyen Age* (Gent and Fukuoka, 1994), pp. 91–125.

Morimoto, Yoshiki: ' "In ebdomada operatur quicquit precipitur ei" (Le Polyptyque de Prüm X). Service arbitraire ou service hebdomadaire?', in Jean Marie Duvosquel and Alain Dierkens, ed., *Peasants and Townsmen in Medieval Europe. Studia in honorem Adriaan Verhulst* (Brussels, 1995), pp. 347–62.

Morimoto, Yoshiki: 'Aspects of the Early Medieval Peasant Economy as Revealed in the Polyptych of Prüm', in Peter Linehan and Janet Laughland Nelson, ed., *The Medieval World* (London, New York, 2001), pp. 605–19.

Moulin, Léo: *Les liturgies de la table* (Antwerp, 1988) [new edn (Paris, 1989)].

Müller, Heribert: *Heribert, Kanzler Ottos III. und Erzbischof von Köln*, Veröffentlichungen des Kölnischen Geschichtsvereins XXXIII (Cologne, 1977), pp. 210–3.

Müller, Heribert: 'Heribert, Erzbischof von Köln', in *Lexikon für Theologie und Kirche*, 3rd edn, vol. 4 (Freiburg, Basle, Rome and Vienna, 1995), cols 1438–9.

Müller, Heribert: 'Heribert, Kanzler Ottos III. und Erzbischof von Köln', in *Rheinische Vierteljahrsblätter*, 60 (1996), pp. 46–71.

Müller, Mechthild: *Die Kleidung nach Quellen des frühen Mittelalters*, Ergänzungsbände zum Reallexikon der Germanischen Altertumskunde XXXI (Berlin and New York, 2002).

Müller, Walter: *Das Problem der Seelenschönheit im Mittelalter* (Bern, 1923).

Muir, Edward: *Civic Ritual in Renaissance Florence* (Princeton, 1980).

Munnynck, Marc de: 'L'esthétique de St. Thomas d'Aquin', in *San Tommaso d'Aquino* (Milan, 1923), pp. 217–39.

Murray, James M.: 'The Liturgy of the Count's Advent in Bruges, from Galbert to Van Eyck', in Barbara A. Hanawalt and Kathryn Louise Reyerson, ed., *City and Spectacle in Medieval Europe* (Minneapolis and London, 1994), pp. 137–52.

Naunyn, Bernhard: 'Anschauungen der modernen Wissenschaft über die sogenannte Nervosität', in Naunyn, *Gesammelte Abhandlungen 1862–1908*, vol. 2 (Würzburg, 1909), pp. 1243–58.

Neeracker, Otto: 'Bader und Badewesen in der Stadt Basel und die von Baslern besuchten Badeorte', Ph.D. Diss. (Basle, 1933).

Nelson, Robert S., ed.: *Visuality before and beyond the Renaissance. Seeing as Others Saw* (Cambridge, 2000).

Nie, Giselle de: *Word, Image and Experience. Dynamics of Miracle and Self-Perception in Sixth-Century Gaul* (Aldershot, 2003).

Nitschke, August: *Kunst und Verhalten* (Stuttgart, 1975).

Nitschke, August: *Historische Verhaltensforschung* (Stuttgart, 1981).

Nitschke, August: 'Vom Wandel des Wirkens. Erläutert an der Tatbestandsaufnahme im Prozeßverfahren am Anfang des 16. Jahrhunderts', in Hans Süssmuth, ed., *Historische Anthropologie* (Göttingen, 1984), pp. 124–40.

Nitschke, August: *Körper in Bewegung* (Stuttgart, 1989).

Nitschke, August: 'Erde – Pflanzen – Tiere. Wie Bauern im Frühen und Hohen Mittelalter die Welt wahrnahmen', in Ernst Schubert and Bernd Herrmann, ed., *Von der Angst zur Ausbeutung. Umwelterfahrung zwischen Mittelalter und Neuzeit* (Frankfurt, 1994), pp. 93–106.

Nivelle, Armand: *Les théories esthétiques en Allemagne de Baumgarten à Kant* (Paris, 1955).

Noble, Thomas F. X.: 'Tradition and Learning in Search of Ideology. The *Libri Carolini*', in Richard Eugene Sullivan, ed., *'The Gentle Voices of Teachers'. Aspects of Learning in the Carolingian Age* (Columbus, OH, 1995), pp. 227–60.

Oberste, Jörg: 'Kölbigk', in *Lexikon für Theologie und Kirche*, 3rd edn, vol. 6 (Freiburg, Basle, Rome and Vienna, 1997), col. 175.

Oexle, Otto Gerhard: 'Memoria und Memorialüberlieferung im früheren Mittelalter', in *Frühmittelalterliche Studien* 10 (1976), pp. 70–95.

Oexle, Otto Gerhard: 'Die Gegenwart der Toten', in Herman Braet and Werner Verbeke, ed., *Death in the Middle Ages* (Louvain, 1983), pp. 19–77.

Oexle, Otto Gerhard: 'Mahl und Spende im mittelalterlichen Totenkult', in *Frühmittelalterliche Studien* 18 (1984), pp. 401–20.

Oexle, Otto Gerhard: 'Conjuratio und Gilde im früheren Mittelalter', in Berent

Schwineköper, ed., *Gilden und Zünfte*, Vorträge und Forschungen, hrsg. vom Konstanzer Arbeitskreis für mittelalterliche Geschichte XXIX (Sigmaringen, 1985), pp. 151–213.

Oexle, Otto Gerhard: 'Armut, Armutsbegriff und Armenfürsorge im Mittelalter', in Christian Sachsse and Florian Tennstedt, ed., *Soziale Sicherung und soziale Disziplinierung* (Frankfurt, 1986), pp. 73–100.

Oexle, Otto Gerhard: 'Memoria in der Gesellschaft und in der Kultur des Mittelalters', in Joachim Heinzle, ed., *Modernes Mittelalter* (Frankfurt and Leipzig, 1999), pp. 297–323 [first published (Leipzig, 1994)].

Oexle, Otto Gerhard, ed.: *Memoria als Kultur*, Veröffentlichungen des Max-Planck-Instituts für Geschichte CXXII (Göttingen, 1995).

Oexle, Otto Gerhard, ed.: *Der Blick auf die Bilder. Kunstgeschichte und Geschichte im Gespräch* (Göttingen, 1997).

Oexle, Otto Gerhard, and Dieter Geuenich, ed.: *Memoria in der Gesellschaft des Mittelalters*, Veröffentlichungen des Max-Planck-Instituts für Geschichte CXI (Göttingen, 1994).

O'Keeffe, Katherine O'Brien: *Visible Song* (Cambridge, 1990).

Ong, Walter Jackson: *Ramus. Method and the Decay of the Dialogue* (Cambridge, MA, 1948) [new edn (Cambridge, MA, and London, 1983)].

Opitz, Claudia, ed.: *Höfische Gesellschaft und Zivilisationsprozess. Norbert Elias' Werk in kulturwissenschaftlicher Perspektive* (Cologne, Weimar and Vienna, 2004).

Ortalli, Gherardo: '. . . pingatur in Palatino'. *La pittura infamante nei secoli XIII–XVI* (Rome, 1979).

Osthoff, Wolfgang: *Theatergesang und darstellende Musik in der italienischen Renaissance*, vol. 1, Münchner Veröffentlichungen zur Musikgeschichte XIV (Tutzing, 1969), pp. 124–69.

Ott, Norbert H.: 'Zum Ausstattungsanspruch illustrierter Städtechroniken. Sigismund Meisterlin und die Schweizer Chronistik als Beispiele', in Stephan Füssel and Joachim Knape, ed., *Poesis et pictura. Festschrift für Dieter Wuttke* (Baden-Baden, 1989), pp. 77–106.

Padberg, Britta: *Die Oase aus Stein. Humanökologische Aspekte des Lebens in mittelalterlichen Städten* (Berlin, 1994).

Paetzold, Hans: *Ästhetik des deutschen Idealismus. Zur Idee ästhetischer Rationalität bei Baumgarten, Kant, Schelling, Hegel und Schopenhauer* (Wiesbaden, 1983), pp. 8–54.

Paissac, Henry: *Théologie du verbe* (Paris, 1951).

Palliser, David Michael, ed.: *The Cambridge Urban History of Britain* (Cambridge, 2000).

Panofsky, Erwin: 'Die Perspektive als "symbolische Form" ', in *Vorträge der Bibliothek Warburg* 4 (Leipzig 1927), pp. 258–331.

Panofsky, Erwin: *Albrecht Dürer*, vol. 1 (Princeton, 1945), pp. 242–73.

Pantaleon, Heinrich: *Warhafftige und fleissige Beschreibung der uralten Stadt und Graueschaft Baden sampt ihren heulsamen warmen Wildbedern so in der hochloblichen Eydgnotschafft inn dem Ergöw gelegen* (Basle, 1578).

Paris, Gaston: *Les origines de la poésie lyrique en France* (Paris, 1892).

Paris, Gaston: 'Les danseurs maudits. Légende allemande du XIe siècle', in *Journal des savants* 64 (1899), pp. 733–47.

Parry, John William: *Spices* (New York, 1969).

Pausch, Holger A.: 'Dialektik des Sehens. Beobachtungen zur Genealogie des Gesichts in der Literatur', in Gerd Labroisse and Dirk van Stekelenburg, ed., *Das Sprach-Bild als textuelle Interaktion* (Amsterdam and Atlanta, 1999), pp. 15–44.

Payer, Pierre J.: *The Bridling of Desire. Views of Sex in the Later Middle Ages* (Toronto, 1993).

Pelikan, Jaroslav: *Imago Dei. The Byzantine Apologia for Icons* (New Haven and London, 1990).

Peres, Constanze: 'Cognitiva sensitiva. Zum Verhältnis von Empfindung und Reflexion in A. G. Baumgartens Begründung der Ästhetiktheorie', in Hans Körner et al., ed., *Empfindung und Reflexion*, Münchener Beiträge zur Geschichte und Theorie der Künste I (Hildesheim, 1986), pp. 5–48.

Perler, Dominik, ed.: *Ancient and Medieval Theories of Intentionality*, Studien und Texte zur Geistesgeschichte des Mittelalters LXXVI (Leiden, Boston and Cologne, 2001).

Perler, Dominik: *Theorien der Intentionalität im Mittelalter*, Philosophische Abhandlungen. LXXXII (Frankfurt, 2002).

Perpeet, Wilhelm: *Ästhetik des Mittelalters* (Freiburg, 1973).

Peters, Hans Georg: *Die Ästhetik Baumgartens und ihre Beziehung zum Ethischen*, Neue deutsche Forschungen. Abteilung Philosophie I (Berlin, 1934).

Peters, Jan: *Mit Pflug und Gänsekiel. Selbstzeugnisse schreibender Bauern* (Cologne, Weimar and Vienna, 2003).

Petry, Klaus 'Die Geldzinse im Prümer Urbar von 893', in *Rheinische Vierteljahrsblätter* 52 (1988), pp. 16–42.

Piponnier, Françoise, and Perrine Mane: *Dress in the Middle Ages* (New Haven and London, 1997) [first published (Paris, 1995)].

Pochat, Götz: *Der Symbolbegriff in der Ästhetik und Kunstwissenschaft* (Cologne, 1983).

Pochat, Götz: *Geschichte der Ästhetik und Kunsttheorie* (Cologne, 1987).

Pochat, Götz: *Bild-Zeit. Zeitgestalt und Erzählstruktur in der bildenden Kunst von den Anfängen bis zur frühen Neuzeit*, 2 vols (Vienna, 1996–2004).

Polet, Caroline, and Rosine Orban, ed.: *Dents et les ossements humains. Que mangeait-on au Moyen Age*, Typologie des sources du Moyen Age occidental LXXXIV (Turnhout, 2001).

Poovey, Mary: *A History of the Modern Fact. Problems of Knowledge in the Sciences of Wealth and Society* (Chicago and London, 1998).

Poppe, Bernhard: *Alexander Gottlieb Baumgarten. Seine Bedeutung und Stellung in der Leibniz-Wolffschen Philosophie und seine Beziehung zu Kant. Nebst einer bisher unbekannten Handschrift der Ästhetik Baumgartens* (Borna, Leipzig, 1907).

Porro, Pasquale: 'Forme e modelli di durata nel pensiero medievale. L'aevum, il tempo discreto, la categoria "quando"', *Ancient and Medieval Philosophy*, Ser. I, vol. 16 (Leuven, 1996).

Posner, Hans, ed.: *Philosophische Probleme des Handelns* (Freiburg, 1982).

Powers, James F.: 'Frontier Municipal Baths and Social Interaction in Thirteenth-Century Spain', in *American Historical Review* 84 (1979), pp. 649–67.

Prescott, Andrew: *The Benedictional of Aethelwold* (London, 1993).

Prescott, Andrew: 'The Text of the Benedictional of St. Aethelwold', in Barbara Yorke, ed., *Bishop Aethelwold* (Woodbridge, 1997), pp. 119–47.

Prevenier, Walter: 'Henri Pirenne et les villes des anciens Pays-Bas au Moyen Age', in Adriaan Verhulst, ed., *La fortune historiographique des theses d'Henri Pirenne. Actes du Colloque 1985*, Archives et Bibliothèques de Belgique XXVII (numéro spécial) (Brussels, 1986), pp. 27–50.

Prizer, William Flaville, II: 'The Frottola and the Unwritten Tradition', in *Studi musicali* 15 (1986), pp. 3–37.

Procaccini, Alfonso: 'Alberti and the "Forming" of Perspective', in *Journal of Aesthetics and Art Criticism* 40 (1981), pp. 29–39.

Prosser, Michael: 'Gesellige Körperpflege als Aspekt der Alltagskultur im spätmittelalterlichen Regensburg. Zugleich ein Beitrag zur Geschichte der Badestuben', in Martin Angerer, Heinrich Wanderwitz and Eugen Trapp, ed., *Regensburg im Mittelalter* (Regensburg, 1995), pp. 293–300.

Quarré, Pierre: 'La "Joyeuse Entrée" de Charles le Téméraire à Dijon en 1474', in *Bulletin de la Classe des Beaux-Arts. Académie Royale de Belgique* 51 (1969), pp. 326–45.

Queller, Donald Edward: *The Office of the Ambassador in the Middle Ages* (Princeton, 1967).

Rabb, Theodore Kwasnik: 'Resolution in Aesthetics', in Rabb, *The Struggle for Stability in Early Modern Europe* (New York, 1975), pp. 100–15.

Radding, Charles: 'The Evolution of Medieval Mentalities', in *American Historical Review* 83 (1978), pp. 577–97.

Rädle, Fidel: 'Das "Tanzlied von Kölbigk' und die Legende vom "Kölbigker Tanz"', in *Die deutsche Literatur des Mittelalters. Verfasserlexikon*, 2nd edn by Kurt Ruh, vol. 8 (Berlin and New York, 1992), cols 616–20.

Raith, Wolfgang: *Die Macht des Bildes. Ein humanistisches Problem bei Gianfrancesco Pico della Mirandola* (Munich, 1967).

Ramseger, Ingeborg: 'Die Städtebilder der Schedelschen Weltchronik', Ph.D. Diss., typescript (University of Berlin, 1943).

Raphael, Lutz: *Die Erben von Bloch and Fèbvre. Annales-Geschichtsschreibung und 'nouvelle histoire' in Frankreich. 1945–1980* (Stuttgart, 1994).

Rapp, Anna: 'Der Jungbrunnen in Literatur und bildender Kunst des Mittelalters', Ph.D. Diss., typescript (University of Zurich, 1976).

Raudszus, Gabriele: *Die Zeichensprache der Kleidung. Untersuchungen zur Symbolik des Gewandes in der deutschen Epik des Mittelalters* (Hildesheim and New York, 1985).

Raulff, Ulrich: 'Chemie des Ekels und des Genusses', in Dietmar Kamper and Christoph Wulf, ed., *Die Wiederkehr des Körpers* (Frankfurt, 1982), pp. 241–58.

Raulff, Ulrich: 'Der streitbare Prälat. Lucien Fèbvre (1878–1956)', in Raulff, ed., *Lucien Fèbvre, Das Gewissen des Historikers* (Berlin, 1988), pp. 235–53.

Raynaud, Christiane: *Images et pouvoirs* (Paris, 1993).

Rebel, Ernst: *Faksimile und Mimesis* (Munich, 1981).

Recki, Birgit: 'Ästhetik', in Werner Schneiders, ed., *Lexikon der Aufklärung* (Munich, 2001), pp. 29–31.

Reckow, Fritz: 'Organum-Begriff und frühe Mehrstimmigkeit', in *Forum musicologicum* 1 (1975), pp. 31–167.

Reichard, Gladys Armanda, Roman Jakobson and Elisabeth Werth: 'Language and Synesthesia', in *Word* 5 (1949), pp. 224–33.

Reichart, Andrea: *Alltagsleben im späten Mittelalter. Der Übergang zur frühen Neuzeit am Beispiel der Stadt Essen (1400–1700)*, Essener kulturhistorische Studien I (Essen, 1996).

Reichert, Folker E.: 'Von Mekka nach Malakka? Ludovico de Varthema und sein *Itinerar* (Rom 1510)', in Xenja von Ertzdorff and Rudolf Schulz, ed., *Beschreibung der Welt. Zur Poetik der Reise- und Länderberichte*, Chloë XXXI (Amsterdam and Atlanta, 2000), pp. 273–97.

Reiners, Adam: 'Die Springprozession zu Echternach', in *Frankfurter zeitgemäße Broschüren* V, 8 (1884), pp. 240–67.

Reith, Reinhold: 'Badstuben', in *Wilhelm Liebhart and Josef Mancal*, ed., *Augsburger Stadtlexikon* (Augsburg, 1985), p. 30.

Rentschler, Michael: *Liutprand von Cremona*, Frankfurter Wissenschaftliche Beiträge. Kulturwissenschaftliche Reihe XIV (Frankfurt, 1981), pp. 36–40.

Renz, Oskar: *Die Synteresis nach dem hl. Thomas von Aquin*, Beiträge zur Geschichte der Philosophie des Mittelalters X, nos 1–2 (Munster, 1911).

Reuter, Hermann: *Geschichte der religiösen Aufklärung im Mittelalter vom Ende des 8. Jahrhunderts bis zum Anfange des 14. Jahrhunderts*, vol. 1 (Berlin, 1875), pp. 183–259.

Reveney, Denis: *Language, Self and Love. Hermeneutics in the Writings of Richard Rolle and the Commentaries on the Song of Songs* (Aberystwyth, 2001).

Richter, Michael: *The Oral Tradition in the Early Middle Ages*, Typologie des sources du Moyen Age occidental LXXI (Turnhout, 1994).

Richter, Michael: 'Die "Entdeckung" der Oralität der mittelalterlichen Gesellschaft durch die neuere Mediävistik', in Hans-Werner Goetz, ed., *Die Aktualität des Mittelalters* (Bochum, 2000), pp. 273–85.

Ricklin, Thomas: *Der Traum der Philosophie im 12. Jahrhundert. Traumtheorien zwischen Constantinus Africanus und Aristoteles*, Mittellateinische Sudien und Texte XXIV (Leiden, 1998).

Rimmel, Eugene: *The Book of Parfumes* (Philadelphia, 1867) [French version (Brussels, 1870); German version (Dreieich, 1985)].

Ringbom, S.: 'Devotional Images and Imaginative Devotion', in *Gazette des Beaux-Arts* 73 (1969), pp. 159–70.

Ritter, Joachim: 'Ästhetik, ästhetisch', in Ritter, ed. *Historisches Wörterbuch der Philosophie*, 2nd edn, vol. 1 (Stuttgart and Basle, 1972), pp. 555–80.

Ritter, Joachim, and Reinhard Romberg: 'Ethik', in Ritter, ed., *Historisches Wörterbuch der Philosophie*, 2nd edn, vol. 2 (Stuttgart and Basle, 1972), pp. 759–810.

Roche, Daniel: *The Culture of Clothing. Dress and Fashion in the Ancien Régime* (Cambridge, 1994) [first published (Paris, 1989)].

Röcke, Werner, and Ursula Schaefer, ed.: *Mündlichkeit – Schriftlichkeit – Weltbildwandel*, ScriptOralia LXXI(Tübingen, 1996).

Röckelein, Hedwig: 'Miracle Collections of Carolingian Saxony', in *Hagiographica* 3 (1996), pp. 267–75.

Roesdahl, Else, ed.: *Wikinger, Waräger, Normannen* (Mainz, 1992).

Roesdahl, Else: 'Dendrochronology and Viking Studies in Denmark. With a Note on the Beginning of the Viking Age', in Björn Ambrosiani and Helen Clarke, ed., *Developments around the North Sea in the Viking Age*, Viking Congress XII = Birka Studies III (Stockholm, 1994), pp. 106–16.

Rösener, Werner, ed.: *Strukturen der Grundherrschaft im frühen Mittelalter*, Veröffentlichungen des Max-Planck-Instituts für Geschichte XCII (Göttingen, 1989) [2nd edn (Göttingen, 1993)].

Rösener, Werner, ed.: *Grundherrschaft im Wandel*, Veröffentlichungen des Max-Planck-Instituts für Geschichte CII (Göttingen, 1991).

Rösener, Werner, ed.: *Grundherrschaft und bäuerliche Gesellschaft im Hochmittelalter*, Veröffentlichungen des Max-Planck-Instituts für Geschichte CXV (Göttingen, 1995).

Rogers, Reginald Arthur Percy: *A Short History of Ethics. Greek and Modern* (London, 1911).

Rogerson, Kenneth F.: 'The Meaning of Universal Validity in Kant's Aesthetics', in *Journal of Aesthetics and Art Criticism* 41 (1982), pp. 301–8.

Rohls, Jan: *Geschichte der Ethik*, 2nd edn (Tübingen, 1999) [first published (1991)].

Rosen, Edward: 'Did Roger Bacon Invent Eyeglasses?', in *Archives internationales d'histoire des sciences = Archeion* N. S. (1954), pp. 3–15.

Rosenberg, Hans: 'Frottole und deutsches Lied um 1500', in: *Acta musicologica* 18/19 (1946/47), pp. 30–78.

Rosenwein, Barbara H.: *Negotiating Space. Power, Restraint, and Privileges of Immunity in Early Medieval Europe* (Ithaca and London, 1999).

Rotberg, Robert I., and Theodore Kwasnik Rabb, ed.: *Hunger in History* (Cambridge, MA, 1987).

Roth, Heinrich: 'Stil II. – Deutungsprobleme. Skizzen zu Pferdmotiven und zur Motivkoppelung', in Roth, ed., *Zum Problem der Deutung frühmittelalterlicher Bildinhalte* (Sigmaringen, 1986), pp. 111–28.

Roth, Helmuth: 'Zum Handel der Merowingerzeit auf Grund ausgewählter archäologischer Quellen', in Klaus Düwel, Herbert Jankuhn, Harald Siems and Dieter Timpe, ed., *Untersuchungen zu Handel und Verkehr der vor- und frühgeschichtlichen Zeit in Mittel- und Nordeuropa*, vol. 3, Abhandlungen der Akademie der Wissenschaften in Göttingen, Philol.-Hist. Kl. 3. F. CL (Göttingen, 1985), pp. 161–91.

Rouget, Georges: 'A propos de la forme dans la musique de tradition orale', in *Les Colloques de Wégimont*, vol. 1 (Brussels, 1956), pp. 132–44.

Rubinstein, Nicolai: 'Le allegorie di Ambroglio Lorenzetti nella sala della pace e il pensiero politico del suo tempo', in *Rivista storica Italiana* 109 (1997), pp. 781–803.

Rudeck, Wilhelm: *Geschichte der öffentlichen Sittlichkeit in Deutschland* (Berlin, 1905).

Rübsamen, Walter: 'From Frottola to Madrigal. The Changing Pattern of Secular Italian Vocal Music', in James Haar, ed., *Chanson & Madrigal 1480–1530*, Isham Library Papers II (Cambridge, MA, 1964), pp. 51–87.

Rüdiger, Otto: 'Die wiedergefundene Handschrift der Zunft der Bader in Hamburg', in *Mitteilungen des Vereins für Hamburgische Geschichte* 8 (1885), pp. 133–42.

Sabine, Ernest L.: 'City Cleaning in Mediaeval London', in *Speculum* 12 (1937), pp. 19–43.

Sabra, Abdelhamid I.: 'Sensation and Inference in Alhazen's Theory of Visual Perception', in Peter Machauer and Robert G. Turnbull, ed.: *Studies in Perception. Interrelations in the History of Philosophy and Science* (Columbus, OH, 1978), pp. 160–85.

Sachs, Curt *Eine Weltgeschichte des Tanzes* (Berlin, 1933) [repr. (Hildesheim, Zurich and New York, 1992)].

Saenger, Paul: *Space between Words. The Origin of Silent Reading* (Stanford, 1997).

Saftien, Volker: *Ars saltandi* (Hildesheim, Zurich and New York, 1994).

Sahlin, Magrit: *Etude sur la carole médiévale. L'origine du mot et ses rapports avec l'église* (Uppsala, 1940).

Salin, Bernhard: *Die altgermanische Thierornamentik* (Stockholm, 1904) [repr. (Stockholm, 1935); another repr. (Wiesbaden, 1983)].

Salmen, Walter: *Tanz und Tanzen vom Mittelalter bis zur Renaissance*, Terpsichore. Tanzhistorische Studien III (Hildesheim, Zurich and New York, 1999), pp. 55–6.

Schadt, Hermann: *Die Darstellungen der Arbores Consanguinitatis und der Arbores Affinitatis. Bildschemata in juristischen Handschriften* (Tübingen, 1982).

Schaefer, Ursula, ed.: *Vokalität. Altenglische Dichtung zwischen Mündlichkeit und Schriftlichkeit*, ScripOralia XXXIX (Tübingen, 1992).

Schaefer, Ursula, ed.: *Schriftlichkeit im frühen Mittelalter*, ScripOralia LIII (Tübingen, 1993).

Schapiro, Meyer: *Words and Pictures* (The Hague and Paris, 1973).

Schasler, Max: *Kritische Geschichte der Aesthetik* (Berlin, 1872), pp. 253–73 [a chapter headlined 'Der Sprung über das Mittelalter'].

Scheller, Robert, and Walter Hans Peter: *A Survey of Medieval Model Books* (Haarlem, 1963) [2nd edn s. t.: *Exemplum. Model-Book Drawings and the Practice of Artistic Transmission in the Middle Ages (c. 900–c. 1470)* (Amsterdam, 1998)].

Schenk, Gerrit Jasper: *Zeremoniell und Politik. Herrschereinzüge im spätmittelalterlichen Reich*, Forschungen zur Kaiser- und Papstgeschichte des Mittelalters XXI (Cologne, Weimar and Vienna, 2003).

Schenk, Günter: 'Die Begründung der Trias "Ästhetik, Logik, Ethik" als normative Wissenschaft durch Georg Friedrich Meier', in Günter Jerouschek and Arno Sames, ed., *Aufklärung und Erneuerung. Beiträge zur Geschichte der Universität Halle im ersten Jahrhundert ihres Bestehens (1694–1806)* (Hanau and Halle, 1994), pp. 106–18.

Schiedlansky, Günther: *Essen und Trinken. Tafelsitten bis zum Ausgang des Mittelalters* (Munich, 1956).

Schieffer, Theodor: 'Gerhard I. von Cambrai (1012–1051), ein deutscher Bischof des 11. Jahrhunderts', in *Deutsches Archiv* 1 (1937), pp. 323–60.

Schier, Kurt: 'Badewesen', in *Reallexikon der Germanischen Altertumskunde*, 2nd edn, vol. 1 (Berlin, 1973), pp. 583–9.

Schild, Wolfgang: 'Geschichte des Verfahrens', in Christoph Hinckeldey, ed., *Justiz in alter Zeit*, Schriftenreihe des Mittelalterlichen Kriminalmuseums Rothenburg ob der Tauber VI (Rothenburg, 1984), pp. 129–224 [2nd edn (Rothenburg, 1989)].

Schiller, Josef: *Abälards Ethik im Vergleich zur Ethik seiner Zeit* (Munich, 1906).

Schivelbusch, Wolfgang: *Tastes of Paradise. A Social History of Spices, Stimulants and Intoxicants* (New York, 1992) [first published (Frankfurt, 1990)].

Schleusener-Eichholz, Gudrun: *Das Auge im Mittelalter*, 2 vols, Münsterische Mittelalter-Schriften XXXV (Munich, 1984).

Schmaus, Michael: *Die Denkform Augustins in seinem Werk De trinitate*, Sitzungsberichte der Bayerischen Akademie der Wissenschaften, Philos.-Hist. Kl. 1962, no. 6 (Munich, 1962).

Schmeiser, Leonhard: *Die Erfindung der Zentralperspektive und die Entstehung der neuzeitlichen Wissenschaft* (Munich, 2002).

Schmid, Karl: 'Unerforschte Quellen aus quellenarmer Zeit II', in Hans Patze, ed., *Festschrift für Berent Schwineköper* (Sigmaringen, 1982), pp. 117–40.

Schmid, Karl: *Gebetsgedenken und adliges Selbstverständnis im Mittelalter* (Sigmaringen, 1983).

Schmid, Karl: 'Unerforschte Quellen aus quellenarmer Zeit [I]', in *Francia* 12 (1984), pp. 119–47.

Schmid, Karl, ed.: *Gedächtnis, das Gemeinschaft stiftet* (Munich and Zurich, 1985).

Schmid, Karl: 'Von den "fratres conscripti" in Ekkehards St. Galler Klostergeschichte', in *Frühmittelalterliche Studien* 25 (1991), pp. 109–22.

Schmid, Karl, and Joachim Wollasch: 'Die Gemeinschaft der Lebenden und der Verstorbenen in Zeugnissen des Mittelalters', in *Frühmittelalterliche Studien* 1 (1967), pp. 365–404.

Schmid, Karl, and Joachim Wollasch, ed.: *Memoria. Der geschichtliche Zeugniswert des liturgischen Gedenkens im Mittelalter*, Münsterische Mittelalter-Schriften LXVIII (Munich, 1984).

Schmidt, Gerhardt: *Die Armenbibeln des 14. Jahrhunderts* (Graz and Cologne, 1959).

Schmidt-Wiegand, Ruth, ed.: *Text-Bild-Interpretationen* (Munich, 1986).

Schmitt, Jean-Claude: 'Macht der Toten – Macht der Menschen. Gespenster-darstellungen im hohen Mittelalter', in Alf Lüdtke, ed., *Herrschaft als soziale Praxis*, Veröffentlichungen des Max-Planck-Instituts für Geschichte XCI (Göttingen, 1991), pp. 143–67 [first published in *Le temps de la réflexion* 3 (1982), pp. 285–306].

Schmitt, Jean-Claude: *Ghosts in the Middle Ages* (New York, 1998) [first published (Paris, 1994)].

Schmitt, Michael: 'Vorbild, Abbildung und Kopie. Zur Entwicklung von Sehweisen und Darstellungsarten in druckgraphischen Stadtabbildungen des 15. bis 18. Jahrhunderts am Beispiel Aachen', in Helmut Jäger, Franz Petri and Heinz Quirin, ed., *Civitatum communitas. Heinz Stoob zum 65. Geburtstag*, vol. 1, Städteforschung. Reihe A, vol. 21 (Cologne and Vienna, 1984), pp. 322–54.

Schmitt, Michael, and Jochen Luckhardt: *Realität und Abbild in Stadtdarstellungen des 16. bis 19. Jahrhunderts*, Beiträge zur Volkskultur in Nordwestdeutschland XXXI (Lippstadt and Munster, 1982).

Schneewind, Jerome B.: *The Invention of Autonomy* (Cambridge, 1997).

Schneider, Marius: *Geschichte der Mehrstimmigkeit* (Tutzing, 1972).

Schneider, Wolfgang Christian: *Ruhm, Heilsgeschehen, Dialektik. Drei kognitive Ordnungen in Geschichtsschreibung und Buchmalerei der Ottonenzeit*, Historische Texte und Studien I (Hildesheim and New York, 1988).

Schneider, Wolfgang Christian: 'Geschlossene Bücher – offene Bücher. Das Öffnen von Sinnräumen im Schliessen der Codices', in *Historische Zeitschrift* 271 (2000), pp. 561–92.

Schneider, Wolfgang Christian: 'Das Öffnen der Codices', in *Zeitschrift für Ästhetik und allgemeine Kunstwissenschaft* 47 (2002), pp. 7–35.

Schnell, Rüdiger, ed.: *Zivilisationsprozesse. Zu Erziehungsschriften der Vormoderne* (Cologne, Weimar and Vienna, 2004).

Schnitzler, Norbert: 'Picturing the Law', in *Medieval History Journal* 3, no. 1 (2000), pp. 1–15.

Schnurrer, Friedrich: *Chronik der Seuchen* (Tübingen, 1823).

Schramm, Percy Ernst: *Kaiser, Rom und Renovatio* (Leipzig, 1929) [repr. (Darmstadt, 1962)].

Schreiner, Klaus: 'Spätmittelalterliches Zisterziensertum im deutschen Südwesten. Spiritualität, gesellschaftliche Rekrutierungsfelder, soziale Verhaltensmuster', in Peter Rückert and Dieter Planck, ed., *Anfänge der Zisterzienser in Südwest-deutschland*, Oberrheinische Studien XVI (Sigmaringen, 1999), pp. 65–6.

Schröder, Edward: 'Das Tanzlied von Kölbigk', in *Nachrichten der Gesellschaft der Wissenschaften zu Göttingen, Fachgruppe IV (Neuere Philologie und Literatur-geschichte)* 17 (1933), pp. 355–72.

Schröder, Edward: 'Die Tänzer von Kölbigk', in *Zeitschrift für Kirchengeschichte* 17 (1897), pp. 126–30.

Schroeder, Jean: 'Zur Herkunft der älteren Fassung der Tanzlegende von Kölbigk', in Michael Borgolte and Herrad Spilling, eds, *Litterae medii aevi. Festschrift für Johanne Autenrieth zu ihrem 65. Geburtstag* (Sigmaringen, 1988), pp. 183–9.

Schroeder, Jean: 'Zur Frage frühmittelalterlicher Kulttänze am Grabe Willibrords in Echternach', in Georges Kiesel and Jean Schroeder, ed., *Wllibrord, Apostel der Niederlande, Gründer der Abtei Echternach* (Luxembourg, 1989), pp. 186–93.

Schubert, Ernst: *Alltag im Mittelalter* (Darmstadt, 2002, pp. 95–107.

Schück, Hendrick: 'En medeltides balladstrof', in *Samlaren* (1908), pp. 56–63.

Schulte, Ingrid: 'Die Badereise der Anna von Weinsberg', in *Parvula manuscula. Festgabe für Franz Irsigler zum 40. Geburtstag* (Bonn, 1981), pp. 29–39.

Schumacher, Josef: *Die seelischen Volkskrankheiten im deutschen Mittelalter und ihre Darstellungen in der bildenden Kunst,* Neue deutsche Forschungen CXL (Berlin, 1937).

Schwab, Ute: 'Das althochdeutsche Lied "Hirsch und Hinde" in seiner lateinischen Umgebung', in Nikolas Henkel and Nigel F. Palmer, ed., *Latein und Volkssprache im deutschen Mittelalter. 1100–1500* (Tübingen, 1992), pp. 74–122.

Schweizer, Hans Rudolf: *Ästhetik als Philosophie der sinnlichen Erkenntnis* (Basle, 1973).

Schwind, Fred: 'Zu karolingischen Klöstern als Wirtschaftsorganismen und Stätten handwerklicher Tätigkeit', in Lutz Fenske, ed., *Institutionen, Kultur und Gesellschaft im Mittelalter. Festschrift für Josef Fleckenstein zu seinem 65. Geburtstag,* (Sigmaringen, 1984), pp. 101–23.

Schwob, Anton: '"fride unde reht sint sêre wunt". Historiographen und Dichter der Stauferzeit über die Wahrung von Frieden und Recht', in Karl Hauck et al., ed., *Sprache und Recht. Beiträge zut Kulturgeschichte des Mittelalters. Festschrift für Ruth Schmidt-Wiegand zum 60. Geburtstag,* vol. 2 (Berlin and New York, 1986), pp. 846–69.

Scribner, Robert W.: 'Das Visuelle in der Volksfrömmigkeit', in Scribner and Martin Warnke, ed., *Bilder und Bildersturm im Spätmittelalter und in der frühen Neuzeit,* Wolfenbütteler Forschungen. LXVI (Wiesbaden, 1990), pp. 9–20.

Scribner, Robert W.: *For the Sake of Simple Folk. Popular Propaganda for the German Reformation,* 2nd edn (Oxford 1994) [first published (Cambridge, 1981)].

Seibt, Ferdinand: *Glanz und Elend des Mittelalters* (Berlin, 1987).

Sennhauser, Hans Rudolf, ed.: *Frühe Kirchen im östlichen Alpengebiet. Von der Spätantike bis in ottonische Zeit,* 2 vols, Abhandlungen der Bayerischen Akademie der Wissenschaften, Philos.-Hist. Kl., N.F. CXXIII (Munich, 2003).

Senninger, Leo: 'Die "springenden Heiligen". Ein Beitrag zur Geschichte der Wallfahrten nach Echternach und Prüm', in *Hemecht* 11 (1958), pp. 33–61.

Shepard, John: 'The Rhos Guests of Lious the Pious', in *Early Medieval Europe* 4 (1995), pp. 41–60.

Siebert, Hermann: *Das Tanzwunder zu Kölbigk und der Bernburger Heil'ge Geist* (Leipzig, 1902).

Siems, Harald: 'Die Organisation der Kaufleute in der Merowingerzeit nach den Leges', in Herbert Jankuhn and Else Ebel, ed., *Untersuchungen zu Handel und Verkehr der vor- und frühgeschichtlichen Zeit in Mittel- und Nordeuropa,* vol. 6, Abhandlungen der Akademie der Wissenschaften zu Göttingen, Philol.-Hist. Kl. 3. F. CLXXXIII (Göttingen, 1989), pp. 62–145.

Siems, Harald: *Handel und Wucher im Spiegel frühmittelalterlicher Rechtsquellen,* Schriften der Monumenta Germaniae Historica XXXV (Hanover, 1992).

Sigal, Pierre-André: 'Le travail des hagiographes au IXe et XIe siècle', in *Francia* 15 (1987/88), pp. 151–54, 178–81.

Simmel, Georg: 'Soziologie der Mahlzeit', in Simmel, *Aufsätze und Abhandlungen. 1909–1918,* ed. Rüdiger Kramme and Angela Rammstedt (Frankfurt, 2001), pp. 140–7 = Simmel, *Gesamtausgabe,* vol. 12 [first published in *Der Zeitgeist. Beiblatt zum Berliner Tageblatt* 41, Festnummer zum hundertjährigen Jubiläum der Berliner Universität (Berlin, 17.10.1910), pp. 1–2; also in Simmel, *Brücke und Tür,* ed. Margarete Sussman and Michael Landmann (Stuttgart, 1957), pp. 243–4].

Simson, Otto von: *Von der Macht der Bilder. Gesammelte Aufsätze zur Kunst des Mittelalters*, ed. Rainer Haussherr (Berlin, 1993).

Skinner, Quentin: 'Ambrogio Lorenzetti. The Artist as Political Philosopher', in *Proceedings of the British Academy* 72 (1980), pp. 3–56 [abridged version in Hans Belting and Dieter Blume, ed., *Malerei und Stadtkultur in der Dantezeit. Die Argumentation der Bilder* (Munich, 1989), pp. 85–103].

Skramlik, Emil von: *Handbuch der niederen Sinne*, vol. 1: *Die Physiologie des Geruchs- und Geschmacksinnes* (Leipzig, 1926).

Slicher van Bath, Bernard Hendrik: *Yield Ratios. 810–1210*, Landbouwhogeschool, Afdeling Agrarische Geschiedenis. Bijdragen X (Wageningen, 1963).

Slicher van Bath, Bernard Hendrik: 'The Yields of Different Crops', in *Acta historica neerlandica* 2 (1967), pp. 26–106.

Smith, Earl Baldwin: *Architectural Symbolism of Imperial Rome and the Middle Ages*, Princeton Monographs in Archaeology XXX (Princeton, 1956).

Snyder, Steven Craig: 'Albert the Great's Analysis of Time in Its Historical and Doctrinal Setting', Ph.D. Diss., typescript (University of Toronto, 1984).

Söder, Joachim R.: 'Albert der Grosse über Sinne und Träume', in *Micrologus* 10 (2002), pp. 239–50.

Soly, Hugo: 'Plechtige intochten in de steden van de Zuiderlijke Nederlanden tijdens de overgang van middeleeuwen naar nieuwe tijd', in *Tijdschrift voor geschiedenis* 97, 3 (1984), pp. 341–61.

Soskice, Janet Martin: 'Sight and Vision in Medieval Christian Thought', in Teresa Brennan and Martin Jay, ed., *Vision in Context* (New York and London, 1996), pp. 29–43.

Spanke, Hans:: 'Tanzmusik in der Kirche des Mittelalters', in *Neuphilologische Mitteilungen* 31 (1930), pp. 143–70.

Speake, George: *Anglo-Saxon Animal Art and Its Germanic Background* (Oxford, 1980).

Spiegel, Gabrielle M.: 'Genealogy. Form and Function in Medieval Historical Narrative', in *History and Theory* 22 (1983), pp. 43–53.

Spieß, Karl-Heinz: 'Zur Wirtschafts- und Sozialstruktur des frühmittelalterlichen Grundherrschaft östlich des Rheins', in *Hessisches Jahrbuch für Landesgeschichte* 41 (1991), pp. 265–76.

Spieß, Karl-Heinz: *Familie und Verwandtschaft im deutschen Hochadel des Spätmittelalters*, Vierteljahrschrift für Sozial- und Wirtschaftsgeschichte. Beihefte CXI (Stuttgart, 1993).

Sprute, Jürgen: 'Hutchesons Grundlegung der Ästhetik', in *Zeitschrift für philosophische Forschung* 56 (2002), pp. 48–71.

Spurrell, Mark: 'The Architectural Interest of the *Regularis Concordia*', in *Anglo-Saxon England* 21 (1992), pp. 161–76.

Starn, Randolph: 'The Republican Regime of the Sala dei Nove in Siena. 1338–1340', in Starn and Loren Partridge, ed., *Arts of Power. Three Halls of State in Italy. 1300–1600* (Berkeley, Los Angeles and Oxford, 1992), pp. 9–80.

Stein, Frauke: *Adelsgräber des 8. Jahrhunderts in Deutschland*, Germanische Denkmäler der Völkerwanderungszeit. Ser. A., vol. IX (Berlin, 1967).

Stein, Karl Heinrich von: *Die Entstehung der neueren Ästhetik* (Stuttgart, 1886), pp. 336–69 [repr. (Hildesheim, 1964)].

Steiner, Reinhard A.: *Theorie und Wirklichkeit der Kunst bei Leonardo da Vinci* (Munich, 1979).

Steneck, Nicholas Hans: 'Albert on Psychology and Sense Perception', in James

Athanasius Weisheipl, ed., *Albertus Magnus and the Sciences. Commemorative Essays*, Studies and Texts. 49 (Toronto, 1980), pp. 263–90.

Steuer, Heiko: 'Der Handel der Wikingerzeit zwischen Nord- und Westeuropa aufgrund archäologischer Zeugnisse', in Klaus Düwel, Herbert Jankuhn, Harald Siems and Dieter Timpe, ed., *Untersuchungen zu Handel und Verkehr der vor- und frühgeschichtlichen Zeit in Mittel- und Nordeuropa*, vol. 4, Abhandlungen der Akademie der Wissenschaften in Göttingen, Philol.-Hist. Kl. 3. F. CLVI (Göttingen, 1987), pp. 131–79.

Steuer, Heiko, et al.: 'Handel', in *Reallexikon der Germanischen Altertumskunde*, 2nd edn (Berlin and New York, 1999), pp. 542–4, 548–52.

Stockmann, Doris: 'Musik als kommunikatives System. Informations- und zeichentheoretische Aspekte unter besonderer Berücksichtigung mündlich tradierter Musik', in *Deutsches Jahrbuch für Musikwissenschaft* 14 (1969), pp. 76–95.

Stolz, Susanna: *Die Handwerke des Körpers. Bader, Barbiere, Perückenmacher, Friseur* (Marburg, 1992), pp. 71–119.

Stolzenberg, Jürgen: 'Das freie Spiel der Erkenntniskräfte. Zu Kants Theorie des Geschmacksurteils', in Ursula Franke, ed., *Kants Schlüssel zur Kritik des Geschmacks*, Zeitschrift für Ästhetik und Allgemeine Kunstwissenschaft. Sonderheft [45.] (Hamburg, 2000), pp. 1–28.

Strasser, Mark: 'Hutcheson on Aesthetic Perception', in *Philosophia* 21 (1991/92), pp. 107–18.

Stratmann, Martina: 'Schriftlichkeit in der Verwaltung von Bistümern und Klöstern', in Rudolf Schieffer, ed., *Schriftkultur und Reichsverwaltung unter den Karolingern*, Abhandlungen der Nordrhein-Westfälischen Akademie der Wissenschaften. XCVII (Opladen, 1996), pp. 97–102.

Straube, R. I.: 'Der Traktat De Clarea in der Burgerbibliothek Bern', in *Schweizerisches Institut für Kunstwissenschaft. Jahresbericht 1964* (1965), pp. 98–114.

Stricker, Wilhelm: 'Zur Kulturgeschichte der deutschen Bäder', in *Zeitschrift für Kulturgeschichte* 1 (1856), pp. 439–42, 2 (1857), pp. 328–34.

Strobel, Adam Walther: *Vaterländische Geschichte des Elsasses*, vol. 3 (Strasbourg, 1843).

Strong, Roy: *Splendour at Court. Renaissance Spectacle and the Theatre of Power* (London and Boston, 1973).

Strong, Roy: *The Renaissance Garden in England* (London, 1979).

Strong, Roy: *Feast. A History of Grand Eating* (London, 2002).

Strömbäck, Dag: 'Den underbara arsdansen', in *Arkiv för nordisk filologi* 59 (1944), pp. 111–26.

Strömbäck, Dag: 'Kölbigk och Hagra', in *Arv* 17 (1961), pp. 1–48, 24 (1968), pp. 91–132.

Studt, Birgit: 'Gebrauchsformen mittelalterlicher Rotuli. Das Wort auf dem Weg zur Schrift – die Schrift auf dem Weg zum Bild', in Ellen Widder, Mark Mersiowsky and Peter Johanek, ed., *Vestigia Monasteriensia*, Studien zur Regionalgeschichte V (Bielefeld, 1995), pp. 325–50.

Sutherland, Jon Nicholas: 'The Mission to Constantinople in 968 and Liudprand of Cremona', in *Traditio* 31 (1975), pp. 55–81.

Sutherland, Jon Nicholas: *Liudprand of Cremona* (Spoleto, 1988).

Sutter, Berthold: 'Der Schutz der Persönlichkeit in mittelalterlichen Rechten', in *Grund- und Freiheitsrechte von der ständischen zur spätbürgerlichen Gesellschaft*, Veröffentlichungen zur Geschichte der Grund- und Freiheitsrechte II (Göttingen, 1987), pp. 17–41.

Swanson, Robert Norman, ed.: *The Use and Abuse of Time in Christian History*, Studies in Church History XXXVII (Woodbridge, 2002).

Symons, Thomas: 'Sources of the *Regularis Concordia*', in *Downside Review* 59 (1941), pp. 15–36, 142–70, 264–89.

Symons, Thomas: '*Regularis Concordia*. History and Derivation', in David Parsons, ed., *Tenth-Century Studies* (Chichester, 1975), pp. 37–59.

Tachau, Katherine: *Vision and Certitude in the Age of Ockham. Epistemology and the Foundations of Semantics. 1250–1345* (Leiden, 1988).

Tatarkiewicz, Wladyslaw: *The History of Aesthetics*, ed. Cyril Barrett, SJ, vol. 2 (The Hague, Paris and Warsaw, 1970) [first published (Warsaw, 1962)] [essentially an edition of selected texts from the Middle Ages].

Tauber, Jürg: *Herd und Ofen im Mittelalter*, Schweizer Beiträge zur Kulturgeschichte und Archäologie des Mittelalters VII (Heitersheim, 1980).

Taubert, Karl Heinz: *Höfische Tanze* (Mainz, 1968).

Taubert, Karl Heinz: *Barock-Tänze* (Zurich, 1986).

Teuteberg, Hans-Jürgen: 'Homo edens', in *Internationaler Arbeitskreis für Kulturforschung des Essens* (1997, 2), pp. 9–27 [also in *Historische Zeitschrift* 265 (1997), pp. 1–28].

Teuteberg, Hans-Jürgen, and Günter Wiegelmann, ed.: *Unsere tägliche Kost*, 2nd edn (Munster, 1988) [first published (Munster, 1986)].

Thirsk, Joan: 'England's Provinces. Did They Serve or Drive Material London?', in Lena Cowen Orlin, ed., *Material London, ca. 1600* (Philadelphia, 2000), pp. 97–108.

Thoss, Dagmar: *Studien zum Locus Amoenus im Mittelalter*, Wiener Romanistische Arbeiten X (Vienna, 1972).

Tiefenbach, Heinrich: *Studien zu Wörtern volkssprachlicher Herkunft in karolingischen Urkunden*, Münsterische Mittelalter-Schriften XV (Munich, 1973).

Tobin, Ronald William Francis: 'Esthétique et société au dix-septième siècle', in *Papers on French Seventeenth-Century Literature* 6 (1976/77), pp. 8–10.

Töpfer, Bernhard: *Volk und Kirche zur Zeit der beginnenden Gottesfriedensbewegung in Frankreich* (Berlin [GDR], 1957), pp. 81–111 [repr. in Klaus-Peter Matschke and Ernst Werner, eds, *Ideologie und Gesellschaft im hohen und späten Mittelalter* (Berlin, GDR, 1988), pp. 139–74].

Trexler, Richard C.: *Public Life in Renaissance Florence* (New York, London, Toronto, Sydney and San Francisco, 1980), pp. 290–330.

Turnbull, David: 'Cartography and Science in Early Modern Europe. Mapping the Construction of Knowledge Spaces', in *Imago Mundi* 48 (1996), pp. 5–24.

Tweedale, Martin: 'John of Rodyngton on Knowledge, Science and Theology', Ph.D. Diss., typescript (University of California at Los Angeles, 1965).

Uhlig, Claus: 'Moral und Politik in der europäischen Hoferziehung', in *Literatur als Kritik des Lebens. Festschrift zum 65. Geburtstag von Ludwig Borinski* (Heidelberg, 1975), pp. 27–51.

Varges, Willi: 'Die Wohlfahrtspflege in den deutschen Städten des Mittelalters', in *Preußische Jahrbücher* 81 (1895), pp. 250–318.

Vayer, Paul: *Les entrées solonnelles à Paris des rois et reines de France, des souverains et princes étrangers, ambassadeurs etc. Bibliographie sommaire* (Paris, 1896).

Vellekoop, Kees: 'Die Orgel von Winchester. Wirklichkeit oder Symbol?', in *Baseler Jahrbuch für Historische Musikpraxis* 8 (1984), pp. 183–96.

Venturi, Adolfo: 'Les "Triomphes" de Pétrarque dans l'art représentatif', in *Revue de l'art ancien et moderne* 2 (1906), pp. 209–21.

Verdon, Jean: *Les loisirs au Moyen Age* (Paris, 1985).

Verdon, Jean: *Le plaisir au Moyen Age* (Paris, 1996)

Verdon, Jean: *Boir au Moyen Age* (Paris, 2002).

Vergers et jardins dans l'universe médiéval (Aix-en-Provence, 1990).

Verhulst, Adriaan: *Der Handel im Merowingerreich*, Antikvariskt Arkiv XLIX, no. 1 (Oslo, 1970).

Verhulst, Adriaan: 'Der frühmittelalterliche Handel der Niederlande und der Friesenhandel', in Klaus Düwel, Herbert Jankuhn, Harald Siems and Dieter Timpe, ed., *Untersuchungen zu Handel und Verkehr der vor- und frühgeschichtlichen Zeit in Mittel- und Nordeuropa*, vol. 3, Abhandlungen der Akademie der Wissenschaft in Göttingen, Philol.-Hist. Kl. 3. F. CL (Göttingen, 1985), pp. 321–385.

Verrier, Paul: 'La plus vielle citation de carole', in *Romania* 58 (1932), pp. 380–421.

Vigarello, *Georges: Concepts of Cleanliness. Changing Attitudes in France since the Middle Ages* (Cambridge, New York and Paris, 1988) [first published (Paris, 1985)].

Visser, Margaret: *Much Depends on Dinner* (Toronto, 1986) [new edn (Harmondsworth, 1989)].

Visser, Margaret: *The Rituals of Dinner. The Origin, Evolution, Eccentricities and Meanings of the Table Manner* (London, 1992) [first published (New York, 1991)].

Vogel, Bernhard: 'Das hagiographische Werk Lantberts von Deutz über Heribert von Köln', in Dieter R. Bauer and Klaus Herbers, ed., *Hagiographie im Kontext* (Stuttgart, 2000), pp. 117–29.

Volkelt, Peter: 'Die Städteansichten in den großen Druckwerken vornehmlich des 15. Jahrhunderts', Ph.D. Diss., typescript (University of Marburg, 1949).

Vollrath, Hanna: 'Das Mittelalter in der Typik oraler Gesellschaften', in *Historische Zeitschrift* 233 (1981), pp. 571–94.

Wacha, Georg: 'Tiere und Tierhaltung in der Stadt sowie im Wohnbereich des spätmittelalterlichen Menschen und ihre Darstellung in der bildenden Kunst', in Heinrich Appelt, ed., *Das Leben in der Stadt des Spätmittelalters*, Veröffentlichungen des Instituts für mittelalterliche Realienkunde Österreichs II = Sitzungsberichte der Österreichischen Akademie der Wissenschaften, Philos.-Hist. Kl. CCCXXV (Vienna, 1977), p. 229–60 [2nd edn (Vienna, 1980)].

Wadle, Elmar: 'Heinrich IV. und die kirchliche Friedesbewegung', in Josef Fleckenstein, ed., *Investiturstreit und Reichsverfassung*, Vorträge und Forschungen, hrsg. vom Konstanzer Arbeitskreis für mittelalterliche Geschichte XVII (Sigmaringen, 1973), pp. 141–73.

Wadle, Elmar: 'Frühe deutsche Landfrieden', in Hubert Mordek, ed., *Überlieferung und Geltung normativer Texte des frühen und hohen Mittelalters*, Quellen und Forschungen zum Recht im Mittelalter IV (Sigmaringen, 1986), pp. 71–92.

Wadle, Elmar: 'Gottes- und Landfrieden als Gegenstand der Forschung nach 1950', in Karl Kroeschell and Albrecht Cordes, ed., *Funktion und Form. Quellen- und Methodenprobleme der mittelalterlichen Rechtsgeschichte*, Schriften zur Europäischen Rechts- und Verfassungsgeschichte XVIII (Berlin, 1996), pp. 63–91.

Wadle, Elmar: 'Zur Delegitimierung der Fehde durch die mittelalterliche Friedensbewegung', in Horst Brunner, ed., *Der Krieg im Mittelalter und in der Frühen Neuzeit*, Imagines medii aevi III (Wiesbaden, 1999), pp. 73–91.

Wähler, Martin: 'Der Kindertanzzug von Erfurt nach Arnstadt im Jahre 1237', in *Zeitschrift des Vereins für Thüringische Geschichte und Altertumskunde* 42 (1940), pp. 72–4.

Waeltner, Ernst Ludwig: *Die Lehre vom Organum in den Musiktratkaten bis zur Mitte des 11. Jahrhunderts* (Tutzing, 1975).

Wagner, Friedrich: *Das natürliche Sittengesetz nach der Lehre des hl. Thomas von Aquino* (Berlin, 1911).

Walser, Ernst: *Poggius Florentinus*, Beiträge zur Kulturgeschichte des Mittelalters und der Renaissance XIV (Leipzig, 1914).

Walter, Michael: *Grundlagen der Musik des Mittelalters* (Stuttgart, 1994).

Warncke, Carsten-Peter: *Sprechende Bilder – Sichtbare Worte. Das Bildverständnis in der frühen Neuzeit* (Wiesbaden, 1987).

Warnke, Martin: *Bau und Überbau* (Frankfurt, 1976) [repr. (Frankfurt, 1984)].

Weber, Thomas: 'Essen und Trinken im Konstantinopel des 10. Jahrhunderts nach dem Berichten Liutprands von Cremona', in Weber and Johannes Koder, *Liutprand von Cremona in Konstantinopel*, Byzantina Vindobonensia XIII (Vienna, 1980), pp. 71–99.

Webster, James Carson: *The Labors of the Month in Antique and Medieval Art to the End of the 13th Century*, Princeton Monographs in Art and Archaeology XXI = Northwestern University Studies in the Humanities IV (Princeton and Evanston, 1938).

Webster, Leslie: 'The Anglo-Saxon Hinterland. Animal Style in Southumbrian Eighth-Century England. With Particular Reference to Metalwork', in Michael Müller-Wille and Lars Olof Larsson, ed., *Tiere – Menschen – Götter. Wikingerzeitliche Kunststile und ihre neuzeitliche Rezeption*, Veröffentlichung der Joachim-Jungius-Gesellschaft des Wissenschaften XC (Göttingen, 2001), pp. 39–62.

Wehle, Winfried: 'Der Tod, das Leben und die Kunst. Boccaccios Decameron oder der Triumph der Sprache', in Arno Borst, Alexander Patschkovsky, Georg von Grävenitz and Karl Heinz Stierle, ed., *Tod im Mittelalter*, Konstanzer Bibliothek XX (Konstanz, 1993), pp. 221–260.

Wehrli, Gustav A.: *Die Bader, Barbiere und Wundärzte im alten Zürich*, Mitteilungen der Antiquarischen Gesellschaft in Zürich. Neujahrsblatt XCI (Zurich, 1927).

Wehrli, Gustav A.: *Die Wundärzte und Bader Zürichs als zünftige Organisation*, Mitteilungen der Antiquarischen Gesellschaft in Zürich. Neujahrsblatt XCV (Zurich, 1931).

Weidinger, Ulrich: *Untersuchungen zur Wirtschaftsstruktur des Klosters Fulda in der Karolingerzeit* (Stuttgart, 1991).

Weidlé, Wladimir: 'Vom Sichtbarwerden des Unsichtbaren', in Weidlé, *Wandlungen des Paradiesischen und Utopischen. Studien zum Bild eines Ideals* (Berlin 1966), pp. 1–9.

Weimann, Klaus: 'Der Friede im Altenglischen'. Ph.D. Diss., typescript (University of Bonn, 1966).

Weissbach, Werner: *Trionfi* (Berlin, 1919).

Weisweiler, Hermann: 'Die Pseudo-Dionysiuskommentare In coelestem hierarchiam des Skotus Eriugena und Hugos von St. Viktor', in *Recherches de théologie ancienne et médiévale* 19 (1952), pp. 26–47.

Weitzel, Jürgen: 'Strafe und Strafverfahren in der Merowingerzeit', in *Zeitschrift der Savigny-Stiftung für Rechtsgeschichte*, Germanistische Abteilung 114 (1994), pp. 66–147.

Welsch, Wolfgang: *Ästhetisches Denken*, 6th edn (Stuttgart, 2003) [first published (Stuttgart, 1990)].

Welsch, Wolfgang: 'Ästhet/hik. Ethische Implikationen und Konsequenzen der Ästhetik', in Christoph Wulf et al., ed., *Ethik der Ästhetik* (Berlin, 1994), pp. 12–13.

Wenz-Haubfleisch, Annegret: *Miracula post mortem. Studien zum Quellenwert hochmittelalterlicher Mirakelsammlungen vornehmlich des ostfränkisch-deutschen Reiches*, Siegburger Studien XXVI (Siegburg, 1998), pp. 126–35.

Wenzel, Horst: 'Partizipation und Mimesis. Die Lesbarkeit der Körper am Hof und in der höfischen Literatur', in Hans Ulrich Gumbrecht and Kal Ludwig Pfeiffer, ed., *Materialität der Kommunikation* (Frankfurt, 1988), pp. 178–202.

Wenzel, Horst: *Hören und Sehen. Schrift und Bild. Kultur und Gedächtnis im Mittelalter* (Munich, 1995).

Wenzel, Horst, ed.: *Gespräche – Boten – Briefe. Körpergedächtnis und Schriftgedächtnis im Mittelalter*, Philologische Studien und Quellen CXLIII (Berlin, 1997).

Werner, Karl Ferdinand: 'Observations sur le rôle des évêques dans les mouvements de paix au Xe et XIe siècles', in Coloman Etienne Viola, ed., *Mediaevalia Christiana XIe – XIIe. Hommage à Raymonde Foreville de ses amis, ses collèges et ses anciens élèves* (Paris, 1989), pp. 155–95.

Wessell, Leonard Paul, Jr: 'Alexander Baumgarten's Contribution to the Development of Aesthetics', in *Journal of Aesthetics and Art Criticism* 30 (1971/72), pp. 333–42.

White, Alan Richard, ed.: *The Philosophy of Action* (London, 1968).

White, John: *The Birth and Rebirth of Pictorial Space*, 3rd edn (London and Cambridge, MA, 1987) [first published (London, 1957)].

Wickham, Chris: 'Problems of Comparing Rural Societies in Early Medieval Western Europe', in *Transactions of the Royal Historical Society*, 6th series, vol. 2 (1992), pp. 221–45.

Wickham, Chris: 'Overview. Production, Distribution and Demand', in Richard Hodges and William Bowden, ed., *The Sixth Century*, The Transformation of the Roman World III (Leiden, Boston and Cologne, 1998), pp. 279–92.

Wiegelmann, Günter: *Alltags- und Festspeisen* (Marburg, 1967).

Wieland, Wolfgang: 'Die Erfahrung des Urteils. Warum Kant keine Ästhetik begründet hat', in *Deutsche Vierteljahrsschrift für Literaturwissenschaft und Geistesgeschichte* 64 (1990), pp. 604–23.

Wieland, Wolfgang: *Urteil und Gefühl. Kants Theorie der Urteilskraft* (Göttingen, 2001).

Wild, Friedrich: *Drachen im Beowulf und andere Drachen*, Sitzungsberichte der Österreichischen Akademie der Wissenschaften, Philos.-Hist. Kl. CCXXXVIII, 5 (Vienna, 1962).

Wilda, Wilhelm Eduard: *Geschichte des deutschen Strafrechts* (Halle, 1842) [repr. (Aalen, 1960)].

Wilhelm, Richard: *Friedrich Justus Riedel und die Aethetik der Aufklärung*, Beiträge zur neueren Literaturgeschichte. N. F. XXIII (Heidelberg, 1933).

Willoweit, Dietmar: 'Die Sanktion für Friedensbruch im Kölner Gottesfrieden von 1083', in Ellen Schlüchter and Klaus Laubenthal, ed., *Recht und Kriminalität. Festschrift für Friedrich-Wilhelm Krause zum 70. Geburtstag* (Berlin, 1991), pp. 37–52.

Willwersch, Matthias: *Die Grundherrschaft des Klosters Prüm*, first and partly printed as Ph.D. Diss. (University of Berlin, 1912) [the full version has been edited by Ingo Schwab and Reiner Nolden (Trier, 1989)].

Wilson, David MacKenzie: 'The Earliest Animal Styles of the Viking Age', in Michael Müller-Wille and Lars Olof Larsson, ed., *Tiere – Menschen – Götter. Wikingerzeitliche Kunststile und ihre neuzeitliche Rezeption*, Veröffentlichung der Joachim-Jungius-Gesellschaft des Wissenschaften XC (Göttingen, 2001), pp. 131–56.

Wimmer, Clemens Alexander: *Geschichte der Gartentheorie* (Darmstadt, 1989).

Winter, Johann Maria van: 'Kochen und Essen im Mittelalter', in Bernd Herrmann, ed., *Mensch und Umwelt im Mittelalter*, 3rd edn (Stuttgart, 1987), pp. 88–100 [first published (Stuttgart, 1986)].

Wiora, Walter: 'Der Brautreigen zu Kölbigk in der Heiligen Nacht des Jahres 1020', in *Zeitschrift für Volkskunde* 50 (1953), pp. 188–201.

Wiora, Walter: *Historische und systematische Musikwissenschaft. Gesammelte Aufsätze* (Tutzing, 1972).

Wiora, Walter, and Walter Salmen: 'Die Tanzmusik im deutschen Mittelalter', in *Zeitschrift für Volkskunde* 50 (1953), pp. 164–87.

Wirth, Alfred: 'Bernburg im Volksreim und der Bernburger Heelechrist', in *Anhaltische Geschichtsblätter* 14 (1938), pp. 59–81.

Wisplinghoff, Erich: *Untersuchungen zur frühen Geschichte der Abtei St. Maximin bei Trier von den Anfängen bis etwa 1150*, Quellen und Abhandlungen zur mittelrheinischen Kirchengeschichte XII (Mainz, 1970).

Wiswe, Hans: *Kulturgeschichte der Kochkunst* (Munich, 1970).

Wize, Kasimir Filip: 'Kants Analytik des Schönen', in *Zeitschrift für Ästhetik und Allgemeine Kunstwissenschaft* [A. F.] 4 (1909), pp. 1–15.

Wohlhaupter, Eugen: *Studien zur Rechtsgeschichte der Gottes- und Landfrieden in Spanien*, Deutschrechtliche Beiträge XIV (Heidelberg, 1933).

Wolfram, Richard: *Schwerttanz und Männerbund* (Kassel, 1936).

Wolfram, Richard: *Reigen- und Kettentanzformen in Europa*, Tanzhistorische Studien V (Berlin, 1986).

Wolfson, Harry Austryn: 'The Internal Senses in Latin, Arabic and Hebrew Philosophical Tracts', in *Harvard Theological Review* 28 (1935), pp. 69–133.

Wolter, Allan Bernard: 'Duns Scotus on Intuition, Memory and Our Knowledge of Individuals', in Linus D. Thro, ed., *History of Philosophy in the Making. A Symposium of Essays to Honor Professor James D. Collins* (Washington, DC,1982), pp. 81–104.

Wood, Ian N.: 'Gregory of Tours and Clovis', in *Revue belge de philologie et d'histoire* 63 (1985), pp. 268–71.

Woodbridge, Kenneth: *Princely Gardens* (London and New York, 1986).

Woodward, David: 'Maps and the Rationalization of Geographic Space', in Jay Levenson, ed., *Circa 1492. Art in the Age of Exploration* (New Haven, 1991), pp. 83–8.

Wormald, Francis: *The Benedictional of St. Ethelwold* (London, 1959).

Wormald, Patrick: 'The *Leges Barbarorum*. Law and Ethnicity in the Post-Roman West', in Hans-Werner Goetz, Jörg Jarnut and Walter Pohl, ed., *Regna and gentes. The Relationship between Late Antique and Early Medieval Peoples and Kingdoms in the Transformation of the Roman World*, The Transformation of the Roman World XIII (Leiden and Boston, 2003), pp. 21–53.

Wright, Lawrence: *Clean and Decent. The Fascinating History of the Bathroom* (London, 1960).

Wunderli, Peter: 'Der Wald als Ort der Asozialität. Aspekte der altfranzösischen Epik', in Josef Semmler, ed., *Der Wald in Mittelalter und Renaissance* (Düsseldorf, 1991), pp. 69–113.

Yu, Jiyuan, and Jorge Gracia, ed.: *Rationality and Happiness. From the Ancients to the Early Medievals* (Rochester, 2003).

Zapalac, Kristin Eldyss Sorensen: *'In His Image and Likeness'. Political Iconography and Religious Change in Regensburg. 1500–1800* (Ithaca and London, 1990).

Zappert, Georg: 'Über das Badewesen in mittelalterlicher und späterer Zeit', in *Archiv für Kunde österreichischer Geschichtsquellen* 21 (1859), pp. 1–166 [separately printed (Vienna, 1859)].

Zeiss, Hans: *Das Heilsbild in der germanischen Kunst der frühen Mittelalters,*

Sitzungsberichte der Bayerischen Akademie der Wissenschaften, Philos.-Hist. Kl., vol. II, no. 8 (Munich, 1941).

Zeitler, Rudolf, ed.: *Les pays du nord et Byzance. Actes du colloque nordique et international de byzantinologie*, Acta Universitatis Upsaliensis, Figura NS XIX (Uppsala, 1981).

Zelle, Carsten: 'Zur Semiotik des Nasenlochs', in *Diagonal. Zeitschrift der Universität-Gesamthochschule Siegen* (1995, no. 1), pp. 131–40.

Ziegler, Philip: *The Black Death* (London, 1997) [first published (London, 1969)].

Zimmermann, Gerd: *Ordensleben und Lebensstandard. Die cura corporis in den Ordensvorschriften des abendländischen Hochmittelalters*, Beiträge zur Geschichte des alten Mönchtums und des Benediktinerordens XXXII (Munster, 1973).

Zimmermann, Robert: *Geschichte der Aesthetik als philosophische Wissenschaft* (Vienna, 1858), pp. 152–153 [brief remarks on Augustine, without further statements on the Middle Ages].

Zimmerman, Robert: 'Kant. The Aesthetic Judgment', in *Journal of Aesthetics and Art Criticism* 21 (1962/63), pp. 333–44.

Zimpel, Detlev: 'Zur Bedeutung des Essens in der "Relatio de legatione Constantinopolitana" des Liutprand von Cremona', in *Historische Zeitschrift* 269 (1999), pp. 1–18.

Zinn, Karl Georg: *Kanonen und Pest. Über die Ursprünge der Neuzeit im 14. und 15. Jahrhundert* (Opladen, 1989).

Zitelli, A., and R. Palmer: 'Le teorie mediche sulla peste e il contesto veneziano', in *Venezia e la peste* (Venice, 1979), pp. 21–92.

Zoepf, Ludwig: *Das Heiligen-Leben im 10. Jahrhundert*, Beiträge zur Kulturgeschichte des Mittelalters und der Renaissance I (Leipzig, 1908).

Doctoral dissertations and other academic publications on the so-called dancing sickness

Binard, François: 'De Chorea', Med.D. Diss. (Lille, 1826).

Bouteille, Etienne-Michel: 'Traité de la Chorée ou Danse de St. Guy', Med.D. Diss. (Paris, 1810).

Braun Christian Friedrich [resp.], Johannes Müller [praes.]: 'De Tarantula', Med.D. Diss. (Wittenberg, 1676).

Brueckmann, Carl Philip: 'Enarratio Choreae Sancti Viti et Epilepsiae' (Frankfurt, 1786).

Dalgairns, William [resp.], George Baird [praes.]: 'De Chorea Sancti Viti', Med.D. Diss. (Edinburgh, 1811).

Ewart, John [resp.], William Robertson [praes.]: 'De Chorea', Med.D. Diss. (Edinburgh, 1786).

Fargues Thomas, [resp.], George Baird [praes.]: 'De Chorea', Med.D. Diss. (Edinburgh, 1811).

Herzog, Eduard August: 'De pathologia morbus quem vocant Chorea Sancti Viti', Med.D. Diss. (Berlin, 1823).

Kinin, Peter [resp.], George Baird [preaes.]: 'De Chorea', Med.D. Diss. (Edinburgh, 1827).

Lockyer Edmund: 'De Chorea', Med.D. Diss. (Edinburgh, 1805).

Martin, Bartholomäus: 'Da casu Choreae Sancto Viti', Diss.D. Med. (Strasbourg, 1730).

Mayer, Georg: 'Über den Veitstanz', Med.D. Diss. (Berlin, 1870).

Mercer, Samuel: 'De Chorea', Med.D. Diss. (Edinburgh, 1805).

Moulson, Richard [resp.]: George Baird [praes.]: 'De Chorea', Med.D. Diss. (Edinburgh, 1816).

Profe, Gottlieb [resp.], Georg Wolfgang Wedel [praes.]: 'Disputatio de chorea Sancti Viti', Med.D. Diss. (Jena, 1682).

Rome, George [resp.], George Baird [praes.]: 'De Chorea Sancti Viti', Med.D. Diss. (Edinburgh, 1831).

Salmon, Thomas Stokes [resp.], George Baird [praes.]: 'De Chorea', Med.D. Diss. (Edinburgh, 1796).

Salt, John Butt [resp.], William Robertson [praes.]: 'De Chorea', Med.D. Diss. (Edinburgh, 1793).

Schwarz Johann Baptist Mathias: 'De Tarantismo et Chorea Sancti Viti', Med.D. Diss. (Vienna, 1766).

Shaw, David [resp.], George Baird [praes.]: 'De Chorea Sancti Viti', Med.D. Diss. (Edinburgh, 1817).

Sinnot, Richard [resp.], George Bard [praes.]: 'De Chorea', Med.D. Diss. (Edinburgh, 1812).

Spangenberg, Peter Ludolf: 'De Chorea Sancti Viti', Med.D. Diss. (Göttingen, 1764).

Stransky, C. J.: *Tractatus de Sancti Viti Chorea* (Vienna, 1822).

Thomson, John [resp.], George Baird [praes.]: 'De Chorea', Med.D. Diss. (Edinburgh, 1807).

Wilhelm, Johann Friedrich [resp.], Carl Gottlieb Küter [praes.]: *De Chorea Sancti Viti dissertatio pathologica* (Leipzig, 1825).

Wolf, Johann Christian [resp.], Georg Wolfgang Wedel [praes.]: 'De morbo spasmodico epidemico maligno in Saxonia, Lusatia, vicinis locis grassato et adhuc grassante', Med.D. Diss. (Jena, 1717).

Index